1840

1P$25.00

CHARLES BOOTH

CHARLES BOOTH

From the portrait by Sir William Rothenstein in the
Library of the University of Liverpool

CHARLES BOOTH

Social Scientist

T. S. SIMEY
Charles Booth Professor
of Social Science
University of Liverpool

M. B. SIMEY

GREENWOOD PRESS, PUBLISHERS
WESTPORT, CONNECTICUT

Library of Congress Cataloging in Publication Data

Simey, Thomas Spensley, 1906-
   Charles Booth, social scientist.

   Reprint of the ed. published by Oxford University
Press, London.
   "Published works by Charles Booth": p.
   Includes bibliographical references and index.
   1. Booth, Charles, 1840-1916. 2. Social
reformers--Great Britain--Biography. 3. Social
scientists--Great Britain--Biography. I. Simey,
Margaret B., joint author. II. Title.
[HV28.B6S5 1980]   361'.92'4 [B]   80-18810
ISBN 0-313-22610-5 (lib. bdg.)

This reprint has been authorized by the Oxford University
Press.

Reprinted in 1980 by Greenwood Press,
A division of Congressional Information Service, Inc.
88 Post Road West, Westport, Connecticut 06881

Printed in the United States of America

10 9 8 7 6 5 4 3 2 1

PREFACE

THE task of writing this book has been undertaken in an attempt to repay to the memory of Charles Booth part of the debt we owe to him, in common with all other social scientists, social administrators, and social workers. In the execution of this task we have, however, incurred many other debts which must now be acknowledged. First and foremost, there is that owing to the members of Charles Booth's family who advised us how we might set to work. and maintained a keen interest throughout the period of our researches. They have helped us by making available much material relating to *Life and Labour in London*, and to the affairs of the firm of Alfred Booth & Co., in which he was a partner; still more important, they have given us access to large quantities of private family correspondence, from which they have allowed us to quote freely. The mere assembling of this material, much of it from remote and more or less forgotten places, has involved them in an infinity of trouble, for which we cannot be too grateful.

We have also to thank Sir Alexander Carr-Saunders for assisting us in many ways, and especially in securing the permission of the Passfield Trustees for our use of Beatrice Webb's papers, and for the publication of extracts from them. The pleasure with which we express our thanks to him is greatly enhanced by reason of the fact that it has given us an opportunity to associate his name, as the first holder of the Charles Booth Chair in Social Science at the University of Liverpool, with that of Charles Booth himself.

We are much obliged to the Librarian of the British Library of Political and Economic Science, at the London School of Economics, Mr. G. Woledge, the Assistant Librarian, Dr. Marjorie Plant, and their colleague, Miss Joshua, for permitting us to use the Booth and Passfield Papers and guiding us in many ways in the course of our researches.

Our indebtedness to colleagues in Liverpool, particularly Mr. J. B. Mays, Dr. W. Scott, Mr. H. Silcock, and Dr. C. Vereker, must also be recorded. Special acknowledgements are due to the Librarian in charge of the Library of the School of Social Sciences and Administration in the University of Liverpool, Miss A. Lythgoe, who, with her colleagues, went to much trouble to obtain books and periodicals for us from a variety of sources. We owe a similar debt to Miss E. Eaves, Secretary of the Department of Social Science and her senior assistant, Mrs. M. Wilson, who with other colleagues undertook the lengthy task of typing the drafts of the book.

We are deeply conscious of the help we have been given by all who, remembering with happiness and pride their acquaintance with 'the Right Honourable', as Charles Booth was so often called, have shared their recollections with us.

T. S. S.
M. B. S.

CONTENTS

KEY TO REFERENCES

Full Title	Referred to as
A. GENERAL	
Charles Booth, a Memoir. (By his widow) Macmillan & Co. 1918 . . .	*Memoir*
Beatrice Webb. *My Apprenticeship.* Longmans & Co. 1926 . . .	*My Apprenticeship*
Manuscripts deposited in the British Library of Political and Economic Science by the Passfield Trustees	Passfield
B. THE INQUIRY	
'The Inhabitants of the Tower Hamlets (School Board Division), their Condition and Occupations.' *Journal of the Royal Statistical Society*, 1887 . .	First Paper
'Condition and Occupations of the People of East London.' *Journal of the Royal Statistical Society*, 1888 . . .	Second Paper
First Edition: *Labour and Life of the People.* 2 Volumes. Edited by Charles Booth (Williams and Norgate, 1889-91)	First Edition i-ii
Second Edition: *Life and Labour of the People in London.* Edited by Charles Booth. 9 Volumes. (Macmillan & Co. 1892-7) . . .	Second Edition i-ix
Third Edition: *Life and Labour of the People in London.* By Charles Booth. 17 Volumes. (Macmillan & Co.)	
First Series: *Poverty* (1902) . .	*Poverty* i-iv
Second Series: *Industry* (1903) . .	*Industry* i-v
Third Series: *Religious Influences* (1902-3)	*Religious Influences* i-vii
Final Volume: *Notes on Social Influences and Conclusion* (1903) . .	*Final*

Note. The second and third editions incorporated the material already published, though some passages were revised and rearranged. A useful abstract of the contents of the definitive edition of 1902-3 is to be found in the *Final Volume*. The names of those who assisted Booth are given on the title pages of the volumes containing their contributions. Where material contained in earlier works was incorporated in the Third Series, reference is made to the latter.

INTRODUCTION

THIS book attempts to describe and to explain how a Victorian man of business, a merchant, shipowner and manufacturer, came to make outstanding contributions to British sociology and social policy; its underlying theme is the problem of social change, and the discovery of methods of bringing it under control. Prominent in its historical background are the changes in the economy of the nation, resulting from the rise of international trade and the development of capitalist enterprise. Equally important, however, is its social setting, established by the expansion of the great cities, the rapid growth of the wealth of the middle classes (and of those above and immediately beneath them), and the increase of the poverty of the unskilled worker and of the unemployed, the sick, the aged, the widowed, and the orphaned. Its moral context is to be found in the exacerbation of the conscience of the wealthy on being confronted by the mass of un-relieved misery in the slums. The story which has to be told originates in the impact of this newly sharpened sense of obligation on the mind and life of Charles Booth. What gives it its significance to the social scientist, the politician, and the administrator of later generations is the fact that here was a man who applied his reason to the problems presented to him by his conscience, and advocated reforms, the necessity and practicability of which were demonstrated by the weight of the relevant evidence, rather than dictated by political dogma, religious or moral belief or personal inclination.

Any attempt to understand Booth's achievement therefore raises a succession of issues that are still of great practical importance in the middle of the twentieth century. The social changes that resulted from the Industrial Revolution were a cause of grave anxiety in his day;[1] in the intervening half-century the development of industrial tech-nology has accelerated, and the need to protect society from its harmful effects is becoming more and more clear to scientists as well as to the statesmen and administrators who are directly responsible for the welfare of the nation. In this sense, the era in which he lived continues today. His problems are also ours; many of the questions they provoke remain unanswered. How, it must still be asked, can a measure of social

---

[1] The Paper which he read in 1886 to the Royal Statistical Society was designed to test the evidence which gave rise to this concern. See below, p. 67.

and economic security be made available to man, without at the same time undermining his incentives to work, and his sense of personal responsibility? What is the true nature of the social problems of an urban and industrial civilization, and can they be relieved by administrative measures of one kind or another? Above all, to what extent (if at all) are the troubles which seem to threaten the existence of society attributable to a lowering of moral standards, and does this, in turn, stem from the weakening of religious influences?

All these questions, and the many others that are associated with them, imply still more fundamental questions that can only be discussed on a philosophical plane; this is often forgotten, or not understood.[1] None of them can be answered without an attempt to some extent at least to explore the ways in which the human understanding is conditioned by feeling and belief, and the generation and application of man's creative energies are influenced by his social relationships. In the course of the past two hundred years, discussion of the issues which this involves has tended to turn on the extent to which reason is or can be made supreme over the emotional, material, and social elements in human experience. In particular, attempt after attempt has been made to develop an 'objective' analysis of psychological and social data, on the supposition that the only means of discovering the truth lies in the development of scientific methods of understanding human nature. From the laying down of the foundations of positivism in France in the middle of the eighteenth century, to the American neo-positivist revival of the middle of the twentieth, there has been a long series of efforts to establish the social sciences in the manner that predominated in the mechanistic sciences up to the end of the Victorian age. There has, however, always been something basically unsatisfactory, or even repellent, involved in the positivist interpretation of human behaviour.[2] Man's social activities and the structure of the society to which he belongs are deeply influenced by his material environment: this is generally agreed. But the question remains to be

---

[1] 'Philosophy is the critic of abstractions. [It is] not one among the sciences with its own little scheme of abstractions which it works away at perfecting. . . . It is the survey of sciences, with the special objects of their harmony and of their completion.' A. N. Whitehead, *Science and the Modern World*, Cambridge University Press, edition of 1953, p. 108.

[2] This has been discussed at length by Lord Lindsay in *Religion, Science and Society*, Oxford University Press, 1943. The physical sciences 'cannot apprehend goodness, courage, pity and love, and therefore (it is asserted) these things do not exist, and a universal debunking of all that was admired and loved and worshipped is the inevitable consequence' (p. 40).

answered precisely how far the fact that they are linked together renders it possible to apply the apparatus of scientific inquiry to the understanding of social problems.

This question lies at the root of Charles Booth's work. The significance of his contribution to the social sciences arises not simply from the fact that he attempted to answer it, but that he was one of the first to recognize that it had to be answered. In effect what he sought to do was to establish the mid-point on the scale occupied at one end by subjective judgement, concerned with such problems as those of evaluation and responsibility, and at the other by impersonal descriptions and analyses of demographic and similar data. Though he inherited the positivist approach from Comte, he only used it in so far as it appeared to him to be proper to do so: it occupied virtually the whole stage in his inquiries into poverty, but played only a restricted part in his examination of religious influences. His starting-point was the moral dilemma in which he found himself, as a rich man in a world whose prosperity seemed to be unavoidably linked with poverty, but this did not compel him to forsake objectivity for speculation. In particular, he was no originator of Utopias; still less was he the creator of philosophical systems, like Bentham, Comte, or Spencer. His first endeavour was to assess the extent of poverty in the society of which he was a member, to lay bare the connexions between poverty and individual character, and to explore the way in which social conditions generally were influenced by industrial organization, but his ultimate aim was to bring about an improvement in the condition of the people. It was, therefore, a problem of critical public importance, that of poverty (for him the Problem of all Problems) which was the central objective of his Inquiry; it was his solution of the specific problem of the poverty of the aged, by the provision of old-age pensions which has secured for him his reputation as a social reformer.

If there was no more to be said than this, Booth's life might be described as that of an extremely successful man of practical affairs, whose sense of moral obligation led him to apply to social problems the qualities upon which his personal prosperity was founded. But this would be by no means the whole truth, for his work can only be understood if it is also regarded as that of a sociologist who sought to introduce some of the objectivity and exactitude of the natural sciences into the study of the unstable world of social relationships. Objectivity and obligation were fused together by him into a new system of thought and inquiry. A basis for social reform could, he recognized, 'be built out of a big theory, and facts and statistics run in to fit it', but this was not the manner in which he elected to work. What he set out to create was 'a large statistical framework', 'built to receive an accumulation of facts', out of which was to be 'evolved the theory and the law and the basis of more intelligent action'.[1] His approach was essentially empirical. He was convinced that theory and experience had to be interwoven if an adequate explanation of the developing pattern of human societies was to be constructed. His aim was to preserve a balance between induction and deduction, and he sought to attain it by exploiting the advantages of both personal observation and statistical measurement, obtaining depth of insight from the former, and certainty and exactitude from the latter. The various methods of inquiry developed by him were, in fact, complementary. It is because of the success which resulted from these pioneering endeavours that he must be regarded today as a founder of empirical sociology.

The value of the contributions thus made by Booth to sociology and social policy has been summed up in the succinct statement that his Inquiry, 'epoch-making' in the history of the social sciences, was as significant in the field of social planning as his survey method was in that of sociological research.[2] Until the results of his researches into poverty had been published, the formulation of social policy had been dependent on speculative deductions drawn from economic or moral laws. In particular, the causes of the sufferings of the poor had been found in individual shortcomings or moral delinquencies, notably drunkenness; after his work had become available to the general public, a new era was inaugurated, in so far as the causes of the prevailing miseries were demonstrated to have arisen in large measure out of deficiencies in the conditions of industrial employment and, in general, in social organization. Looking backwards towards the nineteenth century from the middle of the twentieth, Booth appears to be a true Victorian in so far as he acclaimed the positive values of industrial and commercial enterprise, but sought at the same time to devise methods of combating the evils that had resulted from it. His cast of thought

---

[1] See below, p. 77.

[2] *Encyclopaedia of the Social Sciences*, Vol. XIV, p. 163. The dual nature of Booth's work was emphasized by Beatrice Webb, who regarded him as 'much more than a statistician. He was the boldest pioneer, in my judgment, and the achiever of the greatest results, in the methodology of the social sciences of the nineteenth century' (*My Apprenticeship*, p. 247). But she also thought that he was, within her circle of friends, 'perhaps the most perfect embodiment of . . . the mid-Victorian time-spirit—the union of faith in the scientific method with the transference of the emotion of self-sacrificing service from God to man' (Ibid., p. 221).

was as typical of the social thinking of England in 1900 as Thomas Chalmers' had been of the Britain of 1800.[1] In the century that intervened, the emphasis in the social theories that prevailed had come to be placed on public administration rather than on private benevolence, and on the advancement of social welfare by improving the structure of society rather than by exhorting or compelling individuals to behave more morally. It was Charles Booth who, more than any other person, influenced public opinion towards accepting the new outlook, and was able to change the course of development of the society in which he lived. He did so by analysing its weaknesses with skill, intelligence and courage; under his leadership sociology began to function as the midwife of a new social order, as the eighteenth-century positivists had prophesied.

The precise nature of Booth's contribution was to demonstrate that social structure, social welfare and individual behaviour were interconnected in such a way that, in certain specific respects at least, a general improvement in welfare could be brought about by reforms in structure, providing opportunities for higher standards in behaviour.[2] Chalmers' gloom was therefore matched by a new optimism; this became evident when the collision between his and Booth's attitudes of mind came to a head in the 1890s, during the campaign for old-age pensions. This measure was advocated by Booth as contributing to social security, and stimulating rather than weakening 'the play of individuality on which progress and prosperity depend'.[3] The sharpness of the conflict that developed in this way, and the importance of the basic issues that arose in the course of it, made the old-age pension the symbol of the most urgent moral dilemma of the Victorian era; namely, the reconciliation of collective action designed to remedy social abuses, and promote the well-being of the individual, with the maintenance and encouragement of personal responsibility and initiative.

The significance of Booth's attempt to resolve this dilemma was

---

[1] 'Next to the salvation of their souls, one of our fondest aspirations on behalf of the general peasantry is that they shall be admitted to a larger share of this world's abundance than now falls to their lot. But we feel assured that there is no method by which this can be wrested from the hands of the wealthier classes. It can only be won from them by the insensible growth of their own virtue.' Quoted from *Political Economy*, Vol. II, p. 18, in Henry Hunter, *Selections from the Economic and Social Writings of Thomas Chalmers*, Thomas Nelson & Sons, 1912, p. 341.

[2] Cf. the argument embodied in the *Final Volume*, at p. 208, discussed below, p. 172.

[3] *Pauperism and the Endowment of Old Age*, p. 241.

made manifest in the course of his evidence to the Royal Commission
on the Aged Poor, in 1893. Not less than two-thirds of all unskilled
workers were estimated by him to become paupers in, and because of,
old age. He admitted that they earned enough money in their youth
to provide for themselves in future years, if they delayed their marriage
and saved before it. But, he stated, 'young men do not and will not
do so as a rule. Human nature must be taken as it is found, and while
it remains what it is now, their old age provision will not be made to
any great extent'. In brief, the cause of the pauperism of the aged poor
had to be attributed to 'human nature' on the one hand, and low wages
on the other,[1] and it was possible, and indeed preferable from Booth's
point of view as a common-sense man of business, to treat income (in
the form of a pension) as the object of reform, rather than human
nature, which had resisted the preachings of the self-appointed
improvers of popular morality so stoutly.

The opposition between moral exhortation as a means of social
improvement, and legislation and administration, recurred over and
over again during the Victorian era; it established a theme in public
controversy that is still an outstanding one today.[2] Those who, like
Booth, seek to disburden the citizen of part at least of his material cares
are still open to attack on the ground that they are undermining
personal responsibility, and therefore encouraging immorality. But it
must be replied on behalf both of Booth and those who have followed
in his footsteps that the result cannot but be to leave the citizen as
morally responsible as he ever was, if not more so. He may, indeed,
have to carry an increased burden of moral responsibility in exchange
for the material one, since the ultimate effect must be to endow him
with greater freedom to discharge his obligations. This may well prove
to be the most important characteristic of the new type of citizenship
that came into being after the full implications, both of Booth's
Inquiry and of the old-age pensions controversy with which it was so
closely connected, had been understood, digested, and embodied in
British social policy.

[1] This argument was outlined and commented on by Geoffrey Drage, in *The Problem
of the Aged Poor*, Adam and Charles Black, 1895, especially at pp. 24-5.

[2] A striking example, with which Booth was familiar, occurred immediately before
he began his Inquiry. The passing of the Criminal Law Amendment Act, 1885, designed
to stamp out intolerable abuses connected with prostitution and the international traffic
in women and girls, had been opposed on the ground that improvements could only
come from an increased sense of the value of purity, and the encouragement of honest
pride among the poor.

This being so, it is a surprising fact that no serious attempt has yet been made to describe the origin and nature of Booth's contribution to sociology and social policy. This is all the more strange in view of the importance attached to the great Inquiry into the *Life and Labour of the People in London*, in which his ideas found expression; this must now be recognized as a classic text in both the social sciences and social history, with, it has been said, 'a history of its own, quite independent of the personality and outlook of its writer'.[1] From the moment of the presentation of his first Paper on the subject, what became known as 'Mr. Booth's Inquiry' achieved such fame that no other heading was necessary on the questionnaires which he sent out in search of information. Today, the extent of the debt owed to him by all who are concerned with social administration, or with the carrying out of extensive social researches, is frequently honoured in tribute to his memory. Why, it must therefore be asked, has so little attention been paid to the circumstances out of which the Inquiry was brought to birth? Why has its value, and that of Booth's work in general, never been adequately assessed and its significance established?

Though Booth's name and the titles of his books are common currency wherever the discussion of social problems takes place, few have actually done more than glance somewhat casually at the pages of one or other of the books and pamphlets on the subject of the aged poor, or of the seventeen volumes of the Inquiry which are so familiar an ornament of academic libraries. 'Booth', it has been said, 'is not so much read as he is admired.'[2] The sheer bulk of his published work is certainly intimidating. Its practical relevance half a century later may, in addition, appear at first glance to be somewhat doubtful, since the social changes that have continued throughout this period might seem to those who restrict their attention to the bare results of the Inquiry, rather than endeavour to understand its significance, to have reduced its value to that of a record of past history. These are considerations which do not go to the root of the matter, however. It is more than probable that the lack of curiosity as to what sort of man Booth was, and as to why and how he came to evolve his method of conducting a social survey, should be interpreted as a tribute to the validity of his ideas. His achievements were of such solid worth that attacks on them have always been unthinkable, and Booth, as a man, has passed

[1] Asa Briggs, 'Signpost to the Welfare State', in the *New Statesman and Nation*, 1956, p. 127.

[2] Ruth Glass, *Current Sociology*, No. 4, 1955, p. 46.

unnoticed behind the enduring façade of his work. Moreover, so far as his method of investigating was concerned, the tool of his invention met the public need so aptly that it was immediately accepted as a necessary part of the equipment of the social reformer and the possibilities of adapting and extending his methods have occupied generation after generation of social scientists ever since. The concept of the social inquiry is now a commonplace of everyday social life. We are so used to the idea of the survey, and to being ourselves surveyed, that it is indeed difficult to imagine that there was ever a time—and that so recent—when its invention was matter for long and careful consideration and its achievement a subject for universal astonishment and acclaim.

Booth himself left no record of the processes whereby he arrived at his conclusions; he evidently did not think it necessary to explain at any great length why he had determined to put the preconceptions of his age to the test. He was a modest man; as Beatrice Webb pointed out, it was partly because of this and partly because of his voluminous output, that he 'failed, like so many other successful organizers, to describe his plan of campaign'.[1] His wife's memoir, and Beatrice Webb's well-known account in her autobiography, based on the diaries she kept throughout the period of her apprenticeship as a social investigator under him, constitute virtually all the information which describes either the man or his work as a social scientist.

The present study of Charles Booth has been undertaken as a contribution towards making good this deficiency. His work is described first and foremost in terms of the response of an individual to the demands of his times. This has necessarily restricted the scope of the book. Thus in so far as he was a prominent and successful member of the commercial community, only an outline of his career has been given. The story of the manner in which the independent merchant of the nineteenth century became the company director of the twentieth is a fascinating one, but it is only a necessary part of the present study in so far as it illuminates the sources of the principles and practice upon which his life as a social scientist was founded. These must be considered in detail. In particular, the manner in which he inherited the traditions of Unitarian Nonconformity, on the one hand, and those of British empiricism on the other, must be clearly understood. Both traditions stemmed from the seventeenth century; both were deeply embedded in the way of life of Victorian England. His

[1] *My Apprenticeship*, p. 217.

achievement was to widen and deepen these traditions, and to show that they were directly relevant to the investigation and solution of contemporary social problems.

At the same time, Booth recognized and exploited the opportunities for action which his age made available to him. It was the prevailing climate of thought and opinion that gave *Life and Labour in London* its intellectual content and its public importance, and provided him with the moral energy that enabled him to complete it. Furthermore, the social context in which he lived afforded him many opportunities for carrying out researches that had been denied to the theorists of the preceding century. Effective action had become possible in his day since assistance was available from the social services rapidly being developed in Victorian England. The administrative apparatus of the poor law, public health, the police, and public elementary education gave him a means of collecting large quantities of reliable information which made it possible to formulate hypotheses and plan schemes of research. It was because the current of the times was flowing with him that Booth found himself able to rely on and to exploit the goodwill and understanding of friends, business partners, and his fellow-citizens generally.[1] This permitted him the leisure and gave him the support necessary to the execution of his schemes, just as it aroused in him the personal sense of concern as to the conditions of the poor, and the intense anxiety that drove him forward to find the means to cope with the evils that distressed him, and to launch the Inquiry in his endeavours to do so. This must not, of course, be interpreted as an attempt to explain away the validity of Booth's achievements by suggesting that because his work as a scientist and scholar came to fruition in a specific social context, it was the age rather than the man which produced it. His moral nature, in particular his tenacity of purpose and the probity of his mind, were no doubt influenced by his social relationships, but he repaid in full measure what he had received.

The problem of describing Booth and his work is therefore a complex one. He merits description as an individual in his own right, but what he had to say about the world in which he lived must at the same time be listened to as an expression of the intellectual anguish and moral

---

[1] The doctrine of self-help, for example, had at length come to be understood by his contemporaries to have political and moral implications that were unexpected and far-reaching; for if the workers were to be encouraged to do what they could to help themselves, those in positions of power and responsibility could not escape the burden of an obligation to see that this was made a practical possibility. See Reinhard Bendix, *Work and Authority in Industry*, John Wiley and Chapman and Hall, 1956, pp. 108-16.

doubts of the Victorian era. His contribution to social policy is inextricably linked with his work as a sociologist; both can only be correctly assessed if they are seen in relation to the times in which he lived. The Inquiry, perhaps his greatest work, cannot be regarded simply as a rich man's hobby or even as a scientific way of solving social problems, but must also be appraised as his means of expressing the feelings of obligation derived from the moral tradition in which he was reared. In order to establish him in the place he deserves in our social history it has accordingly been necessary not only to describe the man and his work as seen against the background of his time and place, but also to attempt to capture the essence of the relationships between the two.

To overcome the difficulties which the complexity of purpose necessarily involves, this book has been divided into two parts. In the first, the impressions which the social problems of his day made on Booth's mind are described, and his efforts to understand and to solve them are discussed and analysed as an integral part of his life as a member of the business community of Liverpool, London, and the world at large. The second part contains an evaluation of his contributions to sociology and social policy, and an attempt to estimate the extent of his influence on the subsequent course of British social history. The predominant theme in the first part is that of the interaction between a man and his social environment; the keynote of the second is the evaluation of the significance of his contributions to Western thought in so far as they arose out of the creative processes of an individual mind.

Neither part is complete in itself. It has, up to a point, proved possible to treat the narration of the events of Booth's life and the course of his work apart from the analysis of its nature and significance. But description cannot be kept entirely separate from evaluation. So much of the one is implied in the other that any attempt to break down an account of his life's experiences into its component parts quickly becomes so artificial as to involve the destruction of the entity itself. This division of the subject-matter must therefore be regarded as an arbitrary one, from which it is difficult to eliminate repetition. Imperfect though the result may be, the conviction has nevertheless remained that no other method could have sufficed. Booth's experiences and his contributions to his age must be examined at one and the same time as part of the unique life of an individual, and also as part of an impersonal endeavour, common to all mankind, to widen the boundaries of human understanding. Special attention must be paid to the relationships between the object of social research and the researcher, and between both of these and the society in which the research is carried out. These are aspects of social research and social history which are seldom studied and the importance of which is barely recognized. It is hoped that the result will be to have brought to light the wisdom of a remarkable man. It is also hoped that the truth of his conclusions and the effectiveness of his endeavours have been established and explained in such a way that an addition has been made to the common stock of knowledge available to those who follow after him.

Part I

THE MAN AND HIS WORK

1

The Making of a Liverpool Gentleman

THE economic developments which occurred in Liverpool towards the end of the eighteenth century brought into being a new commercial society in which every man was free to make his own way regardless of the limitations of class or creed. To all Dissenters this indeed stood for freedom, and from all over the north country, young men of this persuasion were attracted in their days of early manhood by the promise which this 'Gateway to the New World', this 'Venice of the North',[1] held out to those who sought to escape from the bondage of conformity to a tradition which they had rejected.

They were not disappointed. They brought to town life the energy and integrity of generations of honest craftsmen, local dealers in corn and timber, builders of small ships. They were hard workers and straight thinkers, reared in the yeoman tradition that to give honest service was an honourable way of life and one worthy of its just reward. Quickly they made a name and a place for themselves in local affairs, establishing themselves in the businesses of their choice, and proceeding to lay the foundations on which the fortunes of subsequent generations were to be so solidly based. These were the men who quite literally made Liverpool. They built its docks and railways. They built the ships upon whose coming and going the very existence of the city depended. They built its town houses, its wide streets and pleasant squares, its chapels and its churches, in an imitation of London which had in it little of envy. Encouraged by their own success they dreamed dreams of public buildings, parks and libraries which would bear witness to the new and nobler way of life of their aspiration.

Their ambitions for themselves and for the new town of their

---

[1] M. B. Simey, *Charitable Effort in Liverpool in the Nineteenth Century*, Liverpool University Press, 1951, p. 7.

creation were fostered by the peculiar requirements of the city's concentration on the business of handling goods in transit. This was essentially a society of merchants, offering little scope to the master craftsman. He who worked in its offices and banks, its custom houses and exchanges, found himself to be a gentleman by virtue of the fact that his occupation required him to wear a white collar and keep his hands clean. Moreover, the essence of success in an industry based on credit lay in the maintenance of confidence: an air of solid security was a necessary part of any merchant's stock-in-trade. The newcomers did not hesitate to follow the example of the small oligarchy of established merchants who had previously set the standard in this matter. Their habitual regard for the things of the mind, and their thirst for the responsibilities of the social status which their non-conformity had long denied them, rendered them apt pupils, and they soon began to play a leading part in the life of the town. The exigencies of commerce no longer requiring that they should live over their business premises, they abandoned to the masses their old houses in the streets running down to the Pool, and retreated to new homes on the higher ground overlooking the docks. Here they settled down to the enjoyment of that combination of culture and commerce which was to become characteristic of their society.

These were by no means the 'newly rich' of a later era for, leavening the whole, keeping the success from becoming too solid and sub-stantial, was the living tradition of the pioneers which was deeply rooted in their character and their religion. The aspiration to gentility of these early Roscoes and Rathbones, Booths, Holts and Bowrings, was based on a solid foundation of moral principle. However rich they might become, they never forgot that commerce was a way of life as well as a means of making money, an opportunity to give honest service to their fellow men in return for which a fair remuneration might properly be expected. They regarded their enjoyment of material wealth as a trust, accepting the obligation to justify their own prosperity by the exercise of a care and concern for those who were less well endowed. At the same time, the very nature of the means of their existence ensured that these qualities would not breed smugness or self-satisfaction. Where the caprices of wind and weather made them-selves so tangibly felt, where the intangibles of credit and luck could play so important a part, where the sinews of daily life ran so far afield that the world of everyday affairs comprised places as remote as the China Seas, the West Coast of Africa and the rebellious States of North

America, no one could dare to be dull or to settle into a rut of complacency. A constant current of fresh ideas blew through men's lives like the wind off the open seas beyond the harbour bar.

Thus regarded, it is difficult to resist the temptation to apply what has been called the varnish of nostalgia to the Liverpool of Charles Booth's early days. By 1840, the anxieties and uncertainties of the first generation of men who had made the move from country to town were over: the drawbacks and the difficulties which maturity was to reveal as inherent accompaniments of urban living were yet to come. The first flush of excitement of the 'boom city' days of the early century had been succeeded by the confidence of success: the men upon whose efforts that success was founded were proudly making way for their sons and grandsons of the second and third generations. It was a good time in which to be young. The infinite resources of a new civilization lay at man's disposal: the delights and responsibilities of a novel way of life awaited exploration. Liverpool at that period was already a substantial city, all the more so because its substantiality was of such recent origin as to be matter for daily remark. Equipped with handsome public buildings in wide streets which cut through the crowded lanes of the old town, the centre of a web of transport serving the industrial north, with trains running out from the imposing station in Lime Street and steam ferries serving the residential suburbs across the river, the town seemed to its citizens to stand on the brink of an era of unlimited progress and prosperity.

This seminal period in English social history is most faithfully reflected in the lives of successive generations of the forefathers of Charles Booth. Charles's grandfather, Thomas Booth, had come to Liverpool from the family farm near Warrington in 1787: his grandfather on his mother's side, Thomas Fletcher, came to Liverpool from rural Lancashire in the 1770s. Thomas Booth set up in business with his brother as a corn merchant, with interests in the ships which carried their grain; Thomas Fletcher entered the trade with the West Indies, although not with very great success, his two daughters being compelled to resort to school teaching as a means of earning a livelihood. Both became what might be called yeomen-merchants, respected and responsible men though not rich, prominent in local affairs, pillars of their respective churches, nonconformist to the backbone.

Though his forbears may thus be regarded as essentially typical of their time and place, it must not be supposed, however, that Charles Booth came of stock which was without individuality. Far from it.

His grandfather on the Booth side married one of a bevy of daughters—
'the talking, the walking, the pretty and the intellectual Misses
Pilkington' of whom 'one was a great traveller and protected herself
by a mythical husband whom she called "The General" '.[1] The sons
of this marriage, of whom one was to become father of Charles Booth,
also made their own mark on the world in which they lived. James was
an eminent legal draughtsman who worked a revolution in the drafting
of private bill legislation for the House of Commons and became
Secretary to the Board of Trade; a pamphlet on *Important Questions
Affecting the Social Conditions of the Industrious Classes* and the fact that
he held 'advanced' views on matters of religion bear witness to his
independence of mind. Henry was even more of an individual,
vigorous and versatile, active in local affairs and of a peculiarly
inventive disposition in regard equally to matters mental and material.[2]
The third brother, Charles, who was to become the father of the
Charles Booth about whom this book is written, was the quietest of
the three, 'a gentle shy little boy', who grew up to be a corn merchant
and a man of singularly attractive character by reason of his 'upright-
ness, sincerity, unaffected goodness and utter unpretendingness'.[3]
Charles Booth thus inherited from his father's side a tradition of
mental activity and a habit of untiring industry which found expression in an ingenuity and variety of interest. His father and his
uncles were essentially men of their times, keenly aware of the possibilities of the age in which they lived, yet never forgetful of the human
issues which social and economic change involved, and of their own
obligations towards the society in which they lived and worked. As
individuals, though they were of a lively disposition, amiable and
interested in all manner of men, they yet maintained an indefinable
reserve which prevented their most friendly of relationships from
developing into intimacy. It is easy to recognize in these men the
personality which was to emerge as characteristic of Charles Booth
himself.

On his mother's side there is equal evidence of a vigorous self-

[1] Harriet Whitting, *Alfred Booth*, Young, 1917, p. 5.

[2] There seems no doubt that the credit for the invention of the new type of boiler
used in the *Rocket* was at least partly due to him, whilst the steam whistle, the yellow
grease used on rolling stock and an ingenious heating arrangment which he installed in
the Renshaw Street chapel at his own expense, were other products of his fertile mind.
Eventually he became chief manager of the Liverpool and Manchester Railway which
owed its existence largely to his energy.

[3] Ibid., p. 36.

assertiveness within the conventional pattern of the society to which the individual belonged. Emily Fletcher was a daughter of the marriage of Anna Enfield, herself a daughter of the well-known Norwich preacher and a friend of the Gurneys, and Tom Fletcher, a son of a Liverpool West India merchant. She was endowed with good looks rather than prettiness, a vigorous intelligence, a well cultivated mind, and a talent for water-colours. The intricate web of relations to which she belonged made up a gay, close-knit little community founded primarily on their membership of the Unitarian chapel, but greatly strengthened by the bonds of intermarriage and of business partnership. They lived in the new streets of middle-class houses on the rising ground behind the city, where the Anglican Cathedral now stands, leading comfortable civilized lives, their modest prosperity offset, it was said, by the 'genuine sympathy and expansive benevolence' with which they fulfilled their social obligations.

This then was the heritage, this the environment, into which the young Charles was born. It constituted an inheritance of which the outstanding features were the vigour and zest with which every experience of life was greeted, and the freshness and inventiveness of mind with which its problems and potentialities were regarded. Here was a society where sincere appreciation of all that was worthy in the tradition of the gentleman was not permitted to exclude a genuine enthusiasm and pride in their calling as men of business. These were in fact the first generation of that new species, the industrial and commercial middle class, specifically the product and the promise of the new urban age to which they belonged.

Charles James Booth was born in Liverpool on the 30 March 1840, at 27 Bedford Street North, the fourth child in a family of five. The house was the sort of pleasantly plain, stucco fronted establishment, one of a terrace with gardens at both back and front, which represented the sensible endeavour of the early Victorian architect to supply the needs of the town-dwelling middle-class family. Presumably his father's management of the family corn business had proved successful, since four years later he began to build himself a larger house in Croxteth Road, fronting on to the then newly laid out Princes Park. To this they moved when Charles was five. Then followed ten happy years. Reviewing the circumstances of Charles's childhood, his life seems to have been singularly free from those frustrations and animosities to which the twentieth century tends to look for explanations of what a man becomes. He was deeply attached to both his parents, and his relationships with his two brothers and two sisters seem to have been unremarkable in their spontaneous affection. This was a loving, happy home in which the children grew up in an atmosphere of material and emotional security.

Of the boy Charley, little direct information is available. At the age of eight, his sister Emily tells us in her 'family chronicle', she and her brother went to a small private school supervised by the unmarried daughters of family friends of the Booths. At ten, Charles and his older brother Tom were entered for the Royal Institution School, which might fairly be described as the local progressive school of its day. The headmaster at that time was a follower of Arnold of Rugby, under whose influence such subjects as English, map-making, and history were introduced into the curriculum. Games were played, including singlestick and cricket, and the boys were 'regularly drilled in the large police shed immediately adjacent'.[1] Of Charles's progress in school, the only record which remains is, significantly enough, of his success in heading the list of an examination of the whole school in arithmetic, although he was still only in one of the middle forms. Nevertheless, his wife assures us that he was not considered to be 'one of the clever ones' although he early showed a capacity for steady application and constancy of purpose.[2] The only event to which any special significance might be attributed was the premature death of his mother when he was thirteen years old. Though this was undoubtedly a source of great grief to the whole circle, the genuine affection which was extended towards Emily's governess when she became their stepmother some four years later would seem to suggest that, as their mother herself had once remarked, their lives were not blighted by bereavement but raised and spiritualized by 'the discipline which brings forth under Providence the good fruit of faith and love'. Certainly the happy relationship which existed between the adolescent boy and his father must have done much to soften the grief occasioned by the loss of his mother.

At sixteen Charles left school, and after a visit to London, Heidelberg and Appenzel in the true finishing-school tradition of the nonconformists, he began his business training in the office of his father's second cousin, Mr. Lamport of the shipping firm of Lamport and Holt. Such an apprenticeship was commonly accepted as a matter of mutual obligation between members of the merchant community, especially

[1] A. T. Brown, *The Royal Institution School*, Liverpool University Press, 1924, p. 97.
[2] *Memoir*, p. 5.

amongst those who belonged to the same church or chapel: it was an obligation which Charles Booth himself was in due course to accept most loyally. Here he stayed for some four years, about which little is known other than may be surmised from the fact that 'the Lamb', as Mr. Lamport was affectionately termed, was reputed to be one of the finest specimens of his kind, in whom were united 'mercantile aptitude with deep reading and ripe scholarship'.[1] No less significant is the fact that he was also an enthusiast for the use of steam engines in ships and materially assisted Alfred Holt in his early struggles as a marine engineer.[2] Outside office hours Charles's particular hobby was sketching, for which he inherited his mother's talent, and in which he already displayed a characteristic preference for the panoramic rather than the romantic point of view: he remained something of an artist all his life. From what is known of his hobbies and interests, young Booth seems to have been an 'exceedingly brickish' sort of lad, to use a boyish expression of his own, actively interested in everybody and everything, gay and healthy.

However, pleasant though this wholesome enjoyment of the pleasures of being alive and young must have been, the harsher realities of life could not be for ever kept at bay. The family had been able to close its ranks with success after the death of the mother, but in 1860 a more decisive blow was struck against their serenity. 'I had a sore throat, beginning on 4th January', writes Emily Booth in an unpublished chronicle, 'which was a very slight attack of scarlatina, but not known at the time. Papa took it on 25th January. He died on 2nd February.' Once again the family rallied round, and for a year or so things ran on much as usual. Anna had by this time married Philip Holt, but Emily was available to keep house for her three brothers, and there was no great shortage of money. For Charles the breaking of the close bond of affection which existed between himself and his father was offset by the happiness of a growing intimacy with 'Tonie Prange, the sister of his school friend Francis, and daughter of a German merchant who had settled with his family in Liverpool. 'Antonia Prange must have been a singularly interesting and charming girl', Charles's wife later wrote, 'and as she grew to womanhood, Charles's feelings towards her rapidly developed into ardent and adoring love. To her, with an intensity of feeling all his own, he gave his heart.'[3]

Having completed his apprenticeship, Charles left Mr. Lamport's

[1] *Porcupine*, 13 November 1869. A local journal published weekly.
[2] F. E. Hyde, *Blue Funnel*, Liverpool University Press, 1956, p. 11.   [3] *Memoir*, p. 7.

office in February 1862, and a month later set sail for Palestine to make a grand tour of the Holy Land and thence through Greece, Italy and Switzerland to Germany, where he proposed to stay for a period of study with Francis Prange. The little pocket-books in which he kept an illustrated record of all that befell him on this tour reveal him to have been a born traveller, even-tempered, readily interested, and with a significant flair for observation. The tour came to a tragic conclusion, however. Arriving in Germany six months later, he was greeted with the news that Antonia was ill with a 'sudden consumption'. After three weeks of sick apprehension, his diary ends with the abrupt entry. 'I heard last night that she had died.' This was not all, however. It had always been intended that Charles should join his eldest brother, Alfred, in the commission business which he had set up in partnership with an American. Moved no doubt by a desire to make a wholly fresh start in life and despite an offer from Mr. Lamport to take him into partnership, Charles accordingly set off for New York immediately on his return from Germany. 'A day or two later', Emily tells us, 'Alfred [then in Liverpool on holiday] got letters telling him of his partner Mr. Walden's illness, and he decided to follow at once. He sailed on the 29th by the *Arabia*. Found the illness very serious, and had to get Mr. Walden into an Asylum. He and Charles were now sole partners.'

The exigencies of the situation in which Charles and his brother found themselves were such as to require of him a concentrated devotion to the business in hand which left him blessedly little time for grief. To add that in the event he found his new life absorbing and satisfying is in no way to question the depth of the feeling roused in him by the death of Antonia Prange or the break-up of his own happy family circle, but rather to suggest that already at this early age he was deliberately cultivating that philosophy of acceptance which was thenceforward to characterize his reaction to the inescapable griefs and frustrations of living. 'Many years had to elapse before his grief was softened enough to make it possible for him again to think of another attachment, whilst, to the end of his life, his feelings towards her memory remained unchanged.'[1] His emotions had run deeply and he never betrayed the loyalties that this implied. But the cost to him must have been great, and the detachment he subsequently displayed may have resulted in part at least from a desire not to give more hostages to fortune.

Charles Booth thus found himself launched upon the world of

[1] *Memoir*, p. 8.

business at the age of twenty-two.[1] Such an event was of course a much more ordinary occurrence 100 years ago than it is today. The independent merchant and the family business were still the main features of the commercial scene, and Charles's life since leaving school had, in fact, been shaped towards this end. The two brothers started out as commission agents, their main interest lying, more by chance than by choice, in the handling of skins, for they had no special knowledge of the trade. They opened offices on the most modest scale in Liverpool and New York: the latter being crowded and expensive they had to be content for some time with accommodation in a basement. Charles enjoyed the push and struggle of life in the upstart New York of the 'sixties, but the development of contacts in Liverpool seemed peculiarly suited to his talents, so it was finally agreed that Alfred should stay in America whilst Charles came home to set up house with Emily. For the first year or two events hung fire. The brothers were highly regarded by the commercial community, and were for that reason able to secure credit when required merely on their personal bond without payment of interest, an asset of which they were justly proud. Nevertheless, their firm was a new one, and clients had to be cultivated with patience. It is evident that this period of waiting was more trying to Charles than any amount of overwork. His eager temperament made him yearn for opportunities of 'active constant work and responsibility' far beyond the limited scope of the existing business. He genuinely enjoyed the 'risks, pleasures and excitements of business', and chafed against the conservatism of his brother, who regarded the firm primarily as a means of securing the financial independence which would permit him to pursue the life of a country gentleman. 'I don't think butter-making would suit me', he assured Alfred.

Charles for his part was very conscious of the world that lay at his feet. Here they were, two young men sound in mind and body, of reputable standing, with capital at their disposal and complete freedom of choice as to what they should do with it. 'We have more capital and more brains (I think) than most young men, and many advantages', he reminded Alfred. The prospect was undeniably pleasing and the only problem was to decide to what end to turn their resources. It was a problem which was solved almost before it was realized. Before

---

[1] The following account is based on the letter-books of A. Booth and Co., except where otherwise stated. For a detailed history of the firm, see A. H. John, *A Liverpool Merchant House*, Allen & Unwin Ltd., 1959.

he had set out for New York in 1862, he had already caught something of the enthusiasm for the use of steam in ships displayed by Anna's brother-in-law, Alfred Holt, who was then struggling to find his feet in business as a marine engineer. By the time he returned to Liverpool, eighteen months later, the whole town was 'talking steam' and Booth immediately began to dream dreams on his own behalf. Philip Holt went into their plans very pleasantly with him, he wrote to his brother in New York, adding:

Alfred Holt said to me today 'don't fritter away your energies. Make a scheme and carry it out' and it just fell in with what I have been thinking and talking to Philip about. If this experiment of theirs answers we must go in for it with all the money we can, and this adds another chance to the probability of our future being connected with steam. I think this is the large scheme to which we ought to work towards, and I would let everything else suffer first. The real plan of succeeding in business is to choose such a course that the tide of affairs is with you—it is that more than individual talent that does it. Then average ability is all you need.

Family tradition has it that, standing in front of a map of the world, he was bidden by the Holts not to go east because they were already there, but to turn in the opposite direction, where he would encounter no other competitor. This he decided to do, and, following what was to become his habitual plan of campaign, promptly asked his brother to collect the basic information in the shape of a record of all the arrivals and departures in New York of ships from the West Indies and Central America so that their plans might be provided with a working basis of fact. Alfred groaned at the work involved, but Charles's appetite for information was insatiable.

I still think I should like to have the Shipping List here and so if it is not very costly please send it. I want to look up the trade with the Windward Islands and Rio Janiero. I made a lot of statistics out about this trade which are very satisfactory. It is a rattling big one. If L[amport] and H[olt] have only pluck to follow it up it will be a smashing big thing one day.

Nevertheless, pleasant though it might be to let his fancy thus mount to success, the normal routine of the business had meanwhile to be carried on if their capital was not to be frittered away on the expenses of daily living. Booth was mortified to discover that he had much to learn, and the letters which he wrote during his first year in charge of the Liverpool office reveal that his self-confidence was undergoing a severe tempering:

My present feeling is that if I could sell all we have without loss, and be quit of the trade for ever with a stroke of my pen, I would do it. . . . I thought we were swells, and I find we were fools. I laughed at the idea that I should have to lose my money to gain experience but so it has been. . . . Business is a bed of thorns.

This setback was not however allowed to overwhelm him. As he vigorously assured his brother, he hated the very idea of taking things as they came and bearing them in a grumbling but Christian spirit. Indeed, to one of his temperament a disaster which called for renewed activity was always preferable to a state of inaction, however secure. Determined never again to experience the painful disillusionment of that first experience in business life, he insisted that in future he would not rely on other men's opinions, but must inform himself as to every last detail of whatever matter was in hand. By way of implementing this resolve, he developed that practice of reducing every situation to terms of simple written facts and figures which was to characterize everything he did from then onwards. 'My "statements" strike you as childish and very often I think they are, but I think they are worth doing', he doggedly insisted in reply to a protest from Alfred against the introduction of method in place of the somewhat slipshod habits of their earlier days. 'We must put an end to this sloppy brotherly way of doing business or we shall pay dearly for it. . . . To leave everything to the other won't do.' Taking his own advice, he set to work to equip himself to master the business to which he had set his hand, paying visits to the tanneries from which the consignments of English hides were received, going down in person to the ships as they came in with cargoes of imported skins in an effort to acquire some skill in judging their quality, getting to know both masters and men and the tricks of the trade, and constantly subjecting himself to a dispassionate criticism of his own manners and methods. 'To learn how to talk to people is an excellent thing, and I am putting myself into training. . . . I am determined to break down this stupid "Booth reserve" in myself and in others so far as I can.'

Soon, however, events began to move more rapidly, and by the end of November 1864 every letter from Charles to his brother once more referred to shipping, bringing a flash of excitement into pages burdened with the anxieties attendant on the slowly developing commission business. Everything now depended on the success or otherwise of Holt's experiments. These proved decisive, and Booth boldly made up his mind. 'As to our scheme . . . I am of the opinion that the risk is worth running. . . . I am too apt to rush into action on my own ideas, but I believe I shall be right now to go ahead on this and I do not wish to lose time. First we get what information we can from Lisbon and on that we decide. . . .' His proposition, which he had reduced to the inevitable 'statement' only after infinite calculations and recalculations of the risks and costs involved and the potential trade and profits, was that he and Alfred should invest all their own capital and that of their sister Emily in building themselves two sizeable ships with which to inaugurate a regular service to the ports of Para, Maranhem, and Ceara in South America. Alfred raised no objection to this: even now, with 100 years between, this young man's combination of logic and enthusiasm is irresistible. 'I am beginning to whistle for the wind', he wrote in January 1865, and it is a striking tribute both to his personal character and to the soundness of his scheme that by the beginning of February he had raised all the money required amongst his own family and friends, and could, indeed, have had more if he had needed it.

So at last, on 18 February 1865, the day came when he was able to report that, 'The boats are contracted for by Hart and Sinnott at . . . a lump sum of £16,000 each. This we think very satisfactory'; this contract was, incidentally, one of the last to be placed with a Liverpool firm of shipbuilders. He had thought himself busy enough before: his days now passed in a whirl of activity, and even he had to admit that passing half the day in Alfred Holt's office always got him into a corner with his other work. 'I am at work on the specifications. I shall go by A[lfred] H[olt]'s advice in everything but at the same time I mean to try to understand the thing from the bottom myself', he assured his brother, bearing in mind his recent resolve. He interpreted his promise in the most literal fashion. In spite of the fact that he had no scientific or technical training, and that he was already engrossed in the task of mastering the intricacies of the business of shipbroking and the skin trade, he now undertook the additional burden of personally planning and supervising the building of two fair-sized cargo and passenger ships on the then new and unfamiliar principle of steam—and what was then regarded as high-pressure steam at that—instead of sail. He had, of course, been brought up in a family which had habitually 'talked steam', whilst his intimate friendship with the Holt brothers had kept him informed as to the latest developments in regard to the use of steam in ships, but even so the feat was an astonishing one. Beginning with the specifications of the ship and the preparation of the contract with the builders, he made himself personally responsible for every detail. Each day he walked to and from his office by way of the yard where the ships were being built, in order that he might keep an eye on all that went on there.

Hart and Sinnott's yard is by the Queen's Dock as perhaps you know, and I think I shall get to know the directest route from there to Princes Park before the nine months are out. . . . I am beginning to understand the rudiments of Iron shipbuilding as I drew out the contracts myself and went to look at ships when I did not understand it. Alf. of course went over it with me to get the scantling and things right and I worked from his last contract for the West India Company's boats and Lloyd's rules. . . .

Inevitably progress was far too slow to satisfy his eager enthusiasm: next week, always next week, he was told in reply to his demands for greater speed. However, eventually all was ready, so that on 4 November 1865 he was able to report that:

We have launched today most successfully. Emily broke the bottle most efficiently in spite of all her declarations that she could not and would not and we all said success to the *Augustine* as she slipped away. A neat little lunch, a few glasses of champagne—The Vessel, The Builders, the Owners, and you in particular and a few appropriate remarks and compliments and back to my work.

The next three months were even more hectic than any that had gone before. 'I am drove very close . . . being at the ship every day and all day gets one's work late.' All sorts of unexpected difficulties arose in the solution of which Booth played an essential part. Finally, his health began to show signs of collapsing: only his enthusiasm kept him going, and his pride in finding himself at the age of twenty-six the owner of a vessel whose construction was in so literal a measure the result of his own effort, and which stood for so bold a venture into the future. Exhausted though he was, he found it impossible to resist the temptation to take his ship for a turn on the river when moving her from one dock to another during her completion, and when at last on 14 February 1866, the *Augustine* set sail for Para, it was inevitable that her owner should be aboard, difficult though it was to leave the Liverpool office to the care of the man and boy who constituted the staff.[1] The immediate financial profit of the trip was small, and though

[1] It should in fairness be added that Booth went on this first trip at least in part because of the unpredictable nature of the new engines, about which he was better informed than anyone else on board, and also because no one else had his grasp of the essential information necessary to the conduct of negotiations with the authorities of the various South American ports for the carrying of their mails.

the prospect for the future of steamships was exciting, the next few years were to be accompanied by considerable anxiety, pleasurable though that anxiety might be to one of Charles's temperament. 'You can have no idea of the intensity of the interest one takes in their business, and how bright Existence would be if they prospered', he informed his brother.

The firm's affairs were now in such a position that important and difficult decisions as to the future policy were urgently required to be taken, and once taken, to be pursued with unfaltering tenacity during the years of constant anxiety and serious financial stringency and risk which ensued before safe waters could be reached. In the development of the many ramifications of the firm's activities in this important period, Charles Booth quickly assumed the leading part. It was a position he retained throughout his life. He it was who conceived and initiated new ventures, who coaxed and persuaded and argued with the other partners, travelling incessantly from office to office and country to country, making new contacts and cherishing old ones, opening up fresh sources of supply and co-ordinating existing services, building up a web of interrelated activity so intricate as to bewilder and amaze the mind of the beholder. The pace was so hard that from time to time others in the partnership dropped out with ruined health, and Booth himself suffered from recurrent 'breakdowns', but the firm's prosperity was eventually established and its reputation for commercial integrity of the highest order was steadily enhanced.

No matter how varied or absorbing his other interests, Booth always regarded himself as primarily a merchant and financier. In 1914, when, over seventy years of age, the outbreak of war gave him an opportunity for taking a more active interest in the affairs of the various subsidiary companies. He wrote: 'The business holds me to its bosom with a charm unbelievable and absurd to most people.' There is, however, no need to pursue the story further here, interesting though it would be to trace the process by which the straightforward business of the nineteenth-century merchant developed into the complex commercial company of the twentieth. The pattern evolved in this early period was to recur over and over again in the years which followed. Infinitely various though the developments of subsequent years were to prove to be, their achievement reflected only the perfecting of the original method, of which the basic elements remained the same throughout. 'His technique in the conduct of affairs', writes Dr. John, 'lay essentially in the analysis of broad trends, as shown by statistical evidence, and the creation of an organization by which the emerging pattern of wants could be met.'[1] The experience of these first few years had, in fact, served to reinforce the natural characteristics of his personality so that what had been a spontaneous approach to the problems of the business became a belief in reason and method as a way of life worthy of deliberate cultivation. They were characteristics which were to stand the partnership in good stead, as on the occasion when he was able to foresee the effect of the discovery of the pneumatic tyre on the Brazilian rubber trade, with which the fortunes of the Booth Steamship Company were, of course, closely bound up. In particular, Booth's flair for building up a comprehensive picture on the basis of detailed information was to prove to be one of their major assets, although it sometimes provoked resentment in those of his associates whose temperament rebelled against what he himself termed his theoretic cast of mind, and who suspected him of collecting facts simply for collecting's sake.

You get hold of figures out of the endless array of statements you want, which do not represent the real facts, and then lecture me about things you really know but little about . . . [wrote his cousin and partner, Tom Fletcher, on one occasion]. Statistics and statements and tabular figures are all very well, but the live interests of the New York business consists in the constant contact with the consumer, and if all the energies of the office staff are to be concentrated in trying to put you who are in Europe in actual possession of every detail, twisted into every variety of figures, I think the result would surely tend to our having less and less business to tabulate and theorize about. . . . You also seem to consider clerks as abstract ideas or puppets to be taken from one place and put in another just as chessmen.

Nothing illustrates better the sweetness of Booth's disposition and the sincerity of his respect for others than the reply he returned to this angry outburst on the part of one who was his junior:

I have just received and read through once your letter of the 17th and I shall read it several times more. I think I need not tell you that nothing in it hurts me at all—nothing you ever write ever does, the credit being yours for that. Nor can I say that I am surprised for I was conscious enough of what I think you mainly complain—a disagreeable and lecturing tone in my letters lately. Oh me it is uncommonly hard to wield the pen rightly.

You will say 'then let it alone' but that could only result in suppressed discontent and still more dangerous misunderstandings. I take to heart all you say and admit that much of it is very true, and if after studying it over again and thinking it over, and looking at everything as much as I can from your point of view, I am able to back down still further, I shall be very glad to do so. I will only say today that I think you think that I mean to *interfere* far more than I have any idea of doing, for I certainly agree that it is an impossible task to attempt to manage the details of any business from across the Atlantic.

I wish it were possible for us to meet this year, for as you say an hour's talk would brush away all sorts of difficulties safely enough when letters are useless or worse. That is not the case with this last letter of yours nor in truth with your letters generally I must say—nor will it be the case with this one I hope— the main object of which is to tell you that I love you and trust you just as much as you could desire and that I beg you to accept all my disagreeableness in proof of this.

It was indeed the qualities of reason and humility with which this letter is infused which redeemed Booth's devotion to method and statistics and roused such feelings of devotion amongst those who worked for him. After a visit to New York in 1862 his brother reported of the clerk in the office that 'Faithful Keppler has fastened C's small photograph up on his desk in front of him so he is still present in the office in that shape'. Though he displayed no false modesty about assuming his position as 'the Chief', his relations with his subordinates were based on a 'frank self-assertion all round with as much good humour as possible', which was a tribute as much to himself as to those who worked for him. Booth was, on principle, a good employer, exacting in his requirements of those whom he employed, but generous in return in his care for those who served him well, treating them as subordinates yet with an unfailing and spontaneous regard for them as individuals. For instance, he expressed the opinion that to give presents in cash as a reward for meritorious service on the part of a ship's officers during an emergency would be an insult. 'We go on the plan of high pay and have stuck to it through bad times and good and shall continue to do so: and I am very anxious that the question of whether this or that service is in the bond, should not be considered an open one. I hope we may soon have the promotion which comes from an increasing fleet as that is the healthiest reward for zealous service.' Throughout his life he was keenly interested in problems of industrial relations and methods of conciliation, and himself introduced one of the earliest profit sharing schemes for the benefit of his staff.

There was, however, a great deal more to Booth's success than the discovery of a commercial trick-of-the-trade or the possession of purely personal attributes, for these were in fact an expression of principles which were of fundamental importance to him, and an integral part of his personality. Commercial integrity was to him a way of life: there could be no distinction between the moral principles to be applied to private affairs and commercial practice. To serve, and to receive just payment for services rendered was his purpose in being in business: money-making as the aim of life he would not countenance.

Tom's idea, and the practice also, adopted in America and perhaps always hitherto in our business, seems based on the idea that it is our object to get the better of the men we sell to [he protested to his brother in 1880]. To let them in for buying what if they knew what we knew they would not buy. I doubt if it succeeds even then; but it injures our business to act on this idea, whether it succeeds or not. It is not our interest to get the better of either the men we buy from or those we sell to—but to do the best we can for each, subject to a moderate remuneration for ourselves—and to give our chief attention to getting the utmost value out of the goods we deal in (1) by proper preparation and (2) by bringing the skins into use for the purposes they best fulfil.

Such service, honourably rendered, merited its due reward, and Booth never hesitated to enjoy the considerable fortune which eventually came his way, permitting his children all that pertained to the standard of living common amongst the upper-class circle in which they moved, and himself spending freely on such objects as seemed to him desirable, amongst which was, incidentally, the Inquiry. At the same time, he never forgot the Unitarian principle that the possession of wealth carried with it obligations as well as privileges. It is noteworthy that for himself he chose to live a life of the greatest simplicity: he never travelled first class until he was over seventy years of age, and then only because he thought he 'ought to do so'. His acceptance of his own prosperity was firmly based on the belief that in so far as he had been more fortunate than others, a responsibility for their welfare had been placed upon his shoulders. His interest in industrial relations was an expression of this 'general feeling that peace on earth and good-will are our business as well as God's'. He accepted as 'the ordinary rule of life which could not be altered' the fact that the rich must pay for the poor, the strong for the weak.[1] This was his answer to the critic of capitalism. A passionate individualist, both by temperament and conviction, his faith in free enterprise and his acceptance of the inequalities he believed to be inherent in human nature were justified in his eyes by this doctrine of the inescapability of the responsibilities of wealth and power. At the same time, his natural modesty never allowed him

[1] Booth, *Pauperism and the Endowment of Old Age*, Macmillan, 1892, p. 217.

to forget that 'life is a lottery',[1] and that it was thanks to no great virtue on his part that his own lot had lain in such pleasant places. His faith in individualism was never shaken: indeed, it might be argued that it was for this very reason that his commercial undertakings were so brilliantly successful. Though he came to accept the necessity for a certain measure of collective action, he never ceased to abhor Socialism and every other scheme for what he once defined to the Webbs as 'the substitution of a new set of consequences for the natural set of consequences following upon a man's action',[2] and was himself prepared to accept the full implications of his own hardy philosophy. 'If I choose a man and he cheats me, I am rightly served and to go crying for redress is to act like a child.'[3]

Thus described, Booth emerges as a typical and most attractive example of the merchant class of which he was a product and to whose tradition and philosophy he owed a lifelong loyalty. 'The important thing', he once wrote regarding the choice of a new partner, 'is that activity of mind and body which Americans call smartness combined with honourable character', and there is no doubt that he sought to achieve this ideal for himself. His financial success was soundly based on moral principles. He regarded the taking of reasonable risks as a necessary and stimulating feature of commercial life, but he steadfastly refused to make money out of 'the business of selling rum' to any peoples open to exploitation and looked askance at an acquaintance who got rich quickly by speculation in the cotton market. Though he had no scruples about working to secure a monopoly of the trade in skins following on the acquisition of the rights of the preparation of patent leather, he was meticulously careful that the firm should regard the power they thus secured as a public trust.

Our place is, and our object should be—to pay *as much* as we can and to sell *as cheap* as we can—not the reverse as it might seem—and to hold the balance as fairly and as steadily as may be between the sellers here and the buyers in America. It is also essential to the running of such a monopoly as we are attempting, that we should be perfectly open at this side with those who sell to us as to the prices we get for their goods which if we aim to get nothing but a commission is quite practicable. If we attempt secrecy, they suspect we are making a lot of money and seek outside for other buyers to set against us. If they don't look for other buyers they expect us to fix the prices fairly without bargaining and this is what we have to do oftener than not.

[1] 'Enumeration and Classification of Paupers, and State Pensions for the Aged', *Journal of the Royal Statistical Society*, 1891.
[2] Passfield.   [3] 'The Colony', 1876. See also below, pp. 33 et seq.

So far as his business was concerned, therefore, Booth was able to formulate quite early in his life the principles which served him, without modification, for the rest of his career. The weight of his responsibilities as a man of business was, in consequence, by no means burdensome to him. The discharge of his social duties as a citizen, on the other hand, involved him in endless doubts and difficulties. In dealing with these, his first inclination was to rely on the same principles which had served him so well in the business, in the somewhat naïve belief that the latter would prove equally successful in social as in commercial affairs. He had much to learn, but he learnt in such full measure that he was ultimately able to make the great contributions to the social sciences and to the social services with which his name has ever since been associated. If the nature of his achievement and the process by which he arrived at it are to be understood, it is apparent, therefore, that attention must be focused on his endeavours to play his part in coping with the wider social issues of his day rather than on the narrower compass of his business activities. It is to this aspect of his life and work that the rest of this volume is accordingly devoted. Nevertheless, although the story of his career as a merchant must in consequence be taken for granted, it is important to bear constantly in mind the fact that Booth always regarded himself as being essentially a man of business, and that in whatever he did he was profoundly influenced by his loyalty to the principles of the commercial community to which he belonged.

2

The Faith of a Liverpool Gentleman

CHARLES BOOTH returned to Liverpool from his first visit to New York in 1864. Nine years later he left for Switzerland in so low a state of mental and physical health that doubt was entertained as to whether he would ever be able to make a full recovery. This despite the consolidation of his position as a merchant during that period, and its crowning success in the shape of marriage to an eminently congenial and charming wife.

Apart from indulgence in consistent overwork, a habit practised by many men of his generation without apparent harm, there would seem at first sight to be no ready explanation for this extraordinary contradiction in the state of his fortunes. The intensity of his devotion to the business during this period by no means implied the exclusion from his life of all other interests. On the contrary, he carried over into his leisure time all, and more than all, of the sparkle and vitality with which he entered into his daily work. The story of his days, as told in Emily's letters to her brother Alfred, is filled with all the bric-à-brac of young Victorian manhood: indefatigable travel at home and abroad, an enthusiastic if somewhat amateur pursuit of drama and the arts, a comprehensive appreciation of the amenities and pleasures of middle-class society. A bit of a dandy, with an eye for style and an indifference to convention, he was an acceptable guest in any household, and a welcome addition to the ranks of the local merchant aristocracy. As time passed, he played an increasingly responsible part in the philanthropic activity for which the Unitarian community in Liverpool was then earning a just reputation. His characteristic enthusiasm for new ideas is discernible in the zest with which he became involved in each of the topical issues of the times as it came to the forefront of public attention. If the attitude in which he approached these various pursuits was marked to a then uncommon degree by businesslike common sense rather than by piety and sentiment, this was in no way remarkable, since it was strictly in accordance with the lead currently being given by the much-respected William Rathbone.[1]

The picture is an eminently agreeable one: here surely was urban living at its best. The impression is confirmed by the business letters to his brother; there is nothing in them to account for the complete breakdown in health which terminated this outwardly auspicious initiation into manhood. His prosperity might surely be taken to constitute demonstrable proof of the validity of the philosophy of life in which he had been nurtured: no cause can here be discerned for an inner conflict so acute as to lead eventually to complete physical collapse.

There in enigmatic obscurity the matter might have remained but for the survival of an alternative source of information in the shape of seven issues of the family magazine, 'The Colony',[2] which cover the years from 1866 to 1871, almost the whole of this phase of Booth's life. The magazine originated in a collective letter to the absent Alfred concocted on the occasion of Charles's twenty-fourth birthday. Edited by Charles, whose spelling incidentally was not always reliable— 'conscienciously' and 'batchellors' are less excusable in an editor than that common enemy 'diarrea'—its contents consisted of an assortment of literary and philosophical essays and poems, some of which were serious attempts to state a point of view, others being trifles written for fun. The title derived from the days when the family had first moved out to the comparative wilderness of the suburbs springing up round Princes Park: it still seemed appropriate to the compact little group of friends and relations which retained its identity in the midst of the bewildering mass of newcomers to the middle classes who now surrounded them.

This type of magazine was a commonplace of Victorian family life, but it is quickly apparent that 'The Colony' constituted much more than the glorified autograph album which such ventures frequently tended to become. Credit for this must certainly be attributed to Booth's influence. Its contributors were, it is true, a lively collection of young men and women. Nevertheless, it was clearly his spontaneous

---

[1] William Rathbone's *Social Duties, or The Introduction of Method into Muddle* (Macmillan), was published in 1869. (See also Simey, op. cit.)

[2] From which the quotations used in this chapter have been taken, except where otherwise stated.

interest in other people and their ideas which provoked them to such an unusually frank expression of their feelings. Moreover, his own inveterate need to clarify his thoughts by committing them to paper led him to use the magazine as a vehicle for the expression of ideas which he would otherwise have had no opportunity to record. The result is a peculiarly valuable source of information as to his own processes of thought and those of his companions which more than compensates for the lack of any other material. It throws a flood of light on this important period in his life, and renders comprehensible the otherwise inexplicable breakdown with which it terminated. Indeed, it is no exaggeration to say that the reading of these pages, intimate as leaves from a diary, is a revelation of what lay behind the outward façade of Victorian middle-class life at this period. The writers were, of course, young, and for that reason might be expected to write a trifle extravagantly about life in general and their elders in particular: there was every expectation that they would (as, in fact, most of them did) settle down in later years when the responsibilities of family and business weighed more heavily upon their shoulders. Nevertheless, there emerges from these poems and essays so acute a sense of the tremendous and inescapable issues with which their times confronted them that one is moved with pity for their youth and in-experience, and with admiration for the courage and sincerity with which they faced their difficulties.

It is at once evident that these young people were acutely aware of and responsive to the crucial nature of the situation in which they found themselves. Though they, and especially the women, were not educated in the modern sense of the word, they were intelligent and well read, and had, in addition, been reared in a tradition of independence of mind and spirit. Eyeing Liverpool thus equipped, they could not fail to be impressed by the all too evident gulf which had developed between ideal and reality in the society to which they belonged. The code of moral principles, based on self-sacrifice, to which their fathers stoutly and with some ostentation affirmed their loyalty, seemed to them to be patently at odds with the materialism of an individualist economy. In Liverpool even more than in most towns, the evident inadequacy of traditional benevolence in the face of the chronic want of the new class of poor constituted a challenge to the established order of life which it would have been impossible to evade even if the whole foundations of conventional morality had not been simultaneously subjected to attack by the great scientific discoveries of the day. As responsible young men and women, the Unitarians amongst whom Booth took his place on his return from New York were acutely conscious of all that these issues involved. They discussed them endlessly together, wholly in earnest even while they derived pleasure from the cut and thrust of argument, and Booth long afterwards recalled as amongst the best that life could offer these early 'discussions on beliefs and doctrines with . . . companions of like age, in which speech is very free, breaking loose from all authority, and the inmost thoughts find utterance and meet with sympathy even from those who most deeply disagree'.[1]

Of this little group Charles very quickly became the hero and the pacemaker, partly because of his natural high spirits and gaiety— 'What a fellow that Charley is!' was Emily's admiring cry—but also because, coming freshly to the scene, he was correspondingly more deeply responsive to what he observed. After being in New York, where he had immensely enjoyed the free-for-all in which every man was given the opportunity to make what he would, or could, of his own affairs, he was forcibly struck by the overriding influence of tradition on English life. Nothing could have been more alien to his own temperament. His brief experience had taught him to take things as they came; it was a philosophy which his habitual curiosity turned into an enthusiasm for every unusual idea or experience which the nineteenth century had to offer. Booth set out to explore this world or new ideas lightheartedly enough. The year or more which he had spent in America had done much to restore his spirits and he had returned to Liverpool in 1864 in a mood of considerable self-confidence. 'Knock all the pleasure you can out of existence and damn the expense', was his injuction to Alfred. 'Take my advice, keep up your spirits and lead a jolly life.' It seemed obvious to him that much of what he and his friends regarded as being amiss with the world might be attributed to the easy assumption that what had been must therefore continue to be. In so far as it referred to his own class in particular, this opinion was confirmed by his discovery towards the end of his first year at home that even he was not the swell he had supposed.

The proposal to extend the franchise to include a whole new class of working men, then very much the topic of the day, struck him as providing an obvious means of remedying the situation. As his close friend and cousin, Tom Fletcher, wrote in the first number of 'The Colony': 'The wish to extend the franchise is not from a worship of

---

[1] *Religious Influences* vii, p. 402.

the ideal working-man of Bright, but from a disbelief in the traditional intelligence of the upper classes so much lauded, and the feeling that as self-interest governs the state, it is but fair that all people should have a chance of taking care of their own.' Confident that so reasonable a point of view must be certain of support, Charles and his friends volunteered to help the Liberals to fight the forthcoming election in 'the Toxteths', two wards in the south end of the city which bore the reputation for being the rowdiest and the most corrupt in all Liverpool. His daily walk from his home on the edge of the Park to the ship-building yard had already familiarized him with the neighbourhood. This consisted of closely-packed courts and alleys, hurriedly run up earlier in the century by speculative builders to house the immigrant labour required for the building of the great new systems of docks and railways, and subsequently filled far beyond their intended capacity by the influx of migrant Irish during the hungry 'forties. There was in these areas literally no room for the civilizing influence of church or school: the Unitarians' own Domestic Mission had found accommodation there only because it dated from the years before the greatest influx had occurred.

Electioneering in such an area in 1865 proved an absorbing and exhausting experience, in the course of which Booth discovered for himself, in terms of living human beings, all that still has power to shock when encountered in the pages of the history books of a century later. His reaction was immediate and forthright. The personal contact with the poor as individuals and the first-hand knowledge he had gained of the struggle for existence which they called life, convinced him that poverty, of the quantity and quality he encountered in the Toxteths, was an evil for which no possible justification could be advanced. He had therefore no hesitation in condemning as hypocrisy and cant the explanations which sought to justify its continued existence put forward by the religious, and was shocked to discover that a community which prided itself on its social sensitivity should countenance such conditions as those endured by the mass of the poor. The fact that the party he supported was rejected by the very people who stood to benefit from the overthrow of the corrupt government of local Tory tradition, enhanced the startled apprehension with which he eyed the world about him.

As yet he was wholly unaware of the implications involved in his wholesale condemnation of poverty. The question as he saw it was primarily an ethical one—namely, that if the poverty of the new poor as he had himself observed it could not be justified, then the religious principles which held that it could were automatically brought into question. The twentieth century is so accustomed to having its customs and habits, beliefs and ideas, submitted to challenge and even to destruction, that it is difficult to comprehend the storm and stress aroused by the mere formulation of such a doubt. Booth and his companions had delighted in discussing the challenge of Darwin's theories to the religious beliefs in which they had been reared, provoked by the publication of the *Origin of Species* in 1859, but they were startled to discover that their own experience bore out this challenge and that the threat to established morality was a very real one. It was incredible to them that this should be so, and yet there seemed to be no alternative. Apprehensive as to the results of their daring, yet too deeply disturbed to abstain, they argued their dilemma with an outspokenness which shocked their elders, but which they claimed stood for an honest effort on the part of 'Young England' to face reality and arrive at an independent judgement.

Unable to forget the poverty that he had seen, yet hardly more able to bear the thought of it, Booth took refuge in an intellectual rebellion against authority and tradition in every shape or form. This led him to adopt an attitude of derisive flippancy towards all accepted customs or ideas. 'I was educated in an atmosphere of "Boyhoods of Great Men" and "Well Spent Hours", but these excellent precepts have not taken root with me', he announced in one issue of 'The Colony'. Elsewhere he devised charades in which he ridiculed the patronizing philanthropy of Lady Christian Consolation and the Reverend Ebenezer Fanatic, or wrote essays in which his mistrust of the 'professions' of middle-class society led him to an extravagantly amused condemnation of the entire fabric of what he dubbed 'the useless shell of an old world society'. Nevertheless, more sober contributions reveal that it was at this time that he first began to fumble his way towards that concept of a 'natural' law as opposed to the supernatural or divine, which was to act like a lodestar to his subsequent thinking: a series of short stories on the subject of ghosts and poltergeists reveal him to have been fascinated by the problem of accounting for the existence of the supernatural within the framework of a rational and scientific explanation of the universe. The façade of flippancy and irreverence clearly concealed a slowly maturing sense of the urgency and importance of the issues at stake, and of his own obligation to face the challenge which they presented.

Booth managed to maintain this uncertain state of mental equi-
librium throughout the following year or so, stifling his mounting
unease in a passionate devotion to the affairs of his firm. It is nevertheless significant that already he was beginning to suffer from the
recurrent bouts of minor ill-health which were to reach a climax in
his eventual breakdown in 1872. In 1868, however, matters came to a
sudden head, and his mood changed from a more or less cultivated
detachment to one of active aggression. There can be little doubt that
the change must be attributed to the fact that it was early in this year
that he first made the acquaintance of the young woman who was
eventually to become his wife.

Mary Macaulay came to Liverpool to visit her cousin, Laurencina
Potter, who had recently married the shipowner, Robert Holt. She
had already made Emily Booth's acquaintance on the occasion of that
marriage at which the bride's young sister, Beatrice, had also been
present. Sophisticated and intelligent, she was promptly admitted
to membership of 'the colony'. As an outstandingly charming
young woman of twenty years of age she was provoked to find
that Charles, the undeniably attractive bachelor whom she there
encountered, was so engrossed in his own affairs as to seem to
be wholly absorbed in business. A letter contributed by her to 'The
Colony' concludes with a spirited protest which may fairly be
assumed to have been directed primarily against its editor: 'You are
all running mad over business, and nobody enjoys himself, and I
can only say in conclusion that if I am asked here again I shall beg
to put off the visit till my hair turns grey and life ceases to be an
enjoyment.'

Charles, however, was by no means as preoccupied as his behaviour
led Mary to suppose. He expressed to Alfred his yearnings for the
companionship which would result from marriage with a woman who
shared his own views, and protested against the conventions of polite
society which made courtship so difficult for 'the man who finds it
impossible to love a girl before he knows her, and who reaches the
point of marriage slowly, with many misgivings'. His indecision was
well founded. Mary Macaulay was not only 'marvellously well-read
and well-informed, and an astonishingly vital person';[1] she was also,
as she was fond of reminding her children, completely different
from Charles both in temperament and because she represented a way
of life so utterly unlike that with which he was familiar. Her father

[1] William Rothenstein, *Men and Memories*, Faber & Faber, 1932, p. 131.

was a senior civil servant at Somerset House,[1] her mother a sister of that Richard Potter who is best known as the father of Beatrice Webb: she was herself a typical member of that new class of intellectuals which emerged out of the Clapham Sect and of which her uncle, Lord Macaulay, was one of the most distinguished. The contrast between the world of literature and public affairs to which she was accustomed, and that of industry and commerce which she encountered on her visit to Liverpool, could hardly have been greater. Of this she was well aware. Writing to 'The Colony' from 'Dullasever Villa' under the pseudonym of 'Frivolity', she was sharply critical of the lives led by middle-class women in Liverpool. Describing as narrow and hypo-critical their devotion to philanthropic work, she concluded:

Covered by the sense of charity and the fluff of flannel, what poisoned darts of gossip may not be innocently flung, what inanities uttered without exciting comment! As Blucher survives to posterity in his boots and Garibaldi will in his shirts, poor Dorcas lives in these societies for circulating gossip.

The freedom with which she expressed such heretical opinions must in itself have been enough to demonstrate that this vivacious and intelligent girl was utterly different from the young women commonly to be encountered in Unitarian circles. Therein, of course, lay the source of much of her charm, since Charles was then in the early stages of discovering in himself a deep dissatisfaction with the tradition in which he had been reared. Therein also lay the source of the vigour with which he now set about the solution of his problems. He was impressed by Mary's sophistication of mind and high intellectual standards, recognizing in her that attitude of mind—essentially critical, essentially reasonable, essentially open to the stimulus of new ideas—for which he had been longing. Although he had been critical of the society to which he belonged, he had never seriously challenged its basic assumptions, and Mary's attacks on them correspondingly disturbed and distressed him. His encounter with her provided both the stimulus and the example that made revolutionary changes in outlook possible.

The sense of guilt and shame with which he had been troubled

[1] Charles Z. Macaulay was Secretary to the Board of Health and Commissioner of Audit (Charles Booth, *Zachary Macaulay: an Appreciation.* Longmans Green & Co., 1934). An attractive picture of family life amongst the Macaulays is given in *The Life of Lord Macaulay,* in which Trevelyan recounts how, on his own marriage to Mary's aunt, he 'used at first to wonder who the extraordinary people could be with whom his wife and his brother-in-law appeared to have lived', because of the family habit of talking in familiar terms of characters from novels. (Longmans Green & Co., edition of 1881, p. 59.)

overflowed in a passion of resentment against both the poverty of the poor and the hypocrisy of those who countenanced it. All affectation of indifference was abruptly cast aside; his feelings now ran too deep for flippancy. Stimulated by the discovery that the doubts whose expression had so shocked those in authority were commonplace matters for discussion in the circles in which Mary moved, his approach to the problems of poverty took on an intensity which it had previously lacked. He began to look at the Liverpool of his daily life in the light of criteria whose validity she took for granted, but which were wholly foreign to his own tradition, for the first time turning on men and conditions that keen scrutiny which was eventually to provide the basis of his social researches. What he observed proved far from being acceptable to him. His previous attempts to display no more than the dispassionate interest of the rational man in the discovery of the natural laws which govern human behaviour was replaced by an indignant repudiation of the unnatural conditions under which some human beings were compelled to live.

I do not hold poverty as ever to be desired—and dependence certainly is not [he announced]. These fashionable qualities for the poor, which delight the soul of Lady Bountiful—humility, respect for those that God had put over them, and the desire to be content with that position to which they have been called—are far from being pleasing to me, and indeed suggest altogether too much the pauper.

Comparing and contrasting his own way of life with that of the crowded streets of the dockside of south Liverpool, he was miserably conscious that there often existed amongst those who were presumed to be his inferiors a brand of Christianity much more in keeping with 'the religion that is read each Sunday in our Churches' than anything ever achieved by his own class. The mixture of envy and regard with which he wrote of the poor was to become perhaps his most individual asset in his work as a social investigator:

They are so uncomplaining, so simple, and so dignified about their sorrows. My warehouseman came to me and said, 'We have trouble at home, sir, the boy died last night—it's the fourth boy we've lost and the girl is ailing now— there is nothing much to do sir, and I thought you'd perhaps allow me half a day to bury him.'
What a fuss we make about our losses by contrast—the house of mourning— the drawn-down blinds—the funeral—the subdued light—the subdued voices and the subdued footsteps of the undertakers carrying gloves—Who does not

know how we try not to hear that knocking—how the drawing-room door is carefully shut—and how we try to hide the sound by talking while that constrained shuffling and whispering passes down the stairs and through the hall.

With sick self-disgust, he realized how little justification there was for the easy assumption of superiority by his own kind, however sincerely they accepted the obligations of their power and prestige. There was inevitably such a want of reality about the so-called charity of the better off,

and about our daily lives altogether, while the lives of the poor are real enough, God knows. The continual contact with the realities of life which the hand to mouth classes experience, the absence of the baize covered doors and well stuffed cushions of existence—these bring with them a train of consequences good and evil, of which the evil only are readily recognized by us.

We see and exclaim against the brutality and indecency of their life—the callousness about death, the lotteries of the burial clubs; but there is something more which springs from this meeting with life as it is. They really feel of how little importance they and their sorrows are. They do not imagine themselves the centre figures in a scheme of providence where God is afflicting and chastening them for some mysterious purpose or other.

Had the existence of poverty been an isolated instance of a false alignment between principle and practice, he might have been able to write it off as a temporary symptom of great social and economic change, arousing interesting discussion and requiring prompt benevolence, rather than presenting a fundamental challenge to an age and a civilization. As religious teaching had been challenged by scientific theory, however, the problem of the existence of poverty in the midst of riches became entangled in the clash between science and religion. Booth was willing, indeed anxious, to believe in a Creator and a Divine Purpose, but look where he would, he could find no evidence of either. Without valid and compelling proof, it was impossible for him to rest content with a blind faith that poverty was divinely ordained. Yet if he denied the explanation that poverty resulted from the working of the 'will of God', then the only alternative was to attribute its existence to the greed of man. Slowly the implications of this conclusion became clear to him: it placed upon him as an individual a burden of personal responsibility for the welfare of his fellow men which was at once so weighty and so unwelcome that he shrank from its acceptance. With the best will in the world, how was it possible for him and others like him, to remedy this appalling situation? In what manner could they hope to discharge this fearful obligation? Wistfully he compared his own situation with that of the poor man, to whom the expression of concern for his fellow-men presented no difficulties, since the love of his neighbours could be interpreted without anguished searchings of the soul in terms of daily bread. Whereas to people like himself, the path of duty was far from clear.

To be generous in giving is almost impossible to us: for even if we admit that we are trustees only of wealth which we hold for the good of mankind, to give it away is a thing we should never think of doing. It would be a breach of the very trust on which we hold it, and as cowardly as the flight of old from the world into a monastery. Yet this which is possible every day to them, to go hungry or ill-clad that others may suffer less, is equally impossible to us, and would be merely adding the scourge of the anchorite to the seclusion of the hermit.

Deeply disturbed by this new concept of his own responsibilities and driven by the memory of the undeserved miseries he had witnessed, inaction became intolerable. Rightly or wrongly, he must make up his mind, and having done so, must at least attempt to put his conclusions to the test. Firmly he took his decision. It was, he concluded, transparently plain that science had destroyed traditional beliefs for ever; the problem of the existence of poverty could no longer be explained by the claim that it had been so ordained by the Almighty, but was to be attributed directly to the working of some 'natural' law whose nature it was the function of science to reveal. The important thing was, therefore, to accept Science and not oppose it, and to devote all one's energies to discovering its laws and living in obedience to them. Away with the belief that one man was rich and another poor because God decreed it, away with patronage and dependence, and instead, set every man free to make what he would of his natural endowments: 'Each for himself and God for us all' was Booth's merry quip, to which rather wryly he added, 'Or is it God for the strongest?'

The two years after he met Mary passed in a whirl of activity which was indicative of the urgency of his state of mind. As he saw it, there was nothing fundamentally wrong with the mass of the people; not for him, therefore, philanthropy in any shape or form which involved the patronage of the poor by the better-off, or their dependence on the charity of others. Instead he looked about him for ways and means by which the working classes might be led to assert their independence and to assume their fair share of responsibility for the management of their own affairs. His disillusionment with 'good works' ran deep, but it did not extend as yet to the world of party politics. The election of 1868 was the first since the extension of the franchise to working men in large numbers; this revived his interest in public affairs. The election promised to be of unusual local importance in that the majority of the newly enfranchised voters in Toxteth were Irish immigrants, whilst the main topic on which the election turned was the Irish land question. The subject of land ownership was one on which he held strong views, maintaining that though the ownership of capital was justifiable, the collection of ground rents by the owners of land was nothing short of bare-faced robbery. The supporters of the Radical cause worked extremely hard and scenes of unusually great excitement ensued. Booth had learnt his lesson in the 1865 election: 'judicious Tory Management' had won the day then, so why should not judicious Radical management win it this time? 'Charley has been organizing the Toxteth wards all this week and has got the machinery into good work', reported Alfred to their cousin, Tom Fletcher, now their partner in New York. Charles himself seems to have been too busy to write, eloquent evidence of how hard he was driving himself. Nevertheless, the result was mortifying in the extreme. 'We got badly beaten on Wednesday and have felt washed out ever since', wrote Alfred. 'Really it has been hard to do office work. . . . Charley is at the office now and then.'

Doggedly, Booth and his friends returned to the fray a year later when the municipal elections took place. It is significant of their mood of revolt that this time they cut adrift from the official party machine and set up a Toxteth Association on their own, with Francis Prange as candidate and a programme consisting wholly of local issues. Booth once more devoted himself to organization behind the scenes. However, although he worked extremely hard, and succeeded in introducing a commendable degree of law and order into what had previously been rowdy and corrupt proceedings, his party never came in sight of winning a seat. Nothing seemed able to shake the Liverpool working man's devotion to the 'beerocracy' which had for so long ruled him, and there must have been gall in the remark of *Porcupine*, the prickly weekly paper, that the election as a whole was lost by Liberal Booby-ism: the Liberals, the Editor declared, 'must cease this constant jabber about the great purity of their principles and practice what they preach'.[1] Booth's disillusionment with politics as a means to social improvement was complete: 'I, for one, can't stand their goings on, from Mr. Gladstone down to Robert Holt', he wrote a few years later. He never again permitted himself to become involved with party politics in any but the most tenuous manner.

The lesson was a sharp one, all the more so as it was reinforced by his experience in other fields. Booth had been for some time interested in the fresh life which was flowing into the trade union movement, about which he was particularly well informed because his cousin Henry Crompton played a leading part in union affairs.[2] The organization of men against masters was a concept he abhorred, but trade union tactics at that time were based on a dislike of strikes and a desire to collaborate with the employers in the improvement of the general standards of the working man, a policy which made an obvious appeal to Booth. Full of optimism as to the possibilities of the trade union movement, he became involved in a scheme for a Trades Hall designed to provide a common meeting place which would 'emancipate the members of trades' societies from the temptation and thraldom of the public house where they customarily met to the exclusion of the more intelligent and responsible members'.[3] Booth devoted much time and thought to its affairs, becoming a director, and greatly enjoying the contacts with the more responsible amongst the working men which the work involved. 'I like the men one gets amongst in this way', he wrote; 'they have a sort of charm about them, being much more simple-minded and unsophisticated than most of us.' Nevertheless, the scheme failed to secure sufficient backing from the unions and its sponsors had to be content with something much less ambitious, providing simply a news-room and reading-room where lectures and classes could be held. The endeavours made by Booth and others to secure trade union support for the settlement of disputes by arbitration and conciliation were similarly unsuccessful, and at

[1] *Porcupine*, 6 November 1869.

[2] There is reason to suppose that Henry Crompton was one of the 'eight Positivists and two Christian Socialists' who comprised the group of young intellectuals which attracted considerable attention in the 1860s by their efforts to act as interpreters of the trade union movement to the public (Sidney and Beatrice Webb, *History of Trade Unionism*. Longmans Green, 1894, p. 229). This is a matter for conjecture, but it is supported by the fact that when in 1869 the legal position of the unions was being hotly debated in and out of Parliament, William Rathbone was advised by Henry Crompton, who drafted a Bill giving legal protection to the unions against the embezzlement of their funds by their officials.

[3] *Porcupine*, 23 October 1869.

least one public meeting called to discuss the subject was forcibly broken up. As for the wider distribution of wealth, which he regarded as eminently within the sphere of the unions, no interest whatsoever was displayed in it by their members.

What Booth made of these experiences can only be surmised from the tone of regret for lost opportunities which may be detected in his writings forty years later. It had been, he recollected, a time of hopeful expectation so far as working men were concerned, but 'they had left it to the philanthropist or the Government official to secure those reforms which should have been their prime concern'.[1] Shortly afterwards, he inaugurated a 'sort of risk fund' for his employees which was partly a bonus scheme and partly an insurance against sickness, but so far as the improvement of standards in general were concerned the whole episode must have been deeply disappointing to him. His own conclusion was that the working man's real inferiority, and the source of that dependence upon the better-off which was the cause of a whole flood of social difficulty, lay in his lack of education. It was because of ignorance that the electors of Toxteth had failed to comprehend where their true interest lay in regard to the 'beerocracy': it was ignorance which suggested to trade unionists that the only improvement that mattered was an improvement in wages. In arguing thus, he was in step with the general trend of public opinion: it was commonly agreed that the working classes should be better educated although there was keen conflict as to how this should be done.

Booth had no difficulty in deciding where he stood in the matter. To him, the spirit of dissension which set the protagonists of the various denominations at each other's throats whenever education was discussed was both a deplorable and an illogical denial of their common Christianity. He accordingly joined Chamberlain's Birmingham Education League and threw himself with zest into supporting its campaign for a universal secular system of education.

In view of the forthcoming legislation on the subject, he and his friends determined to test public opinion by launching a pilot scheme in Liverpool. His own preference would have been for one which was entirely secular, but support for such a principle 'appeared so far off, and the need of action so urgent' that he reluctantly agreed to a compromise. The proposal as it eventually emerged was eminently reasonable. It was estimated—one cannot but believe that the calculation was made by Booth—that there were at least 25,000 children in

[1] *Industrial Unrest and Trade Union Policy*, Macmillan, 1913, p. 1.

Liverpool who were neither at school nor at work. The aim of the proposed society was to persuade and if necessary to assist parents to send their children to school by making a grant to the schools concerned of 5s. per child per annum. In this last clause lay the dynamite. Many were prepared to agree that for the children of the poor to be educated was a good thing, but the scheme deliberately gave no heed to the fact that the existing schools were all denominational and that consequently the subscriptions of the Protestant supporter might well be spent on the education of the Catholic child and *vice versa*.

Moved by the 'vigour and earnestness' of the young organizers, William Rathbone consented to support the scheme at a public meeting held in May 1869, organized by Booth and his friends jointly. Booth did all he could to ensure that the subject should be discussed on a reasonable plane, and that the meeting should be as representative as possible. In spite of these precautions, sectarian controversy quickly broke out, 'an element of personal vituperation was introduced', and the temperature of the meeting grew so warm that the police had to be called in to remove at least one fanatical opponent from the room. The newspapers next day devoted full-page articles to the reporting of the 'miserable exhibition of sectarian jealousy', and a spirited correspondence ensued, in the course of which the scheme was variously denounced as impractical, absurd, and a barefaced insult to the Reformed Church.[1]

Booth declared himself satisfied that though he and his friends had 'failed to commend the proposed society to those from whom they had anticipated a possibility of opposition', at least they had secured a firm declaration of principle which was of great value as an indication of public feeling. Nevertheless, he was sufficiently disturbed by the reactions of the public to devote a great deal of time to the work of the Birmingham League, serving on the local committee and actively assisting in the organization of meetings. The campaign reached its climax in 1870 when what the press described as a 'noble meeting' brought between three and four thousand people to the Theatre Royal: at this, interruptions took place on such a scale that 'the newspapers had to report it with the largest possible allowance of interjectional parentheses'.[2] Any hopes which Booth may still have entertained of securing support for the progressive point of view were finally dashed by the passing of Forster's compromise Education Act later in the same

---

[1] *Liverpool Daily Courier*, 27 May 1869.   [2] *Porcupine*, 5 February 1870.

year. His disappointment must have been rendered doubly painful by reason of the fact that the failure to secure a full, free and non-sectarian educational system was generally attributed to the unyielding opposition of the nonconformists.

These were sobering experiences. To most of Booth's generation, the discouraging reception accorded to their well-intentioned efforts at reform was enough to reduce their ardour to something like conformity. In his immediate circle, his sister Emily, for example, took refuge in charitable activities which ultimately led to her election as one of the first of Liverpool's women Guardians of the Poor, whilst his brother Alfred retreated into dreams of country life. Not so Charles, to whom the opposition he had encountered simply served to clarify and confirm his original conviction that the 'headlong race after wealth' and the degeneracy of life amongst the poorest classes were wrong and must be abolished. Though he was forced to admit that 'our modern civilization has brought evils with it which almost counterbalance its advantages, and which repression seems powerless to check', he refused to abandon his belief that the human race was nevertheless capable of improvement and tended, however slowly, towards perfection.

There was, however, one respect in which his opinions had undergone drastic revision, with results which were to be of lasting duration. This concerned the means whereby the change of heart in both masters and men on which he was convinced that all chance of improvement depended, might be brought about. For whereas he had originally assumed that reason alone would be enough to carry conviction, his experiences had forced him to conclude that the only way in which the thoughts and habits of the people in general could be influenced for the better was by means of an organized religious influence. He was convinced that the old morality was powerless to provide this, in view of the altered circumstances of contemporary times, even though people might be more religious than ever before. The fashionable 'undogmatic Christianity' was equally inadequate because it dared not say to Science: 'Teach us to live—experience is our only law.' Nor, passionate individualist though he was, did he believe that the current faith in the freedom of the individual was likely to prove any more effective because 'in experience we find every day how many things must be controlled by a strenuous exertion of public opinion'. What was required, he concluded, was a means of influencing public opinion for good, which would be based upon a knowledge of science and the natural laws governing human behaviour. In other words, hope for progress in the future rested on an understanding of sociology, which he defined as comprising the study of 'the relations between the individual man and the rest of humanity'.

In reaching these conclusions, Booth's thinking reflected the strong influence exerted on his mind by Positivism, to which he had been introduced by his cousins and lifelong friends, Albert and Henry Crompton.[1] The Cromptons had been early converts to the Positivist faith as taught in England in the early 'sixties by Comte's disciple and translator, Henry Congreve. In common with many others of the more 'rational' amongst the young intellectuals of the day, they were attracted by the hope that Comtism provided a formula which would unite explanations of the working of natural laws in terms of human behaviour with principles of moral action and social endeavour. Their whole-hearted enthusiasm would in itself have been enough to provoke Booth's interest: its attraction was greatly fortified by the relevance of Comte's teaching to the situation in which he found himself, and his contributions to 'The Colony' reveal the extent to which he was influenced by it. 'Science must lay down afresh the laws of life', he declared in an outspoken essay in 1870. 'I feel assured that the principles of Positivism will lead us on till we find the true solution of the problem of government. We are on the right road, let us advance with a good heart.'

This was all very well in theory but provided little comfort in practice. He spoke with deep feeling of the perplexity which beset those whose minds were loosened from the old ways of thinking but who were unprepared for the new and could find no rest in it. He himself was not prepared to accept 'the exact scheme of a Utopia' put forward by Comte. Wistfully he looked about him for some escape from this irrevocable choice, some 'temporary religion which would accept science and assist progress and satisfy the heart of man for a time at least'. One thing only seemed beyond dispute. Tormented as he was by a profound dissatisfaction with himself and his kind, the

---

[1] The Cromptons were outstanding supporters of the Positivist movement. Henry was a leading member of the group which met in London: Albert, when he came to Liverpool in 1872 to act as cashier to Philip Holt, immediately set about the formation of a Positivist Club, with which Booth was strongly urged to identify himself. Their sister Emily married the Dr. Beesly who translated one of the four volumes of Comte's work, and played a prominent part in the international socialist movement: she and her husband became intimate friends of the Booths after they moved to London. Albert's daughter was one of the first children to be 'presented' for acceptance by the Church of Humanity in England.

self-assurance of the 'Toxteth set'[1] could no longer be endured. Their calm assumption that Unitarianism could and did provide an answer to all the attacks of science on religion stood in his eyes for nothing less than complacent blindness to the painful realities with which their lives were encompassed. This quarrel with the faith of his fathers involved, to one of his loving and loyal temperament, a fearful rejection. Nevertheless the implacable paradox of widespread poverty in the midst of unparalleled prosperity goaded him on towards the destruction of his old faith and the acceptance of the new one, Positivism.

No compromise is possible [was his final despairing conclusion]. It must be war to destruction between the old thought and the new, until the mind of man, freed from the trammels of this last form, as it has been of each previous form of theology, turns aside from destruction and finds new food for its faculties of worship in the recognised order around us and the great example of progress in order presented by the Human Race.

His family stood aghast before the growing isolation which separated them from the beloved Charley of earlier days. Alfred piously expressed the hope that 'with wide differences of opinion on the deepest subjects, we shall not gravitate to bitterness amongst ourselves', but the differences between Charles and the companions of his youth went too deep to be bridged by good intentions, however sincere. He was often lonely and depressed, exhausted by his long agony of indecision in face of the moral dilemma with which he was confronted, and cut to the heart by the realization that he was no longer at one with those whose affection and esteem he so highly valued. His only escape lay in an almost frenzied absorption in 'The Fight', as he called the duel between the ships of the Booth Line and those of the rival firm of R. Singlehurst and Company which was then reaching its climax. Finally, in June 1870 he decided to withdraw from all public work and 'merely stand by and look on'. Significantly enough he reached this conclusion only a matter of months after his enthusiasm for the campaign for secular education had been quenched by the introduction of what he regarded as Forster's disappointing Education Bill. Depression, he wrote, 'now takes effect at once in my head and so prevents me from working altogether, being past fighting against'.

It was in these circumstances that he found his thoughts turning to Mary Macaulay with an ever-increasing urgency. He had hesitated to

---

[1] So called by reason of their membership of the Ancient Chapel of Toxteth.

propose to her in the first instance because of his keen awareness of the differences between her way of looking at life and his own. The accumulating sense of strain between himself and his family circle now made him realize that it was the very fact that she was so utterly unlike anything in his familiar setting which made her companionship essential to him. For the same reason she on her side was at first led to ask her father to convey to him her rejection of his entreaties. Driven by the desperation of his need for her companionship, Booth flatly refused to accept his dismissal, insisting on being allowed to plead his cause in person. This he did with a vehemence and a disregard for convention which moved Mr. Macaulay to deem him 'a most extraordinary young man'. So determined a courtship could not be denied, and after the briefest of engagements, the marriage took place at Teignmouth on 29 April 1871.

More Macaulay than Potter, and much influenced by her father, Mary had developed a speculative and philosophical bent of mind. The intrusion of the keenly sharpened doubts of the young Charles Booth into this somewhat detached intellectualism proved singularly disturbing. She was now repaid in her own coin, for she had herself played a decisive part in the stimulation of Booth's fervent questioning. Her mind was 'startled out of its previous position', to use her own phrase. The barrage of criticism to which her every conviction was submitted by him, threatened the very foundation of her existence. Half eagerly, half reluctantly, she found herself accompanying her husband on his search for a new creed to fit the circumstances of contemporary living.[1] Small wonder that the first few years of their married life should have been far from easy, all the more so because of the increasing uncongeniality of the background against which they were lived. The forebodings which had provoked such hesitations in both of them before their final decision to marry, proved amply justified. 'I could almost pray that if life holds another such epoch of suffering as I have gone through, in store for me among its dark secrets, I may be taken away before its time draws near', Mary Booth assured

---

[1] More particularly, and possibly for the first time, she became acutely aware of the difficulties that her sex could not surmount in that particular conjunction of time and place. For though Booth never openly supported the emancipation movement, it is evident that he sought from his wife the companionship of an equal rather than the acquiesence of Victorian tradition. His ideal for her, as for himself, comprised an active participation in the world's affairs: she must translate her ambition to *be* good into one to *do* good, and there is more than a suggestion that it was at his instigation that, after her marriage, she contemplated the preparation for publication of the literary studies which she had previously pursued in the discreet anonymity then expected of her sex.

her husband in later years. It was upon this experience of difficulties shared and eventually overcome that the ultimate and enviable security of Booth's marriage was founded, but at the time it often seemed to them as if there were no solid ground beneath their feet.

When she married him, Mary found Charles in bad shape. 'Over-work at his business, leisure hours too closely filled with political and philanthropic work, scanty time for meals and scanty hours of sleep', she wrote, 'had made inroads into the strength which he had thought unlimited, and he had become subject to a distressing form of nervous indigestion. He could take but little food unless he rested before and after, and for a long time he met the difficulty characteristically, by going without.'[1] Little could be done to mend matters for some time, however. Plans for a holiday were delayed by the birth of their first child early in 1873. This was a girl, whom they named Antonia in one of those gestures of sentiment which the twentieth century finds hard to comprehend, but in which Mrs. Booth participated in a way which bears testimony to her remarkable endowment of mingled sense and sensibility. Finally, however, and with some difficulty, occasioned by the absence of anybody competent to take his place, Booth managed to withdraw from active participation in the business, and in December 1873 set out for Switzerland with his wife and child, with no other object in life than the restoration of his health and spirits.

[1] *Memoir*, p. 10.

3

The Problem of All Problems

THE Swiss holiday was not a success. It was perhaps hardly to be expected that the answer to what Mary Booth aptly described as the 'problem of all problems' would be found in the solitude to which Booth retreated with his wife and baby daughter. This was—

a quiet and secluded house at a little distance from Bex in the Canton de Vaud. Here his eldest boy was born and here he sat out in the shady wooden galleries surrounding the house, or took tiny walks in the woods which rose behind it. Charles Booth loved nature, and the spot which he had chosen for his retreat was very beautiful. In the spring and early summer the glories of the wild flowers and blossom delighted him, and in the rich autumn he revelled in the glow of colour, brilliant and delicate beyond any that he had known under our English skies.[1]

Had Booth's breakdown resulted simply from the exhaustion of his physical energies by the efforts of the previous years, here surely was the ideal setting in which to recuperate. Yet his wife tells us that:

The experiment of an entire rest did not bring the hoped for improvement. He continued to suffer and to lose weight. There was much disappointment, and for a time he thought that recovery was unlikely. . . . He could read but little. Any mental exertion brought on the miseries of his disorder. His wife used to hide from his sight the books and periodicals sent out from home, to save him from being tantalized by what he was unable to enjoy. But though he could not grapple with the thoughts of others, he could lie and brood, and during the time he spent abroad the ideas which he developed later grew and took shape.[2]

Booth's normal practice when faced with an intractable situation would have been to assemble on paper all the available facts on which a comprehensive view could be based, but no trace of any such

[1] *Memoir*, p. 11.   [2] Ibid.

memorandum has come to light. The process of repair therefore cannot be discussed. Nevertheless it did in fact take place in some measure, and such information as is available points to the conclusion that credit for this should be attributed to Mary's influence. His breakdown ran its course in her company, their association becoming steadily more intimate as the months went by. Eventually, they returned to London in the summer of 1875, well enough but with a sense of failure at the time so far as the restoration of Charles's health was concerned. 'Though ever more delighted with each other's company, they felt it would not do, and that they must face the world again', one of their daughters recollects, but it is significant that the world to which they returned did not comprise life in Liverpool. Booth 'was still an invalid, and no thought could be entertained of his undertaking a regular office life. He took a house in London, and, though still unequal to mixing in society generally he saw a good deal in an informal way, and as he could bear it, of his friends and cousins, and those of his wife.'[1]

Mary Booth now came into her own. The hopes she had begun to entertain of publishing her literary studies having apparently suffered some rebuff, she wholly abandoned the difficult enterprise of seeking to make an independent reputation for herself. With all the impulsiveness of her 'Highland' temperament, she determined in future to devote her considerable talents to a meticulous performance of her wifely duties which later provoked her cousin, Beatrice Potter, to somewhat acid comment. The health and welfare of her 'chicks' became her prime concern. She filled the house with visitors and was assiduous in fulfilling her social obligations, though she ruefully confessed to a regret that she derived so little pleasure from the company of her own kind. A sparkling conversationalist with a phenomenal memory, she was domesticated more from a sense of duty than from inclination, except when a sudden half-exasperated awareness of the differences between her own household and those of other less intellectually-minded women swept her into a gale of enthusiasm for the latest thing in Morris wallpapers or for wholesale reconstruction of the domestic premises.

To Charles and Mary, their new sense of companionship was doubly precious after the trials and tribulations of the early years of their marriage. Mary was one of the very few who were able to overcome the characteristic 'Booth reserve' which Charles regretted in himself; he could think of no better way of expressing his happiness when his

[1] *Memoir*, p. 12.

son George joined the firm than by saying, 'It is like having your mother in the business'. Though Booth never ceased to deplore her withdrawal from independent creative work, his wife's decision placed talents at his disposal without which he would have been ill-equipped to undertake the work he thenceforth proceeded to accomplish. It was in letters to her that he 'thought aloud' about the problems of the business which took him away from home. It was in 'argufying' with her that he felt his way towards the conception of the Inquiry, arguments so vigorous as to stop short only of the point at which they could no longer speak to each other, though it is recorded that their efforts to study J. S. Mill's books together were defeated by the heat of their discussion. She read widely on his behalf. She acted as universal critic and amanuensis, making herself responsible for everything he wrote, whether it concerned his business interests or those of his leisure, correcting and re-writing with the confidence and freedom of one who shared his innermost thoughts. So far as the business was concerned, her children believed that she knew more about it than his partners.

Perhaps most important of all at the moment of their return to London, she was able, as a daughter of the Macaulay family, to introduce her husband to a circle of friends and relations whose way of thinking even more than their way of living was characterized by precisely those attributes whose absence from Liverpool society Booth had so deeply regretted. The Macaulays were integral parts of that remarkable network of eminent Victorian families which constituted the new intellectual aristocracy of the towns, in direct contrast to that of the traditional rural society.[1] In such company, Booth rediscovered the liberalism of mind and interest, and the combination of intellectual detachment with social responsibility, which had first attracted him to his wife; this constituted for both of them the mental climate in which they were at their greatest ease. Here he encountered a keen discussion of the contemporary conflict between science and religion and its implications in terms of nineteenth-century life which, though it provided no solution for his personal doubts, did more to soothe his mental anxieties and to stimulate his thoughts than all the confident assertions of the Unitarianism of his upbringing. Gradually the

[1] N. G. Annan, 'The Intellectual Aristocracy', in *Studies in Social History*, Ed. J. H. Plumb. Longmans, 1955. His wife's *Memoir* tells us that 'in later years he was wont to say that his intimacy with his father-in-law in particular had a greater effect on him than any other single influence in his life' (p. 9).

spriteliness of mind with which he had once participated in the 'challenging debates' of his young manhood came back to him, and for the first time in years his spirits began to revive. 'We are having a perfect round of dissipation, dining out every night', he told his brother Alfred in 1875. 'I suppose it won't last very long and it is better it should not, but in the meantime it does not seem to suit us amiss. Mary has been uncommonly well.'

Amongst those of his wife's relations with whom Booth now became acquainted were her cousins, the daughters of Richard Potter, one of whom years later described his first visit at this time to her father's house.

I recall with some amusement the impression made on a girl's mind by this interesting new relative [Beatrice Webb wrote in her autobiography]. Nearing forty years of age, tall, abnormally thin, garments hanging as if on pegs, the complexion of a consumptive girl, and the slight stoop of the sedentary worker, a prominent aquiline nose, with moustache and pointed beard barely hiding a noticeable Adam's apple, the whole countenance dominated by a finely-moulded brow and large, observant grey eyes, Charles Booth was an attractive but distinctly queer figure of a man. One quaint sight stays in my mind: Cousin Charlie sitting through the family meals, 'like patience on a monument smiling at'—other people eating, whilst, as a concession to good manners he occasionally picked at a potato with his fork or nibbled a dry biscuit. Fascinating was his unselfconscious manner and eager curiosity to know what you thought and why you thought it; what you knew and how you had learnt it. And there was the additional interest of trying to place this strange individual in the general scheme of things. No longer young, he had neither failed nor succeeded in life, and one was left in doubt whether the striking unconventionality betokened an initiating brain or a futile eccentricity. Observed by a stranger, he might have passed for a self-educated idealistic compositor or engineering draughtsman; or as the wayward member of an aristocratic family of the Auberon Herbert type; or as a university professor; or, clean shaven and with the appropriate collar, as an ascetic priest, Roman or Anglican; with another change of attire, he would have 'made up' as an artist in the Quartier Latin. The one vocation which seemed ruled out, alike by his appearance and by his idealistic temperament, was that of a great captain of industry pushing his way by sheer will-power and methodical industry, hardened and sharpened by an independent attitude towards other people's intentions and views—except as circumstances which had to be wisely handled —into new countries, new processes and new business connexions. And yet this kind of adventurous and, as it turned out, successful profit-making enterprise proved to be his destiny, bringing in its train the personal power and free initiative due to a large income generously spent.[1]

[1] *My Apprenticeship*, p. 219.

Charles Booth had left Liverpool a sick and possibly a dying man; he returned to London with no plans for the future, no hopes, nor even any clear idea as to what he had made of life so far or would like to make of it in the future. Only one thing was certain, that for financial reasons if for no other he must make up his mind as to what he proposed to do with the rest of his life. The business had settled into a routine during his absence from which only routine profits resulted, and Booth's share in these, diminished by reason of his inactivity, was inadequate to maintain his growing family. He had, however, reached the lowest point in his fortunes, and it was not long before they began to improve. A year later, though still far from well, and still uncertain as to the future, he went with his wife to Brazil in one of the Company's ships, nominally for the purpose of testing the possibility of effecting economies in fuel consumption by reducing the speed of cargo steamers. The results he obtained were inconclusive, but the trip proved immensely successful in that the renewal of the life he loved brought about an astonishing rebound of his spirits. It became obvious for the first time that he had passed a turning point in his career. Restored to something approaching his old vitality, he set out for Liverpool to meet his partners and discuss with them both his own future and that of the business. New ideas speedily emerged. So far as the firm was concerned, he was convinced that the only hope lay in abandoning the policy of opportunism then current, in favour of a consolidation of its interests on a long-term basis. He was even more clear that the foundations of his personal life had to be completely relaid. The sojourn in Switzerland and the decision to set up house in London had confirmed the existence of a gulf between himself and his old circle of friends and relations. Whatever else remained uncertain, the conviction had overwhelmed his mind beyond any possibility of argument that Liverpool stood for a way of life on which he had for ever turned his back. His wife wholeheartedly supported him, urging him in their daily exchange of letters[1] to adopt a policy of complete honesty with his partners in regard to the question of his return there.

You must not seek to explain your not doing so by ill-health or give the slightest encouragement to the idea that good health would mean Liverpool. What you really will have to do, heaven only knows—you and I must talk it over but as far as the world goes, we have chosen our part, and our part is

---

[1] This series, which is one of the main sources on which this book is based, starts in 1876.

London. I am sure that this is the right line, but I want much to see you, and talk things over.

His partners yielded to his insistence on both scores, and returning to London, he set up what was euphemistically known as 'the London office' in a single room with a desk for his own use. Circumstances allowed him little opportunity to regret his decision. After an active year spent familiarizing himself with the English end of the trade in skins, difficulties on the American side reached such a climax in 1878 with the illness of Tom Fletcher, as to demand the presence in New York of another of the partners. Charles undertook to go, in a mood of considerable diffidence: what had he to show for the past that he should now presume to pick up the threads of the disordered skein of the business and set it right?

In the event, his visit lasted for seven months, and proved decisive. After a miserable Atlantic crossing during which he strove in vain to keep seasickness at bay with alternate draughts of champagne and the novels of Trollope, Booth arrived in New York to find Fletcher and his family dangerously ill with scarlet fever, and the affairs of the leather factory, whose fortunes were bound up with their own, chaotic almost beyond recovery. Characteristically, the very seriousness of the situation served to stimulate Booth to quite remarkable achievements. Holding a watching brief over the New York office and the unfortunate Fletchers, he spent most of his time at the glove factory at Gloversville, personally and completely reorganizing its administration, including its accounting system. The story is one which it would be a delight to tell at length by means of quotations from his letters. Set against the early colonial background of the Mohawk Valley, the account of his firm but friendly handling of the one-time owner of the factory and his staff, the details of the problems he encountered and the means he devised for overcoming them, is intrinsically of the greatest interest, quite apart from the fact that these letters constitute a revealing record of the growth in his stature and the development of his character which accompanied this experience.

Working from dawn till midnight every day of the week, returning for a private session in the office on Sunday mornings, he lived frugally on bread and butter, vegetables and cider, depriving himself of all such luxuries as the indulgence of his fancy for white waistcoats for which the laundry charged as much as 25 cents. He had to learn the trade as he went along: this included not only the buying of skins and the making of gloves, but the development of the invention of patent leather which the firm was then pioneering. The nominal head of affairs having collapsed, Booth assumed responsibility for the entire administration of the business, supervising the work and the workers in the factory, 'playing besom' with courage and conviction, re-organizing every last detail of its administration. His only relaxation lay in occasional drives about the lovely countryside, and talking till far into the night with Kuttner, a German who became one of his most trusted employees and who shared his own keen interest in working-class movements, 'though not in Karl Marks (—is that the name?—) and the ultra set'. And at some point in every day he released the 'congealed chatter of his soul' by writing down at length in letters to his wife all that he had seen and done, letters which bear witness to his natural talent for observation, and which sparkle with his in-credulous delight in the fact that this should really be his own self about which he wrote. The experience was certainly one he enjoyed; but it was also sobering, for he was acutely conscious of the importance of succeeding. Failure would bring consequences for himself and for other members of the partnership too serious to be lightly contem-plated. Though he grasped his nettles bravely, he could never blot out from his heart the harshness of some of the decisions which necessity forced upon him. The duty of making clear to the bankrupt owner of the factory the seriousness of his position was exceedingly difficult for him, but he faced it boldly and humanely. 'When I came home and had my supper', he told his wife, 'I felt so badly for Kent's misery at it and conscious how hard I had had to be, that I put on my coat and went to his house and told him so.'

The lead which he assumed in the family business from this time onward brought with it a heavy burden of responsibility, and for the next few years he knew little leisure, even his Continental trips taking the form of 'skin hunts' in pursuit of new sources of supply. He had much to learn; as he remarked himself, his efforts to cope with the various interests of the firm made him feel 'like a conjuror spinning plates'. Some years passed before his policy began to justify itself financially, and it almost seemed at one point as if the London house would have to be given up as being beyond his means. Eventually, however, his work began to bear fruit, and on returning to New York two years later in 1880 he was surprised to find himself received with a new respect. 'I am a little taken aback at my own importance and *awfully afraid* of making some mess with my hasty tongue and stupid thick head,' he confided to his wife, adding that his new role of senior partner and successful man cost him extra dollars in hospitality and tips, but this he regarded as wise expenditure. Though he made it lightheartedly, the comment is a revealing one which demonstrates the extent to which he had achieved maturity under the stress and strain of the preceding years. He himself remarked on the fact to his wife: 'It is astonishing how much older I feel than when I crossed the Atlantic two years ago—and I am—and for once I believe it is mostly gain.'

The years of his misery of indecision and self-disparagement were now finally behind him. Though his estimation of his own worth remained a singularly modest one throughout his life, it was never again to sink to the dangerously low level which had threatened his very existence during what his wife referred to as 'the gritty period'. It is clear that in the few years after his return from Switzerland he had come to terms with himself, accepting his strengths and his weaknesses for what they were, and resolving quite simply to make the best of life with such gifts as were at his disposal, without allowing his questioning intellect to hamstring his sense of purpose. 'I got an attack of depression with the last of the [sea] sickness', he wrote whilst crossing to New York in 1880, 'but thrust off both together, and am now blessed with a heart brave enough, and see my life before me as a smiling land over which I can surely make my way till I come to that river we know of —and not as a prickly wilderness through which man can neither walk nor see.' Beatrice Webb's description of the Booths at this date merits quotation:

The last six weeks spent in London, with friends and sisters. The Booths' house dark and airless, but the inmates exceedingly charming and lovable. Mary, really a remarkable woman, with an unusual power of expression, and a well-trained and cultivated mind. She makes one feel, in spite of her appreciative and almost flattering attitude, 'a very ignoramus'. To me there is a slight narrowness in her literary judgements; they are too correct, too resting on authority? Hardly the result of original thought? Perhaps it is this very orderliness of mind and deference to authority which makes her so attractive as a woman; for, added to this culture and polish of the intellect, there is a deep vein of emotion, of almost passionate feeling.

Charlie Booth has a stronger and clearer reason, with a singular absence of bias and prejudice. It is difficult to discover the presence of any vice or even weakness in him. Conscience, reason and dutiful affection, are his great qualities; other characteristics are not observable by the ordinary friend. He interests me as a man who has his nature completely under control; who has passed through a period of terrible illness and weakness, and who has risen out of it, uncynical, vigorous and energetic in mind, and without egotism. Many delightful conversations I had with these two charming cousins, generally acting as a listening third to their discussions.[1]

In what lay the secret of this remarkable achievement of peace within himself was a subject Booth never discussed. His manifest success as a merchant, and the genuine pleasure he derived from the conduct of the business, must obviously have contributed to it; it seems reasonable to suppose that, as in the case of many of his contemporaries, he found ease for his hurt mind in the pursuit of the practical affairs of useful living. One gets the impression that his experiences in Gloversville brought him back into contact with a reality which restored his sense of perspective and enabled him to escape from his previous mood of intense absorption in the problem of the meaning of life. In so doing, he had come to realize that so far as he at least was concerned, the eternal mysteries must remain unsolved. It is significant that it was at this point that he finally repudiated his tentative support of the Positivist faith and that his wife also abandoned the search for a new creed, returning to the fold of the Anglican Church, from which she had strayed in her endeavour to accompany her husband in his pursuit of truth. Though he never lost his intense interest in every form of religious belief, and in fact became more rather than less convinced of the importance of its influence on human progress, from now onwards he was able to rest content with that philosophy of 'reverent unbelief'—to use a phrase of his own—which sustained him until his death.

There is no doubt that he was increasingly happy. Though business affairs were troublesome, they provided him with endless variety of interest, involving constant meetings with new people, constant journeys to new places. He divided his time between the London and Liverpool offices, and paid an annual visit to the New York connexions. Domestically he much enjoyed his status as a householder and the head of an increasing family, and his wife's letters to him are full of the detail of the lives of their children. To the tenancy of the London house Booth was now able to add that of a country home, and the hunt was already on for a congenial 'place' which was to lead to the discovery of Gracedieu Manor in Leicestershire in 1886. The choice was a revealing one. Socially, the locality was deplorable. The

[1] *My Apprenticeship*, p. 221.

population constituted one of the old-established mining communities of the Midlands, originally stocked by Irish immigrants but now half-derelict, with a decayed and dissipated appearance which deeply impressed the Booth children on their first arrival. Uncared for and unlovely, its people excluded from the tidy society of rural Leicestershire, this had been one of the last areas where common land had been enclosed. For that reason, Gracedieu had no rich neighbours, no 'society', no squirearchy. The house itself was in need of extensive repair, a comfortable enough stucco mansion to which Pugin had added a wing but otherwise undistinguished except for a reflected beauty derived from the deep woods in which it was embedded. Though an odd choice judged by the standards of the society in which they moved, Gracedieu met the Booths' needs exactly. Here Booth could find the peace and solitude so necessary as a counter to the intensity with which he lived his days: here his wife could escape from the exhausting obligations of polite society which were a necessary part of the role she had chosen to play. To all this he loved to escape during the hard years of work on the Inquiry. Later, 'Satur-Monday' parties of friends and relations became a regular feature of his life, and social contacts were established with neighbouring landowners from which resulted joint 'shoots' for the benefit of his sons and guests, in which, incidentally, he never participated himself. Nor did he play any part in the affairs of the local church, his unorthodox views having to be explained to successive incumbents, though his wife became a regular communicant.

Freed at last from the cramping preoccupations of the years of mental and physical ill-health through which he had passed, and of the financial anxieties which had accompanied them, Booth was once more able to take a practical interest in the problems of the world about him.[1] The moment was peculiarly opportune. As a merchant, he had necessarily been all too familiar with the mood of depression which, throughout the 1870s, had shaken the security of the urban middle classes for the first time. The experience was a common one, but Liverpool had been particularly badly hit: a large number of merchants had failed to meet their commitments, unemployment had extended into the white collar classes, and the reports of those whose business took them into the poorest parts of the city had revealed the existence

[1] Though his health steadily mended, Booth was never again to be a robust man. 'I seem to be settling down into vegetarianism', he wrote in 1881. 'I have had no meat to speak of for six months and am much better for the new diet.'

of an apparently chronic poverty on a horrifying scale.[1] It was a situation which was matched in every large city, not least in London. A variety of causes and cures for this alarming state of affairs was canvassed, but there was fairly general agreement that the clue to the whole situation lay in what Carlyle comprehensively called the 'Condition of the People' problem. The middle classes took the poverty of the mass of the people very much to heart, regarding it as both a threat to their own security and a reproach to their good intentions. But what to do about it? Moving as he did between Liverpool and London, where he habitually encountered those who were pre-eminent figures in the field of social reform and practical philanthropy, Booth could not fail to be impressed by the conflict of principle and practice to which the situation gave rise.

It was a time which offered a good deal of interest [Mary Booth records]. People's minds were very full of the various problems connected with the position of the poor, and opinions the most diverse were expressed, remedies of the most contradictory nature were proposed. The works of Ruskin, the labours of Miss Octavia Hill, the principles and practice of the C.O.S., all contributed to this upheaval of thought and feeling. The simple, warm-hearted, and thoughtless benevolence of former ages was held up to reprobation. Those who desired to help the poor were exhorted not to give money, still less food and raiment, but to give themselves, their time and brains. They were not so much to try to relieve hunger and cold, as to raise a flag and establish a standard; but what flag, what standard was it to be?[2]

His energies now fully restored and his appetite whetted by the mounting seriousness of the situation, all Booth's old interest in social questions rapidly revived; insisting that copies of *The Times* be regularly sent to him on his American visits, he assured his wife of his passionate interest in public affairs. It was, as Herbert Spencer remarked, a period when everybody was very much in earnest about something and Booth took full advantage of the opportunities which came his way of meeting people in every walk of life who cherished ideas on the subject of the cause and cure of poverty.

He made acquaintance with many of those who were engaged in attempts of all sorts to ameliorate the life of the people, whether by actual work and experience among them, as in the case of Miss Octavia Hill and the Barnetts,

[1] Simey, op. cit., Chapter VII.
[2] *Memoir*, p. 13.

or by seeking in the study an intellectual basis for an improved state of things. Foremost among these came the exponents of the various sections of opinion among the Socialists, and at Toynbee Hall and Oxford House were many who combined practical work with research into the causes of the evils which oppressed those among whom they laboured.

He had talks with Mr. Hyndman of the Social Democratic Federation, attended the meetings of that body, listening eagerly to addresses, and on one occasion giving one himself on the best principles of land ownership. He was heard most courteously, but a certain amazement showed itself and grew as his quiet voice advanced points of view so widely different from those usually taken before that audience.

Among his friends at this time were several working men of Socialist opinions, and two of these were invited to spend three evenings at his house for a sort of symposium; they expounding the advantages of their system, whilst Booth himself and his friend and cousin, Alfred Cripps, suggested difficulties. These talks were prolonged for many hours on each occasion, and were of the most friendly character throughout.[1]

However, though this interest in social problems was a revival of his earlier enthusiasm, nothing better demonstrated the dramatic change which had come over Booth's whole cast of thought than the attitude he now adopted towards them. Starting from the assumption which he had always cherished as to his own responsibility and that of others like him towards the poor, his concern had become the wholly practical one of discovering ways and means of expressing this obligation, leaving altogether out of account the ethical question of why one man should be rich and another poor. Consequently, though he was still deeply interested in all the 'movements' of the day, his interest focused on the practical possibilities of whatever proposal they embodied. Moreover, his success in the handling of the firm's affairs had fortified his loyalty to the individualism in which he had been brought up. Like many of his contemporaries in the world of industry and commerce, he found himself disturbed by the 'slow but continuous retreat of individualist forces before the annual increments of Socialistic legislation and administration'[2] which marked the period. The letters which he exchanged with his wife when he was in America reveal the concern aroused in their minds by what they regarded as grave errors of judgement on the part of Gladstone; any limitation on the freedom

---

[1] *Memoir*, p. 15. Mary Booth elsewhere described this gathering as consisting of her husband's 'set of intelligent and enlightened unwashed friends who discussed positivism and social dynamics in the dining-room'.

[2] *My Apprenticeship*, p. 184.

of the individual was anathema to Booth.[1] His views on social problems were, in consequence, governed by a firm determination to justify as well as improve the existing state of affairs, rather than to introduce radical alterations in the structure of society.

This strictly realistic approach permitted full scope for his characteristic flair for grasping the essentials of a situation as a whole. As a businessman, his practical decisions were invariably founded on a careful and comprehensive review of the facts of the situation under consideration. What more natural than that he should apply the same method to the problem of poverty? The consequence was inevitable: Booth quickly realized that all too many of the various proposals for dealing with the poor had been prepared without regard to the facts. From this it was but a short step to the suspicion, which gradually became a conviction, that the basic information was lacking and that no one really knew the truth about how the poor lived. Who were 'the people of England'? How did they really live? What did they really want? Did they want what was good, and if so, how was it to be given to them? To such questions no one could give him any satisfactory answer. As he was to put it later, the lives of the poor

lay hidden from view behind a curtain on which were painted terrible pictures: starving children, suffering women, overworked men; horrors of drunkenness and vice, monsters and demons of inhumanity; giants of disease and despair. Did these pictures truly represent what lay behind, or did they bear to the facts a relation similar to that which the pictures outside a booth at some country fair bear to the performance or show within?[2]

At what point Booth determined to undertake the task of attempting to answer these questions himself is not known. Years later he declared that he owed his original inspiration to Canon Barnett, and a letter written by Mary Booth in 1878 certainly bears this out. In it she describes a visit to the Barnetts in Whitechapel in the course of which she had a 'most interesting long talk with Mr. Barnett about work and waiting and enthusiasm', the burden of which concerned the respective merits of immediate if uninformed social action as against 'holding your hand till you were quite sure'. One of Booth's own letters reveals

[1] Booth's dislike of socialism was to come to a head in his disapproval of Fabianism; his condemnation of it was so sharp that it is still remembered by his children. But the origins of his strong opinions lay far back in his life, and his attitude to socialism was fundamentally the same in 1884 as it had been years before, and as it came to be in later years.

[2] *Poverty* i, p. 172.

that by the following year he had already developed the habit of exploring the East End:

I have been studying the ways of the people this evening having supped at a Coffee palace and then gone to the nearest music hall to hear the Jolly Nash, &c. The coffee palace was next to a mission hall with a door through, but is not the one you aided to inaugurate. It is however bedizened with texts and when I add that the victuals provided are inferior to those to be had at the secular establishments I have been to at Liverpool and elsewhere, you have a clincher. Good food might excuse the texts, but the texts do not excuse bad food. However, I did not do so badly after all and must admit that nothing could equal the atrocity of the beer at the Music hall where there were no texts. Oh, for the delicious lager of other lands. Now I have chattered nonsense enough and will read a chapter of *Persuasion* and then with calmed mind proceed to bed.[1]

However, dearly though he delighted in such voyages of discovery, Booth was well aware of the deficiencies of this method of securing information, if only because his own love of 'statements' naturally turned his thoughts to the reduction of facts to figures. Too many people had already sought to introduce an element of reality into the discussion of social problems by making personal visits to the slums, and, startled and shocked by what they there encountered, had rushed to relieve their feelings by telling the world of their experiences. Of these, *The Bitter Cry of Outcast London*, published in 1883, was the outstanding example. This pamphlet originated in a sober enough endeavour on the part of the London Congregational Union to discover which districts were most suitable for missionary work,[2] but its revelations profoundly shocked public opinion. Issue after issue was promptly sold out, and in every large city similar 'commissions of inquiry' were appointed to report on conditions in the local slums.[3] Booth regarded all of this with increasing doubt and distaste.[4] His

[1] An equally interesting letter written during his visit to America describes a visit to a religious revival meeting at Ocean Grove in terms which clearly anticipate similar descriptions included in the Religious Influences Series (*Memoir*, p. 60).

[2] J. A. R. Pimlott, *Toynbee Hall*, Dent, 1935, p. 25.

[3] Booth cannot have avoided reading a pamphlet entitled *Squalid Liverpool*, which told a story no less dramatic than that recounted in the London prototype: its impact on local public opinion was equally profound. See Simey, op. cit., pp. 99ff.

[4] Booth welcomed some of the effects that were being made to bridge the gulf between rich and poor in the East End of London, especially the founding in 1884 of Toynbee Hall, and, later in the same year, of Oxford House, inspired by his friend, Octavia Hill.

determination to undertake investigations on his own behalf has in fact been attributed by some of his later colleagues to the effect on him of reading *The Bitter Cry*, though no evidence in support of this claim has been discovered. He was prepared to accept the motives of those who conducted such investigations without criticism: on the other hand he believed the impression their writings conveyed to be wholly erroneous and potentially dangerous. Certainly some of 'the people' lived in conditions which could not be tolerated by any decent society, but was it therefore justifiable to condemn the way of life of the entire working class? Judging by his own experience, the mass of the people who lived in what were dubbed 'the slums' were by no means all wretched and unhappy and in need of succour.

What alternative method of describing and appraising the social landscape was there? In that day and generation there could be only one reply: the application of the scientific method. Booth's final rejection of Comtism had in no way affected his enthusiasm for science, which in him as in so many of his contemporaries, amounted to 'an almost fanatical faith'.[1] This current of opinion had, of course, been flowing for many years, and Booth was by no means alone in resolving that 'the most hopeful form of social service was the craft of a social investigator'.[2] Many people were conscious of the need for accurate information of the kind that he had decided to seek and some experiments in the 'scientific' investigation of social problems had already been made. These had, however, all been somewhat tentative and restricted,[3] and the problem of their elaboration and extension so as to make it possible to produce reliable accounts of the 'working classes', let alone of society as a whole, had defied solution. This was obviously a problem after Booth's own heart. His experiences in Liverpool had cured him of any desire to play the philanthropist; he had abandoned philosophy and theology as being beyond his powers. But the preparation of statements, the translation of facts into figures, the collection and analysis of information relating to a given situation,

[1] *My Apprenticeship*, p. 130. 'In these latter days of deep disillusionment', Beatrice Webb wrote in her autobiography in 1926, 'it is hard to understand the naïve belief of the most original and vigorous minds of the 'seventies and 'eighties that it was by science, and by science alone, that all human misery would be ultimately swept away.'

[2] Ibid., p. 150.

[3] There was, for instance, the inquiry into the educational attainments of the children employed in his stocking factory, conducted by A. J. Mundella, Member of Parliament for Sheffield. Booth appears to have heard of this when Mundella visited Liverpool to speak in support of the Birmingham Education League campaign (W. H. G. Armytage, *A. J. Mundella*, Ernest Benn, 1951, p. 56).

were accomplishments of which he could claim to be a past master. It was, therefore, to the practical implications of the application of scientific method to social problems that he increasingly devoted his attention. Precisely how, he asked himself, were the inquiries he envisaged to be carried out and what difficulties would be encountered?

The publication in 1883 of the Reports based on the Census of 1881 suggested a possible line of development. It seemed to Booth probable that examination of these would enable him to discover whether the 'Condition of the People' question could be reduced in some degree at least to the precise language of arithmetic, and so to refute what he regarded as exaggerated statements as to the situation of the poor. It is significant that at this stage his purpose was not, as it later became, simply to collect facts about the existing situation but also to attempt the more elusive task of estimating the extent to which conditions had been influenced by the social and industrial changes introduced during the nineteenth century. The task proved to be a laborious one, involving extensive calculations. To accomplish it he sought the assistance of Jesse Argyle, a member of his office staff, who continued to serve as secretary to each of his succeeding investigations. As the work progressed, he was, however, disappointed to discover that not only was it impossible to find the information he sought in the pages of the Census Reports, but also that such statistics as they did contain were often singularly unsatisfactory. He discussed these deficiencies with characteristic frankness in a Paper which he set about preparing for presentation to the Royal Statistical Society.[1] In this he bluntly declared that official census statistics seemed to him to be often meaningless. Some were, he alleged, the result of an accident or defect of enumeration: he condemned the 'want of fixity of principle or method as between succeeding censuses' and he deplored the enormous total of false information deduced from the Census Tables by a trusting public.

Booth was confident that his criticisms of the way in which the Registrar-General's department did its work could be justified, though he was under no illusions as to the 'amount of soreness' to which they would probably give rise, but he was also well aware of the fact that his Paper shed little light on the problem of the condition of the people. The Census having failed him, he would have to devise an alternative means of securing accurate information, and an entry in Beatrice

[1] 'Occupations of the People of the United Kingdom, 1801-81.' *Journal of the Royal Statistical Society*, 1886. Booth had joined the Society in 1885.

Potter's diary for August 1885 reveals them to have been deeply absorbed in discussion of this problem.

> Delightful two days with the Booths, and C. and I long walk among Pines and Spanish Chestnuts. Discussed the possibilities of social diagnosis. He, working away with clerk on the Mansion House Enquiry into unemployed —and other work of statistical sort. Plenty of workers engaged in examination of facts collected by others—personal investigation required. Pall Mall have started this—but in the worst possible way—shallow and sensational.[1]

Meanwhile, the gathering force of the social unrest which marked the whole decade of the 1880s reached such a pitch as to provoke general alarm. The winter of 1885 brought renewed distress amongst the poor, and out of a welter of talk 'the unemployed' emerged as a bogy of horrifying dimensions. In the mind of the public, supposition and surmise turned to fear before the outbreaks of violence on the part of the masses: the rush to contribute to successive Mansion House Funds owed its inspiration to panic rather than pity. In the face of the ensuing confusion, Booth's long consideration of the problem of poverty crystallized out into what has since become the classic analysis of the situation and of the logical conclusions which had to be drawn from it:

> It is the sense of helplessness that tries everyone; the wage earners, as I have said, are helpless to regulate or obtain the value of their work; the manufacturer or dealer can only work within the limits of competition—the rich are helpless to relieve want without stimulating its sources—the legislature is helpless because the limits of successful interference by change of law are closely circumscribed. From the helpless feelings spring socialistic theories, passionate suggestions of ignorance, setting at naught the nature of man and neglecting all the fundamental facts of human existence.
>
> To relieve this sense of helplessness, the problems of human life must be better stated. The *a priori* reasoning of political economy, orthodox and unorthodox alike, fails from want of reality. At its base are a series of assumptions very imperfectly connected with the observed facts of life. We need to begin with a true picture of the modern industrial organism, the interchange of service, the exercise of faculty, the demands and satisfaction of desire.[2]

Late that autumn fuel was added to the bonfire of public opinion by

[1] Passfield. Of the Mansion House Enquiry, to which this entry refers, no more is known. The 'other statistical work' was presumably the preparation of the paper based on the Census Report referred to above, which Booth presented to the Statistical Society the following May, whilst the 'shallow and sensational' investigation sponsored by the *Pall Mall Gazette* was that conducted by W. T. Stead into the traffic in women which had just been published under the title of *The Maiden Tribute of Modern Babylon*.

[2] First Paper, p. 376.

the publication of the results of an inquiry conducted by the Social Democratic Federation under the inspiration of F. D. Hyndman. This inquiry was directed towards 'the condition of the people in the working-class districts of London, in order to determine how large a proportion of the wage-earners were receiving as their weekly remuneration an amount of payment insufficient, under the conditions in which they lived, to keep themselves in proper physical health for the work they had to do . . .'.[1] The Federation's claim that their investigations showed as many as 25 per cent. of the population to be living in conditions of extreme poverty provoked considerable dissension, and those who conducted it were widely denounced as 'deliberate falsifiers of facts and exaggerators of the poverty of the mass of the people', to quote Hyndman's own account. The *Pall Mall Gazette* sprang to the Federation's defence, publishing in successive issues the results of their own house-by-house scrutiny of the inhabitants of certain supposedly typical streets. Shortly afterwards, rioting again broke out in the West End, and it was commonly rumoured that the unemployed had been incited to these extremities by Hyndman in person.

Provoked beyond bearing by what he was convinced was sensationalism of the cheapest and most reprehensible order on the part of the socialist movement, Booth determined upon action. What he believed to be illfounded and exaggerated claims could no longer be allowed to pass unchallenged. Characteristically, he first called on Hyndman in order to be able to tell him in person what he thought of his actions, and what steps he himself proposed to take in order to disprove the results of the Federation's survey.

One day [Hyndman wrote in his autobiography] Mr. Charles Booth, then quite unknown to me, came to our house with a letter of introduction from Greenwood, who was editing the *St. James Gazette*. Mr. Booth was very frank. He told me plainly that in his opinion we had grossly overstated the case. He admitted there was great poverty in the metropolis among the workers, but he maintained that to say that there were not fewer than twenty-five per cent. who existed below the line of reasonable subsistence was to make a statement which could not possibly be substantiated over the whole area. I knew how thoroughly we had done our work—I think I may claim for myself that I have never yet been shown to be wrong in my statistics, even when handling them alone, while here I had the help of capable friends—and I at once said I was quite sure that the more thorough any examination might be the more completely would

---

[1] F. D. Hyndman, *Record of an Adventurous Life*, Macmillan, 1911, p. 331.

our figures and statements generally be verified. Mr. Booth, who, by the way, is a Conservative, again assured me that he himself intended to make, at his own expense, an elaborate inquiry into the condition of the workers of London: the wages they received and the amount of sustenance they could obtain for the money remuneration they were paid, he being quite certain he would prove us to be wrong. I welcomed this as a very useful thing to do, and congratulated Mr. Booth upon his public-spirited attempt to establish the truth beyond all question by putting the real facts and the deductions from them in such a manner and on such a scale as to carry conviction to all.

This inquiry was . . . entered upon, as I say, with the idea on Mr. Booth's part that we had very considerably exaggerated the proportion of the working people who lived below the line of decent subsistence, Mr. Booth even going as far as to denounce me in a quiet way for putting such erroneous, and as he then termed them 'incendiary' statements before the people.[1]

Within a month of this meeting Booth had summoned to his aid such friends as he deemed likely to be interested in his project for an intensive inquiry into the life and labour of the people of London.

[1] *Record of an Adventurous Life*, p. 331. Though no precise date is attached to Hyndman's account, there seems little doubt that this interview took place in February 1886. Beatrice Potter was also moved to protest, writing a letter to the Editor of the *Pall Mall Gazette* in the same month (18.2.86), which was published under the title of 'A Lady's View of the Unemployed of the East'. This was her first appearance in print.

4

The Craft of an Investigator

IT is tantalizing in the extreme that a man who habitually expressed his thoughts on paper should have left so little record of his major achievement in life as did Booth. Such clues to the process whereby he arrived at the principles and practice of his chosen craft of social investigator as are scattered throughout the mass of papers, pamphlets and books which resulted from his activities consist of no more than incidental references to the subject. Other sources are no less unhelpful. His letters to his wife contain almost no mention of the Inquiry, presumably because when he was engaged about its business he was necessarily within easy reach of her, whilst when he was abroad, his attention was concentrated on the affairs which had taken him there. Few of his contemporaries seem to have thought their conversations with him worthy of record; one can only suppose that his essentially businesslike point of view was something of an anomaly in the society of such thinkers, administrators and reformers as he encountered. This sense of difference was, of course, intensified by his natural detachment and reserve: his outward air of mild eccentricity was deceptively unintellectual.

The one exception to this generalization was that of Beatrice Potter, his wife's cousin, who seems to have discerned the essential quality of the man from the moment of their first acquaintance.[1] Her autobiography contains frequent references to both Charles and Mary Booth, which are doubly valuable because she was herself associated with the early stages of the implementation of Booth's hopes and plans. This association was the outcome of a friendship which dated from the days of the Booths' return from Switzerland. Beatrice had discovered in their unusual attitude to life and its problems an antidote to the personal

[1] See above, p. 55.

difficulties which beset her when, as a young woman of exceptional
intelligence, she found herself launched upon conventional society.
She was then, recorded Mary Booth in 1879, 'as odd as ever she can
be but a good sort of girl. She is dreadfully bothered with the
"weltschmerz"; the uselessness of life, etc., etc., and fancies that no one
ever went through the like before. I sympathized and comforted as
well as I could.' In the years that followed, Beatrice had been an eager
party to the constant 'argufying' about social problems which went on
between Charles and Mary, at first as a silent listener, but gradually
intervening with characteristic comments of her own as her wide
reading gave her confidence. Though she was much younger than they
were, her interests were closely similar to theirs, and it is significant
that by 1882 she too had arrived at the conclusion that her main
interest in life lay in the analysis of social problems rather than in
practical philanthopy.[1]

The comments in her diary throw a revealing light on the relationship which existed between Charles and Mary Booth, and make plain
the fact that their outward conformity with convention concealed an
enviable similarity of interest and parity of esteem. 'The visit to the
Booths has recovered my spirits', reads one entry.

The beautiful old place, filled to overflowing with happiness and youth,
checked my egotistical suffering. The Booths' home life at 'Gracedieu' is
perfect. Mary says her life is one continual sunshine. Charlie has the three sides
of his existence complete—profession, home, intellectual interest. His business
he says is the most important of the three—but I expect he underrates the
constant happiness of satisfied affection.[2]

Beatrice declared that she derived from the Booths' example much
of the inspiration which, after some years of doubt and indecision,
eventually led her to reject the prospect of marriage as offered to her by
Joseph Chamberlain.[3] Having thus come to the conclusion that she
must abandon the 'feminine' possibilities of her life and absorb herself
in a stern intellectual discipline, it was therefore only to be expected
that she should turn to them for advice and help in carrying into effect

[1] *My Apprenticeship*, p. 50. Beatrice had, in fact, tried the 'religion of science' in her
'six years of irresponsible girlhood' from 1876 to 1882, and had found it wanting. Ibid.
p. 92.

[2] Passfield.

[3] The story of her relationship with Chamberlain is a revealing one, but it is only
relevant here in that its outcome led her to devote herself to intellectual pursuits. The
episode was finally terminated by Chamberlain's unexpected marriage to an American
bride in 1888.

her intention. 'They and their family are the bright spot in my life', she wrote in her diary, 'a continual source of strength—an everlasting, up-springing interest'; in their company she sought relief from the 'agony of strong but useless feeling' through which she subsequently had to pass.[1]

It was in these circumstances that Beatrice Potter came to be associated with Booth at the moment when he was approaching the stage at which discussion of his theories had to yield to their translation into practice. Inevitably she found herself caught up in his enthusiasm and her career as his 'industrious apprentice'[2] may be said to date from this moment. She had everything to learn, and her responsibility for the care of her father severely restricted the extent to which she was able to participate in the execution of the Inquiry. Nevertheless, the recurrent entries in her diary suggest that Booth found in this intellectually mature young woman a stimulating and receptive audience for his ideas: her youth and sex dictated that she should be his lieutenant, whilst her intellectual ability constituted her his equal, a perfect combination in an apprentice. One would give much to know the extent to which the brilliant discussion of the principles and practice of social investigation given in her account of these years in her life owed its inspiration to conversations with Charles and Mary. It can be no coincidence that they reflect the contents of the letters written to her by Booth at the start of his investigations, letters which, incidentally, constitute the only written record of his principles.[3] Certainly the intensity of the interest which her own account reveals her as having focused upon the subject of the investigation of social problems, must have given great encouragement to Booth in the initial stages of his venture, and it is perhaps not too much to suggest that it may indeed have served as a decisive influence in bringing his plans to fruition. Emotionally exhausted as she then was, she, for her part, found in his characteristically altruistic devotion to the work in hand an inspiration to the subordination of self which must have been of inestimable assistance to her at this difficult period in her life.

That this friendship should have been brought about was entirely due to the love and understanding of Mary Booth. The precise nature of her contribution to her husband's undertaking is difficult to define, but its importance cannot be over-emphasized. Like Beatrice, Mary also sought, and in large measure found, a means of resolving her personal problems in her association with the Inquiry. Outwardly she chose to

[1] Passfield.   [2] See below, p. 102.   [3] See below, pp. 82 et seq.

maintain a façade of dutiful tolerance of activities on the part of her husband which polite society assumed she could not like; the fact that she actually participated in them remained for long a family secret. She did her utmost to keep hidden the fact that her husband submitted every page of the manuscript to her almost as he wrote it and that her disapproval was accepted by him as reason enough for changing or abandoning any doubtful passage. Perhaps even his staff never realized the extent to which he encouraged her to correct and even to re-write such portions of their work as she saw fit: 'they must never know' was her strict injunction to her husband. She firmly resisted every attempt to draw her into public discussion of the Inquiry, and expressed annoyance that a certain Macaulay sweep of the pen rendered those sentences which she herself had inserted into the manuscript irresistibly attractive to reviewers for purposes of quotation.[1] Nevertheless, she proved to be an active and fertile contributor to the conception and gestation of the whole great scheme, her wide cultural background and critical approach providing an essential frame of reference for the narrower specialisms of her husband and cousin.

It is a tribute to the genuineness of Booth's indifference to convention that it was on the basis of the sympathy and support of these two women that he should have contemplated the launching of so considerable an undertaking. In fact, such hopes as he had originally entertained of securing the assistance of other interested people were quickly dispelled. His original intention had been to constitute a Board of Statistical Research to which his plans could be submitted and for this purpose a meeting of those likely to be interested was called in March 1886. The response was discouraging. 'Charlie plods on with a moderate amount of success', Mary Booth reported to her cousin, 'but was yesterday rather depressed because nobody except himself turned up at the Friday meeting, when his proposals and general scheme of work and aims were to be commented on.' None the less, Booth remained undefeated by this lack of enthusiasm; as his wife once remarked, his optimism in regard to the extent to which other people

---

[1] One is indeed tempted to attribute to her the more caustic and highly coloured of those passages in the Inquiry whose tone seemed to those who knew him to be oddly inconsistent with Booth's character. More than one reviewer commented on the unsuspected idealism which led him to conclude the Final Volume with the much quoted reference to Blake's 'Jerusalem' (*Final*, p. 216). The sentence was in fact the work of Mary Booth who insisted throughout successive sets of proofs that it must end with an exclamation mark. On receiving the parcel containing the published volume, she at once looked at the last page where she discovered to her extreme annoyance that the exclamation mark had again, and this time irretrievably, been omitted.

would respond to what he regarded as 'reasonable expectations' was so unquenchable as to amount at times to a fault. He was, however, extremely busy with the firm's affairs, and another month passed in which the only visible progress was the recruitment to the 'board' of Maurice, the younger son of the publisher, Kegan Paul.[1] Eventually, in April, a second attempt was made to get together the little group of potential investigators, this time with better success, for on the 17th of the month a meeting took place which may be regarded as the official birthday of the Inquiry. Once again, the only record was that made by Beatrice in her diary:

April 17th. Charles Booth's first meeting of the 'Board of Statistical Research' at his city office.

Present: C. Booth, Maurice Paul, Benjamin Jones (Secretary to the Working Men's Co-operative Society), Radley (Secretary to a trade Society) and myself.

Object of the Committee to get a fair picture of the whole of London society—the 4,000,000! by district and by employment, the two methods to be based on Census returns. We passed C. Booth's elaborated and detailed plan of the work; and a short abstract of it for general purposes.

At present C. Booth is the sole worker in this gigantic undertaking.[2]

After this single if epoch-making appearance, the Board of Statistical Research rapidly faded from the scene. Incidental references suggest that Booth did not abandon hope of its active support for some months; he was encouraged by the fact that Alfred Cripps, one of Beatrice's several brothers-in-law, accepted an invitation to join, but it is significant that of the original band, Beatrice Potter's is the only name to appear in the final list of contributors to the first volume of the Inquiry. Possibly Booth had been over-optimistic as to the staying power of his volunteers: equally possibly he may have failed to foresee the difficulties which the process of decision by committee would present to one used, as he was, to making up his own mind for himself. For their part, the members of the Board may well have been taken aback

[1] Maurice Paul was at that time combining the study of medicine with active voluntary work as an auxiliary to Octavia Hill's rent-collectors, of whom Beatrice Potter was one, and his personal experience of how the poor lived (he actually lived in lodgings 'on the job' for a time), must have made him a welcome addition to the manpower of the proposed Inquiry.

[2] Passfield. This quotation from the typed copy of the diary deposited in the British Library of Political and Economic Science at the London School of Economics and Political Science differs slightly from the version given in *My Apprenticeship* (p. 287). In her autobiography Mrs. Webb replaced the numeral 4,000,000, by the phrase '. . . that is—of the four miles!'

by the scheme to which Booth proposed they should commit themselves. On further reflection, there must have appeared a great deal to be said for the point of view so forcibly expressed by Canon Barnett when he lunched with Beatrice Potter the day after this first meeting: 'He threw cold water on CB's scheme', runs the entry in her diary. 'Said it was impossible to get the information required and was evidently sceptical of the value of the facts when there.'[1] However this may be, his wife tells us that 'he soon made up his mind that it was not possible in this manner to obtain sufficient cohesion in the work . . . if it was to be accomplished at all, it must be, like an executive department of the State, by a number of helpers to be gradually trained to the work, and acting under the orders of a chief'.[2]

There can have been singularly little indication at the time of the magnitude of the final achievement which was eventually to result from so inauspicious a start. Mary Booth spent the summer with the children at Gracedieu Manor, which she and her husband were then trying out as a possible halfway home between London and Liverpool. Her days passed in a long round of difficulties with workmen, leaking roofs and quarrelsome domestics. She was too much alone with the children, her husband finding himself compelled to undertake more rather than less responsibility for the firm's affairs, contrary to his expectations. The weather was often wet and cold, the neighbourhood as yet strange and unfriendly. 'I suffer from a strange access of moral blight', she wrote to Beatrice, who was also in the country and also struggling with a heavy burden of domestic responsibility, for which she had little taste. To neither could Booth's 'gigantic undertaking' have possessed any reality other than as a day-dream.

Booth continued unperturbed with the preparation of his detailed plans. His aim had always been as much to devise a method of investigation capable of universal application as to secure specific results, and the defection of the members of the Board simply meant that the scope of his plan must be curtailed, not that the scheme must be abandoned.

I don't think from what I hear, [Mary told Beatrice] that Charlie will not be able to hold on to his little pot for the present. He says that though little is done over a long time, the thing is alive and that he thinks the men he has got hold of by no means lose their interest in the idea; so I hope he will last out

1 Passfield.

2 *Memoir*, p. 17. It is characteristic of Booth's modesty that when the Inquiry was finally published, the opening sentence nevertheless contained a tribute to 'those friends who helped me at the outset in laying down the principles on which the inquiry has been conducted'.

for some time yet, and that you when your free time comes, will find, not probably a perfected instrument but a usable one. By the way, he proposes himself to dine with you on Wednesday if you can have him; he has a great deal to talk to you about.[1]

Booth's approach was essentially that of a man of affairs. When discussing with Beatrice in July of that year the article which she was then preparing on the subject of 'social diagnosis', he robustly refused to be drawn into academic argument as to whether the 'hen' of theorizing preceded or followed the laying of the 'egg' of fact-finding.

As to deductive and inductive methods I seem to need both eternally and never could separate them in my mind nor decide which moved first—no induction is possible (I should say) without preceding deduction nor any deduction without preceding induction. If induction does not promptly lead to further deduction, it is barren, and if deduction be not humble and modest, leaning on induction first, and demanding increasingly inductive proof for every step it takes forward, it will assuredly go wrong. I think Political Economy needs badly to step back just now—we have had too many hasty deductions and too much cutting out of complicating considerations—which are never cut out in nature. Perhaps I need to say that by deduction, or the deductive method I here mean having or finding a theory or law.

I am doubtless out of my depth here and I will swim no further lest a cramp o'ertake me. . . .[2]

Though he might feel himself to be out of his depth in abstract argument, there was not the slightest doubt in Booth's mind as to what was most urgently required so far as the immediate present was concerned. In his search for the answer to the 'problem of all problems', he had encountered far too many people who were so possessed by enthusiasm for some great theory or system of society that they were prepared remorselessly to force every known fact to fit into it. What he had sought for in vain, and what he was sure was essential to the solution of the social problem, was a detached and impartial presentation of the situation as it actually was, not as it ought to be or might become.

A framework can be built out of a big theory and facts and statistics run in to fit it—but what I want to see instead is a large statistical framework which is built to receive accumulations of facts out of which at last is evolved the theory and the law and the basis of more intelligent action.

[1] Passfield. Beatrice was only able to play an active part in the Inquiry during her periodic rests from the responsibility of caring for her invalid father.

[2] Passfield.

Amongst all the complicated relations of the facts dealt with they must have *one* in common, which is their place in the framework—without this they are of no use for the purpose in hand.[1]

The erection of this framework, and the accumulation of the facts with which it was to be clothed, was the task to which he now turned. In his opinion, previous efforts to analyse social phenomena had been narrow in conception and abortive in execution; this had rendered their results unreliable and often mutually contradictory. 'The facts of the figures may be correct enough in themselves,' he assured Beatrice, 'but they mislead from want of due proportion or from lack of colour.' The flood of personal impressions which had appeared in papers and pamphlets during recent years provided ample evidence of the distortion which could result from the high-lighting of single factors without due reference to the subject as a whole. Tables of statistics could equally well be a source of the wildest misinformation however accurate each individual figure might be, as his examination of the Census had demonstrated to his complete satisfaction. This was, indeed, the aspect of his paper on 'The Occupations of the People, 1841-1881' which attracted most attention when he presented it to the Statistical Society in May 1886.[2] On this occasion, his optimism as to the trend of social progress in the country as a whole passed unchallenged, but his criticisms of the value of the Census Tables evidently disturbed his hearers; not surprisingly, perhaps, in view of the typical disregard for anything but the truth with which he drafted and presented his paper.

Booth's safeguard against the errors he thus recognized was a simple one. He proposed to make use of all the available methods of collecting information, playing each off against the other in a process of cross-verification which he hoped would provide a view of society denied to those who relied on a single perspective. He made this clear in a letter to Beatrice.

As to methods of inquiry, I think I should say that the statistical method was needed to give bearings to the results of personal observation and personal observation to give life to statistics. . . . It is this relative character, or the proportion of facts to each other, to us, to others, to society at large, and to possible remedies, that must be introduced if they are to be of any value at all in social diagnosis. Both single facts, and strings of statistics *may* be true, and demonstrably true, and yet entirely misleading in the way they are used.[3]

1 Passfield.   2 *Journal of the Royal Statistical Society*, 1886. See also above, p. 67.
3 Passfield.

Profitable though all this preliminary discussion proved to be, Booth's patience was wearing thin, and he was rapidly coming to the conclusion that further argument and talk would get him nowhere. 'Trying to do it over and over again is the best plan,' he remarked to Beatrice. 'The theory and practice must go hand in hand and there is no better key than a little ignorant self-confidence—humble quality compared to proud reserve and much more useful.'[1] His plans were, in fact, in an advanced state of preparation by this time. A sheet of paper has been preserved amongst the records of the Inquiry which there is reason to suppose was the actual note prepared for consideration by the 'Board': neatly written out in pencil in Booth's own writing on a double sheet of ruled foolscap, much creased along the folds as if from frequent consultation, here in outline is the plan of the whole endeavour as its originator first conceived it. It reads:

General Aim. To connect poverty and wellbeing with conditions of employment. *Incidentally*, to describe the industrial peculiarities of London (and of modern towns generally) both as to character of work, character of workers, and of the influences which act upon both.

Then follows what was evidently a preliminary list of the headings under which the information was to be analysed. The essentially twofold nature of this scheme makes it plain that Booth was determined to practise what he had preached: this was to be no narrowly exclusive analysis of the social scene but one which would comprehend the labour as well as the life of the people, and comprise a picture of their condition as well as an account of the influences to which they were subjected.

Certain practical decisions remained to be taken. His experience in preparing the paper on the Census had convinced him that he must drastically restrict the scope of his investigations, but this presented no great difficulty, since he was satisfied by this time that the clue to the problems of his times lay in the study of urban life.

It is not in country but in town that 'terra incognita' needs to be written on our social maps. In the country the machinery of human life is plainly to be seen and easily recognized; personal relations bind the whole together. . . . It is far otherwise with cities, where as to these questions we live in darkness, with doubting hearts and ignorant unnecessary fears, or place our trust with rather dangerous confidence in the teachings of empiric economic law.[2]

[1] Passfield.   [2] *Industry* i, p. 18.

This was, of course, in accord with his own personal preference. Though he turned to the countryside for rest and relaxation, his greatest interest lay in the life of the big city. 'New York's the place for me', he once wrote to his wife:

There seems something subtle, an essence, pervading great metropolitan cities and altering everything so that life seems more lively, busier, larger, the individual less, the community more. I like it. It does me good. But I know it has another aspect and I am not surprised when people feel crushed by the wickedness of it, the ruthlessness, heartlessness of its grinding mill, as you did in Paris. . . . What place for the individual, is the question. Call the roll, close your ranks, forward march.

If this natural predilection for life in a metropolis, and his personal familiarity with the life of the London street made the choice of the subject of his first exploratory study seem to him an obvious one, he nevertheless realized that his selection of the East End called for explanation:

My only justification for taking up the subject in the way I have done is that this piece of London is supposed to contain the most destitute population in England, and to be, as it were, the focus of the problem of poverty in the midst of wealth, which is troubling the minds and hearts of so many people.[1]

It was less easy to decide on which sources of information to rely. He believed that much of the data he required was already available in one form or another,[2] if only he could discover it; this had inspired his first examination of the Census Returns. These having proved unsatisfactory, he was faced with the problem of discovering what alternatives were available, and there is reason to suppose that he reviewed for this purpose the possibilities of co-operation with the Poor Law Unions, charitable societies, and the clergy. Ultimately a suggestion from Joseph Chamberlain,[3] conveyed to Booth by Beatrice, gave him the idea of utilizing the records kept by the School Board Visitors. 'The School Board Visitors perform amongst them a house to house visitation', he wrote:

[1] First Paper, p. 374. The fact that he never again made his home in Liverpool after his breakdown in 1873, his visits there being strictly confined to business, must also have influenced his choice of subject for his first inquiries. But see below, p. 120.

[2] *Final*, p. 32.

[3] In his evidence before the Royal Commission on the Housing of the Working Classes, 1885 (*Minutes of Evidence*, p. 443), Chamberlain referred to a recent inquiry into overcrowding in Birmingham which was based on information secured by the School Board Officers in the course of their ordinary duties.

Every house in every street is in their books, and details are given of every family with children of school age. They also begin their scheduling two or three years before the children attain school age, and a record remains in their books of children who have left school. Most of the visitors have been working in the same district for several years, and thus have an extensive knowledge of the people. . . . Thus their work keeps them in continual and natural relations with all classes of people.[1]

Booth recognized the possibilities of the situation, and was planning to pursue them when the death of the head of one of the subsidiary businesses in America necessitated an unexpected visit to New York. Though his appetite for work was undiminished, even he began to wonder whether a twenty-four-hour day could possibly contain all the things he hoped to do, whilst Mary Booth was frankly doubtful whether the whole idea of the investigation would not have to be shelved. As she wrote to Beatrice:

I have been luxuriating [in the summer beauty of Gracedieu] with just the drawback of regret for poor Charlie, forced to post across the Atlantic and go in for what will be a very wearing, agitating fortnight of arrangements and decisions, listening to what all the maritime interests have to say; and picking his way as best he can towards a wise conclusion. Mr. Kent's death will make a good deal of difference to him in the future as well as just now, making it necessary for him to go back to the oar to an extent that he had hoped to avoid. He was very low about this before leaving, fearing it would be difficult to give much time to the new work. This country life also becomes more doubtfully wise if he is as much tied to his desk as he fears he may have to be—so as to be able to spare very little time for being with us in the country. But time must show us our way. One can't decide much just yet. This neighbourhood would not be a bad centre in some ways for the 'personal observation' part of your scheme. We have a fearfully poverty-stricken population; left behind in the race, their special industries being partly superseded, partly better done elsewhere—a violent Irish element, disorderly.[2]

These doubts do not seem to have lasted long. As so often happened, the more there was to be done, the more Booth seemed able to do: his temperament was such that he gave of his best when at his fullest stretch. Accordingly, the trip to America having been concluded swiftly and successfully, he was back in London at the end of July, absence having apparently merely whetted his appetite for the task which awaited him. Beatrice was then at home with her father in the country, and the events of the next few weeks had therefore to be

[1] First Paper, p. 327.   [2] Passfield.

reported to her by letter. She fortunately kept these letters, and they are worthy of quotation not only for the information they contain as to the earliest stages in the launching of the Inquiry, but also for the witness they bear to the 'working intimacy' into which the two now entered to their mutual benefit. Beatrice was possibly the only one amongst his colleagues who shared his passionate interest in the method of the Inquiry, as distinct from its results, and there is no doubt that it was on the basis of this common interest that their friendship developed along such profitable lines.

We are very fond of each other [she wrote in her diary in 1887]. A close intimate relationship between a man and a woman without sentiment (perhaps not without sentiment, but without passion or the dawning of passion). We are fellow-workers, both inspired by the same intellectual desire. Only in his life it is an etc.: in my life if it becomes anything, it would become the dominating aim. . . .[1]

'Dear Beatrice', his letters baldly begin, and with no more ado plunge into discussion of the matters in hand, ending with an equally bare minimum of polite salutation or personal news. The first letter in the series was written from London on 27 July 1886:

I humbly beg to report as follows: I returned to this country on Monday the 21st and after visiting my wife and children, and my partner in Liverpool, I came hither, reaching London yesterday afternoon. I found my secretary and his assistant sore distraught for lack of work from which trouble I pray Heaven they may soon be relieved—but I am in truth still in some difficulty as to this, as will appear.

I lost no time in calling on Mr. Mather of the School Board, but found that worthy just about to start on a holiday or some such diversion, which will last he tells me till the end of August. Under these circumstances I conceive that it is best that I should also take a holiday myself which I am most willing to do, and so I count to return to Gracedieu at the end of this week and have agreed with Mr. Mather to begin work with him on the 1st of September. I have also seen Maurice Paul and find him overhead in examinations and also about to make holiday, being invited for some part of the time to [stay with you].

So all seems to point to a further interval before we get to close quarters with our work.[2]

---

[1] Passfield. Elsewhere she commented: 'Charlie and I make admirable fellow-workers: he has the cautious, careful, intellect with an ingenious touch of detail, while I paint in broader colouring, caring more for the general effect of the picture than for *exactness* in representation.' Ibid.

[2] Passfield.

This enforced holiday over, not a moment was lost in getting to work, and the first interviews took place at seven-thirty on the evenings of 1 and 2 September 1886. The results were duly reported to Beatrice by Booth:

We had two successive evenings with Mr. Mather on the School Board figures. At the first we got a rough idea of what sort of information was to be had: at the second we made a definite effort at the statement of the facts concerning certain streets. The first evening dealt with very much more picturesque facts than the second, but the second served well enough, and the sort of streets dealt with are probably more frequently to be met with than the sinks of iniquity and hells upon earth which were described to us by old Mr. Orme, the first visitor we met.[1]

Then followed an eager discussion of the use to be made of the information which these interviews had revealed the School Board Visitors as possessing. First, how was this to be extracted?

The information will have to be got by personal interview with each visitor and a good many hours of it for each—more than can be had without paying for it—but I think the work may be divided and we shall relegate any female visitors to your care. Once get the system arranged and any one of us may tackle his visitor and thrash out his district filling up so many sheets of figures and so many pages of remarks. I enclose a letter from Mr. Paul. If we can *get* the information we shall manage to classify it.[2]

Not that classification would be easy. The two interviews had clearly confirmed Booth's hope that the School Board Officers would be able to supply him with information as to both the material condition and the occupations of the people whom they visited in the course of their duties. The problem was to decide how this unorganized mass of experience and fact should be handled so that it might not only be reduced to order, but to an order which would enable it to be compared and contrasted with the results of the parallel inquiries which it was hoped would be undertaken elsewhere. Going over the notebooks of the two officers, he had sat, pencil in hand, ready to enter each family under the appropriate heading in the schedules of income and of occupation which he and Beatrice had previously roughed out together; if this system of classification worked, the condition of every person would be comparable with that of all others in the same neighbourhood and the same trade. With some satisfaction he reported that the results of this preliminary trial had been more than

---

[1] Passfield.   [2] Ibid.

encouraging, but even as he wrote his mind was reviewing the adjustments which the brief test had shown to be necessary:

As to the system of classification you will see that I have abandoned to some extent the division by earnings and have fallen back on that by trades. We can get from the visitors an *opinion* on the earnings of each man and I should like to find some way of noting this down for averages; but I feel that at the end it is only an opinion and I hesitate to make it the basis of our classification. The character of employment is at any rate a fact and I think that we may so arrange and deal with the information as to this as to make it yield the facts as to Earnings in a way that can be proved if disputed. I should like to have the School Board Visitors' view as one item of evidence. What is needed is that the Employments should be so arranged as to be capable of research by other means into the facts of income of each class and this will need a good deal of thought.[1]

Reading this long letter, one feels very close to the secret of Booth's success. Though it glows with the intensity of the interest he took in the whole project, he wrote with a sobriety which reveals that his first attempt to come to grips with the practical problems of conducting an inquiry had made very real to him the difficulties of what he proposed to do. Nevertheless, his decision to proceed remained unshaken. Closer examination had revealed the necessity for certain emendations to his plans, whilst the defection of his friends on the 'Board' required a reduction in the scale of the enterprise. But any idea that he should retreat was simply not entertained. His decision to embark on an inquiry had been taken months before, deliberately and after most careful consideration: once taken, there could be no question of turning back. However, though he was determined to press on with the work, his natural caution did not desert him, and the letter to Beatrice describing the first exploratory interviews ends on a note of reflection:

We ought not to make a false start and I have told Mr. Mather that I shall delay one or two weeks before beginning the work—I have also called a committee meeting for next Thursday to consider the points. I only fear that nobody will come except Paul and if so we must go on as best we can. I wish you were in London. Could you come up for a day? Anyhow you will write your views. Alfred Cripps is no doubt away now and of the others I know nothing.[2]

---

[1] Passfield. The difficulties that Booth faced in applying the earnings and industrial classifications are dealt with below, pp. 183-4, 200-3.

[2] Ibid.

As he expected, the meeting consisted only of Paul and himself, but, he wrote to Beatrice, 'we have decided to go ahead'. He wasted no more words on the lapsed 'Board'. Minor adjustments were made, and at long last on 10 September his plans were ready to be put into operation.

> The two plans to collect information as to conditions and occupation will thus absolutely converge and will fit in as well as can be contrived with the Census Returns. The scheme thus becomes complete and every bit done will be so much towards the whole statement for London. I don't think the whole work is beyond our reach and I think it *might* be completed in three years. The district figures will be classified according to occupations, and the trade figures, starting naturally with occupations, will be classified according to earnings also.
>
> We shall start in earnest next week. Paul, Argyle and I doing one visitor together and then dividing our forces so as to each take one, and by and by others can come in to the work if they will.[1]

It was characteristic of Booth that he should thus quietly set to work without any preliminary flourish of trumpets. As he once remarked, his instinct in tackling any enterprise was 'after getting a start, to work in silence and in darkness and never mind anybody'.[2] Two months later, the work was in full swing. Up in London for a two-day visit to the Booths, Beatrice wrote in her diary: 'Charlie absorbed in his inquiry, working all his evenings with 3 paid secretaries. I have promised to undertake the Docks in my March holiday. Dear sweet little Mary, with her loving ways and charming motherhood. They become each year more near to me. Perhaps they are the only persons who really love me.'

Once started, he and his assistants worked hard and fast. 'At first, nothing seemed so essential as speed. The task was so tremendous; the prospect of its completion so remote; and every detail cost time.'[3] And there was every reason for haste. Public confidence had been gravely shaken by the events leading up to the so-called West End riots, and it seemed only too probable that the continuing state of unrest amongst the poor would end in more violence.

The long months, and indeed years, during which Booth had

[1] Ibid.

[2] In defence of those who have succeeded him in the twentieth century it should be remarked that Booth was able to afford an independence utterly beyond the means of those who have to depend on grants in aid of research, and must publicize their ambitions if they are to achieve them.

[3] *Poverty* i, p. 25.

ruminated over the possibilities of conducting an inquiry into human affairs now bore fruit. He moved into action like an experienced campaigner who has methodically prepared himself for every eventuality. Details might require amendment, and the skill with which he and his assistants set about their work naturally improved as the work went on, but the principles on which the whole scheme was built proved sound from the very start. In consequence, only six weeks after the interviewing of the School Board Officers had begun early in September, he was able to invite criticism from Professor Alfred Marshall, the Cambridge economist, on his method of classifying the first batch of information relating to the people living in the St. Paul's sub-registration district. The letter in which he did so is worth quoting in full since it summarizes in his own words precisely what he was trying to do: it is dated 18 October 1886:

I am now engaged (with some others) on an attempt to describe analytically the industrial and social status of the population of London, that is, to state the proportions in which different classes exist, with the actual present conditions of each.

It is a very difficult undertaking and any results obtained will be much open to criticism of all kinds.

What I wish to ask for from you is criticism, *in advance*, on the method adopted.

It is proposed to place together information from as many different sources as possible, so as to make the evidence check and complete itself so far as possible. The frame-work of the inquiry will be found in the facts obtainable from the School Board Visitors, who, among them, provide something very like a house-to-house visitation in the poorer districts, and who usually know the occupation and something of the condition of life of every family where there are school children, in the lower middle class and all below it.

As a trial I have completed a preliminary analysis, from School Board information, of a sub-registration district in the East End of London with 20,000 inhabitants and it is this analysis which I desire to submit to you before going further with the work, as much depends on the soundness of the system adopted.

What reply was received to this letter is not known. It was presumably encouraging since Booth promptly extended his inquiries to cover the whole of the Tower Hamlets district. The collection of the material proved an arduous but comparatively straightforward task. As he had expected, his belief that much of the required information was already in the possession of one or other of the many people actively concerned with the condition of the poor proved justified. The School Board Visitors responded nobly, each of the thirty-four submitting to some twenty hours of cross-examination on the information recorded in their routine notebooks. In order to ensure uniformity, Booth interviewed the first of these in company with Paul and Argyle, then the only workers in the Inquiry. After this each continued to work separately, Booth taking his fair share of the work. In these interviews they discussed with individual Visitors every inhabitant of every house in every street of each district, verifying the facts by reference to the Visitor's daily records. As the interviews proceeded, the information secured was entered into forty-six small notebooks, prepared on an identical plan so that any one of the entries could be compared with any other. The name of the street was given at the head of each page; every house in it was noted and the occupants of each room were enumerated; particulars were recorded of the occupation, and probable income, of every inhabitant, together with the number of children in each family.

At the outset we shut our eyes, fearing lest any prejudice of our own should colour the information we received. It was not till the books were finished that I or my secretaries ourselves visited the streets amongst which we had been living in imagination. But later we gained confidence, and made it a rule to see each street ourselves at the time we received the Visitor's account of it. With the insides of the houses and their inmates there was no attempt to meddle. To have done so would have been an unwarrantable impertinence.[1]

Working from these notes, Booth and his assistants then proceeded to classify the entire population on the double basis of their employment and their apparent means.[2] For this purpose a list had been prepared of all the known occupations of the people of this part of London, divided into thirty-nine 'Sections'; every family was allotted to the appropriate 'Section' in it, according to the occupation of its head. The families were then again analysed on the basis of their apparent 'means and position' into eight Classes, which extended from Class A, the lowest class of occasional labourers, loafers and semi-criminals, through the various groups of casual and regular wage-earners to Classes G and H, the lower and upper middle classes. On the basis of this double classification, tables were then constructed which Booth

---

[1] *Poverty* i, p. 25.

[2] See Appendix IV for a fuller discussion of the question as to the extent to which Booth took 'means' into consideration in deciding whether or not a given family was to be classified as 'poor'.

GCB

hoped would enable him to compare and contrast his results concerning the life of the people with those relating to their labours.[1]

All of this was logical and orderly in theory. In practice, obstacles were immediately encountered. Allowance had, for example, to be made for the existence of unmarried men and women and for children over or under school age, of whom the School Board Officers had no direct information. Again, the classification of the population according to means compelled him to define what he meant by 'poverty'. How, for example, should a family be classified whose miserable condition was due to drink rather than to lack of means? The problem proved a surprisingly difficult one: it was in the course of his search for its solution that Booth invented the concept of the Poverty Line, perhaps his most striking single contribution to the social sciences.[2] Another difficulty of which Booth was well aware, was that the information provided by the School Board Visitors was basically a matter of opinion and not of fact. To offset this he took infinite trouble to make use of every opportunity to amplify and verify the material they supplied by checking it against evidence obtained from other sources such as the police records of inmates of registered lodging houses, Poor Law statistics, and of course, the Census.

These troubles having been overcome to the best of his ability, Booth then proceeded to implement the statistical data by careful and detailed verbal descriptions, in accordance with his declared intention not to rely on any single method of analysis. Class by class, section by section, he outlined the salient characteristics of each of his categories, and justified the distinctions he had made between them. In addition, an account of the life of each neighbourhood was prepared, largely on the basis of his own observations, in order to provide a general background against which the detailed results might be set.[3] Though he regarded these descriptive notes as being of the greatest importance, Booth was doubtful of his talent for writing them. 'I cannot hope to make the rows of figures in this Table as luminous and picturesque to every eye as they are to mine and yet I am not content without making an attempt to do so',[4] he remarked. In fact, they were to prove immensely attractive to his public, his descriptions of the individual

---

[1] See Appendix III.

[2] First Paper, p. 328. See below, pp. 184 et seq.; also Appendix I V.

[3] Booth had hoped to provide parallel descriptions of the characteristic trades of the East End which would throw light on the statistical analysis of the people according to their occupations, but this proved to be beyond his resources at this stage.

[4] First Paper, p. 361.

classes making a specially deep impression on his readers. Combined with the statistical information they constituted an account of the life and labour of the people 'in the round' which appealed both to the intelligence and the emotions in a way which has hardly been equalled, and never surpassed, since he wrote.

By the middle of the following May, only eight months after work had been begun, the Inquiry was so far advanced that Booth felt able to submit his findings to the test of scrutiny by the Royal Statistical Society. As he assured its members, 'he felt very great doubt whether he could go on with the work by himself without going wrong, and he wanted to bring it to the touch of public discussion'. 'The In-habitants of the Tower Hamlets (School Board Division), their Con-dition and Occupations (1887)'[1] was based on information relating to nearly half a million people. It consisted in the main of the statistical and descriptive analysis of the occupations and conditions of the in-habitants, but also included brief notes on five subjects of topical and local interest, on which Booth felt that the information he had acquired threw some light. Of these, 'Employment at the Docks' incorporated material collected by Beatrice during her spring 'holiday' from the care of her invalid father: it inevitably turned on the question of casual labour which Booth deplored because of its effect on the character of the men.[2] The other four notes covered 'The Jewish Settlement and Immigration', 'The Sweating System and Middlemen', 'Working Women', and 'The Unemployed'.[3] The Paper concluded with some comments on the accuracy of his figures in which he attempted to disarm criticism by a plain statement of the assumptions on which his calculations were based, and with some general remarks on the results to be obtained by this form of inquiry if carried further.

In summing up the conclusions to be drawn from his work, Booth studiously avoided the sensational, whether as to its method or its content, his practice always being to incline towards understatement. He had undertaken the Inquiry, he explained, simply in order to give a specimen, though a very imperfect one, of what could be done to

[1] *Journal of the Royal Statistical Society*, 1887, pp. 326–91. The area covered was that of the five Poor Law Unions of Whitechapel, St. George's-in-the-East, Stepney, Mile End Old Town, and Poplar, and included the London Docks, Millwall Docks, and both the East and West India Docks.

[2] This paper was presented in a much extended form under her own name in *The Nineteenth Century*, October 1887.

[3] Although these notes were presented in the context of the discussion of poverty, they must be regarded as Booth's first attempt to investigate the structure and organization of industry.

describe the lives of the people of London and their occupations: 'I have had no foregone conclusions and it is rather to the method here employed, than to the results yet shown that I pin my faith.' This method he hoped would make possible the co-ordination of all the miscellaneous information which he believed to lie hidden in such records as those kept by the School Board Visitors. In evolving it, he had been guided by his belief that 'every social problem must be broken up to be solved or even adequately stated'[1] and he presented his own work primarily to demonstrate that this could be done.

As for results, the only conclusion which he was prepared to put forward at this stage was that an unexpectedly high proportion of the total population, 35 per cent., had been found to be living 'at all times more or less in want'. Booth refused to say anything more on this point than that the figures had come as a surprise to him. Having regard to the fact that his survey had thus justified Hyndman's estimate rather than his own expectations, one might have supposed that the situation thus created called for comment and appraisal, to put it mildly. However, he refused to be drawn into controversy and took refuge in reassurances addressed perhaps as much to himself as to his middle-class audience:

This is a serious state of things, but not visibly fraught with imminent social danger, or leading straight to revolution. That there should be so much savagery as there is, and so much abject poverty, and so many who can never raise their heads much above the level of actual want is grave enough; but we can afford to be calm, and to give attempts at improvement the time and patience which are absolutely needed if we are to do any good at all.[2]

At this stage, he wished to emphasize only one point:

The question of those who actually suffer from poverty should be considered separately from that of the true working classes, whose desire for a larger share of wealth is of a different character. It is the plan of agitators and the way of sensational writers to confound the two in one, to talk of 'starving millions', and to tack on the thousands of the working classes to the tens or perhaps hundreds of distress. Against this method of agitators who class all the working classes together as starving millions I strongly protest, and I do so all the more that I am deeply in earnest in my desire that the conditions under which the mass of the people live should be improved, as well as that of those who now suffer actual distress. To confound these essentially distinct problems is to make the solution of both impossible; it is not by welding distress and aspirations that any good can be done.[3]

---

[1] First Paper, pp. 327, 375.   [2] Ibid., p. 375.

[3] Ibid., p. 376. The passage 'Against . . . distress' was drastically cut when the Paper was reprinted in Volume One of the first edition of the Inquiry (p. 155).

The report of the discussion which followed the reading of the Paper reveals the almost total lack of precise information concerning the problem of poverty. The audience might be members of a learned society, but when they were given an opportunity to discuss the nature, cause and cure of the problem of poverty in the midst of plenty, it soon became apparent that their guess was as good—or as bad—as that of the man in the street. As for Booth's statistical methods, they expressed themselves with all the dubiety of experts faced with the brash thinking of a younger man, though to do them justice, they elected Booth to serve on their Council shortly afterwards. Nevertheless, some very useful points were made by the members of the Society who had read the Paper with care; Professor Levi, for instance, wondered

whether the paper gave an accurate idea of the word 'poor'. Who was a poor man? . . . The author had not mentioned the causes of poverty, such as gambling and drink, nor had he touched upon the average wages of the community with which he dealt. . . . It would be of great value if Mr. Booth would add as an appendix budgets of the earnings and expenditure of as large a proportion as possible of the classes with whom he dealt.[1]

These remarks, and others which echoed them, were listened to with due attention by Booth, with important results in his subsequent work. In replying to the discussion, he dealt with them specifically:

It would not only be important [he said], but a necessity . . . to insert something like a budget of the expenditure of the people referred to. The question of earnings he had dealt with in the paper by urging that the information could only be got by a trade inquiry. . . . The moral question would form a third set of inquiries.[2]

One is immediately struck by the fact that this reply contains the whole Inquiry in embryo. As a result of his trial investigation, Booth seems already to have achieved a comprehensive grasp of what he intended to do. He had described his intention as being to erect a gigantic framework into which detailed information could be fitted as and when it came to hand and this was precisely what happened: the work of the seventeen years which lay ahead was in effect a monumentally patient filling-in of the structure he envisaged at this early stage. Thus the Poverty Series contained an analysis of the causes of poverty and an attempt to deal with the problem of budgets, the 'question of earnings' inspired the Industry Series, whilst in the seven

[1] First Paper, p. 394.　　[2] Ibid., p. 401.

volumes of the Religious Influence Series, Booth was to grapple with 'the moral question'. The undeviating nature of his devotion to this early concept of the Inquiry was to introduce a certain element of rigidity into the conduct of his subsequent investigations, but one cannot fail to be impressed by the far-sightedness which enabled him to grasp so clearly what most men would only have been able to discover by experience.

The press were much less critical than the statisticians. In fact, they were only too ready to regard Booth's paper as grist to their mill. Most of what the journalists wrote, it is true, amounted to an expression of the blankest astonishment, but this was regarded by editors as 'news', as was evidenced by the fact that one 'very remarkable and sensational' article about his work, entitled 'London's Suffering Millions', appeared in newspapers all over the world. That any one, especially any private individual, should succeed in throwing light on the conditions and habits of the hitherto inaccessible and incomprehensible peoples of the East End rightly struck them as quite remarkable. Moreover, they saw in Booth's achievement a most welcome sign that here at long last was promise of the discovery of solid ground on which a stand might be taken against the fearful threat of poverty: as he himself remarked, it was the sense of helplessness caused by the almost total lack of factual information which baffled and depressed all those who attempted to deal with the chronic poverty of their times. 'A very curious and interesting inquiry has just been completed in East London', wrote the *Morning Post* in a review which may be taken as typical of all the rest:

It is extraordinary that a private individual should not only have dared to take in hand, but should have been able to successfully carry out, an elaborate investigation as to the occupations, earnings, and social condition of half a million of persons, or no less than one-eighth of the inhabitants of the Metropolis; and this in the very poorest districts, where the circumstances of the population present more difficulties. Yet this is what has been done by Mr. Charles Booth, and we venture to say that the facts and figures which he laid before the Royal Statistical Society last week, as the first results of the inquiry in question, are more valuable than a ton of the average blue-books on pauperism, or an ocean of sensational writing on progress and poverty. . . . Such hard facts as have been collected in this inquiry form the best basis for the efforts both of the legislator and the philanthropist.[1]

Only the *Pall Mall Gazette*, reviewing a subsequent reprint of the

[1] *Morning Post*, 26 May 1887.

Paper, criticized what he had to say with any severity. If Booth had not exactly stolen its thunder, he had made it more difficult to produce the storms which the editor had made an almost personal concern of his own. Booth was, accordingly, sharply put in his place in a leader entitled 'Under the Black Flag', in which exception was taken to his entire pamphlet on the ground that it read 'too much like a complacent and comforting *bourgeois* statement of the situation'.[1]

In general, however, Booth could congratulate himself on having cleared his first hurdle safely—and gratifyingly. Speed seemed doubly essential now that public attention had been so extensively drawn to the Inquiry, and expectations as to its results so generally aroused. The widespread notice taken of the Paper on the Tower Hamlets had simplified the task of explaining the nature of what now became commonly known as 'Mr. Booth's Inquiry': the experience gained in the use of the technique of social investigation which he had invented gave Booth and his assistants added confidence in tackling the second instalment of his plan. The area selected this time was the Hackney School Board Division, which comprised the districts of Shoreditch, Bethnal Green, and Hackney. Booth had intended to turn his attention to some quite different part of London, but declared himself to be so dissatisfied with the incompleteness of his first effort that he felt impelled to make a thorough job of the East End before moving to any other district. It seems fairly clear that he was in fact much more disturbed by the results of his first inquiries than he cared to admit. Possibly he hoped that a more complete examination of a similar area would show that he had over-estimated the bulk of poverty and that a closer analysis of its causes might suggest some solution of the problem.[2] In a sense, this was a major turning-point in Booth's work, for he must be regarded as having rejected a number of profitable alternative lines of advance when he decided to apply his methods of inquiry, virtually

[1] *Pall Mall Gazette*, 13 October 1887.

[2] It is noteworthy that Booth had the figures relating to St. George's-in-the-East reworked before they were re-presented in his second paper. This was the first district to be surveyed; it was 'very imperfectly done', and was 'the *corpus vile* of our experiments' (Second Paper, p. 277). As first published, the figures showed that that district was the poorest in the Tower Hamlets, and it may be that the criticisms had had the effect of causing him to institute a check. But the result was to demonstrate that there was even more poverty in the district than had originally been thought; though the percentage for those in chronic want was slightly reduced from 17·17 to 16·36, that for those in poverty was increased substantially, from 26·2 to 32·23. This must have been a considerable reassurance to Booth at this stage in his work; it provides, moreover, an indication of his ability to give careful attention to criticism, but to reject it if it appeared not to be justified.

unaltered, to ever-increasing numbers of the population. Instead of going over the same ground again and again, and getting much the same results, he might have asked himself whether and if so why it was that the work already done demonstrated a correspondence between poverty and type of employment. However, this fact had been obscured by his revelation of the startlingly high proportion of the population living in poverty, and in any case it is perhaps true to say that the experiment had to be repeated over and over again before the results could be generally accepted as true. Whatever the reason, the wide horizons that Booth had originally held in view were drastically narrowed, and for the time being at least the Inquiry became a survey of poverty in the East End.

The lines on which the work now continued necessarily repeated those originally laid down. The notebooks of the School Board Visitors, the volumes of the official Census, and the inquiries made by his staff[1] were once more the sources of his information: the basis on which the facts were classified was as before. The only innovation was the preparation of what became known as the Poverty Map, on which the character of each street was marked according to its classification in a variety of colours 'varying from pink, through violet and blue, to black'. This was displayed in Toynbee Hall and Oxford House for examination by anyone with expert knowledge of the neighbourhood; Booth was gratified to find that few corrections had to be made as a result.

In May 1888, exactly a year after his first Paper to the Royal Statistical Society, Booth presented his second report on the progress of his Inquiry, 'The Condition and Occupations of the People of East London and Hackney, 1887'. [2] This did for the whole of East London what the previous Paper had done for the Tower Hamlets only: the material already published was repeated in order that the account given might be a complete one. 'In submitting the whole thing again', he pleaded in self-justification, 'I run the risk of being considered tedious in the hope of being thorough.' Thus was established a practice whereby new material was grafted on to old, which was to grow on him as his results accumulated.

The notes on 'special subjects' were, however, kept strictly within

1 Who these assistants were can only be surmised from the list of names which eventually appeared on the title page of Volume One of the First Edition of the Inquiry: the only two who are shown by the evidence to have worked with him during this period were Jesse Argyle and Beatrice Potter.

2 *Journal of the Royal Statistical Society*, pp. 276–331.

the narrower field of problems concerning poverty. The first consisted of a 'Comparison of the East End with the Rest of London', in which Booth attempted to forecast the total amount of poverty which an extended Inquiry might be expected to reveal. It was followed by a discussion of 'The Question of Poverty' which dealt with some of the points raised when the First Paper was presented. So far as the first of these is concerned it is only necessary to remark that the forecast was ultimately shown to have been over-optimistic. Greater interest was aroused at the time by the defence of his definition of poverty[1] with which his second section dealt. In this he compared the Very Poor who were 'at all times more or less in want', with the Poor of whom he wrote: 'their lives are an unending struggle, and lack comfort, but I do not know that they lack happiness'. He also defined more explicitly his distinction between poverty, want and distress. 'Want, as I use the word, is an aggravated form of Poverty, and Distress an aggravated form of Want.'[2] At the same time, he made it clear that he regarded income as merely one factor amongst many to be taken into account in assessing the condition of a household. In order to throw light on the nature of these factors, Booth sought the aid of the School Board Visitors in making a special analysis of the causes of poverty in 4,000 of the cases classified as Poor or Very Poor. He again presented his results as tentative examples of how the subject might be explored rather than as precise conclusions; nevertheless, they pointed to a continuing shortage of work as the dominant factor in regard to poverty, and he reviewed the situation thus disclosed with some alarm.

Industry will not work without some unemployed margin—some reserve of labour—but the margin in London to-day seems to be exaggerated in every department, and enormously so in the lowest class of labour. Some employers seem to think this state of things is in their interest—this argument has been used by dock officials—but this view appears to me short-sighted, for labour deteriorates under casual labour more than its price falls.[3]

The mere fact that this second inquiry corroborated the almost unbelievable conclusion of the First Paper, that one-third of the population of London was 'sinking into want', would have been shocking enough, but in addition, Booth's expression of his own opinions was much more forthright than on his previous appearance before the Royal Statistical Society. He had admitted then that his findings had

[1] See Appendix IV.   [2] Second Paper, p. 294.   [3] Ibid., pp. 297-8.

surprised him, and it is evident he was profoundly moved by the corroboration provided by the second investigation. There could be no suggestion now that he failed to comprehend the true meaning of a life spent in poverty: 'I shall not regret it if, in spite of my "middle-class complacency", I have in this instance painted things darker rather than brighter than they truly are.' Abandoning both his intention to content himself with the role of providing information upon which better men could act, and his dislike of interference with the freedom of individuals, he went on to urge the need for greater regularity of employment, and for the organized use of the leisure enforced by casual labour. Finally, overcome by the magnitude of the problem constituted by such widespread poverty, he ended with a plea for drastic and even Draconian remedies. Discussing the large numbers whom he classified as being chronically in want, his Classes A and B, he wrote:

To the rich the very poor are a sentimental interest: to the poor they are a crushing load. The poverty of the poor is mainly the result of the competition of the very poor. The entire removal of this class out of the daily struggle for existence I believe to be the only solution of the problem of poverty. Is this solution beyond our reach?

He himself believed it was not: 'the individualist community on which we build our faith, will find itself obliged for its own sake to take charge of the lives of those who, from whatever cause, are incapable of independent existence up to the required standard, and will be fully able to do so'. Economically, there was everything to be said for this, but was it a practical proposition? Here he halted, no doubt aware of the storm his very suggestion would provoke.

However slowly and kindly it may be done, it is not a pleasant process to be improved off the face of the earth, and this is the road along which we have as I think to travel. I do not venture to make any definite proposals; I only say that it seems time that we should find some means to carry voluntarily the burden which otherwise we have to carry involuntarily round our necks.[1]

Such a statement by one of the most liberal employers of the day inevitably whetted the public interest and it was obvious that a vastly wider public than that of the Royal Statistical Society was keenly interested in what he was doing. Unassuming as ever, Booth's only concern was that his methods of inquiry should be more fully exploited by others than he had been able to do himself, and he expressed

[1] Second Paper, p. 308.

the hope to the Society that parallel inquiries would be undertaken elsewhere, specifically mentioning the one already started in Manchester by a Mr. Frederick Scott. For his own part, his intention was to complete the work he had begun. 'I am glad to say', he assured the Royal Statistical Society at the end of the discussion on his second Paper in 1888, 'that I have obtained some very valuable co-operation, and can now see my way to the completion of my task by the end of the present year, when I hope to gather together the various fragments in one volume.'

5

The Life of the People

So began the great Inquiry into the *Life and Labour of the People in London* which was to culminate in the seventeenth and final volume published in 1903. Whether Booth, now about to enter upon his fiftieth year, realized the magnitude of the task to which he had committed himself, is not known. True to form, he started with a methodical reorganization of his own affairs. 'My idea', he wrote to his brother Alfred from Gracedieu Manor—

is to transfer the whole of the ordinary London work to Christopher Garland so as to make my presence when in London that of a visitor at the office. The business statistics and private business correspondence, which have always been a large part of my personal work, and which tend to increase, I shall work from home—here in Summer, London in Winter—and shall employ young Pearson as clerk for it, being myself at London or Gracedieu about 3 days and at Liverpool about 4 days every week. So far as I can see this will work when it gets into shape—at any rate I am ready to try it for 18 months.

On paper this reads very well, but one cannot but be taken aback by the hardihood which could accept as convenient a triangular base of which one point was so remote from a station, let alone a main line, as Gracedieu.[1] One is, moreover, startled to observe that no place is allotted to the Inquiry in this schedule. It is salutary for the twentieth-century social scientist to realize that to this heavily burdened business-man, research, even on so ambitious a scale, was simply a leisure-time interest which had to be fitted into spare moments mainly in the evenings and at the week-ends.

[1] His children recollect that he was sometimes mistaken for a retired grocer on these cross-country train journeys by reason of the fact that in order to put the time thus spent to good use, he would perch a row of candle-ends along the carriage window-sill by which to read.

From now onwards, and for many years to come, Booth led not one but several distinct lives in which fantastically hard work was only relieved by fantastically hard play. His investigations were at first conducted from his office in Talbot Court off Gracechurch Street, but in 1893 the Inquiry staff was moved into the spare premises of the Royal Statistical Society in Adelphi Terrace. On this dual basis, he controlled the complicated business with one set of staff, the growing survey with another. The heavy burden of responsibility which he carried as principal partner in the business, absorbed his days: the hour after dinner was, nominally at least, devoted to conversing or reading with his wife and family, though it became a standing joke that he tended to spend most of it comfortably asleep. Only at ten o'clock at night would he consider himself free to turn his attention to what he regarded as simply a personal hobby, sometimes setting off to walk the London streets, sometimes meeting friends and colleagues for discussion, more often, as time passed, settling down to a hard stretch at the work of organizing and writing up the material collected by his staff of assistants. His wife from time to time urged him to limit this late-night stint to three hours: 'I think I could do it in less time but I daren't risk it,' was his reply. It rarely proved possible for him to take time off from the business in order to devote himself wholly to his investigations.

The pattern of his life was, of course, frequently disturbed by the necessities of the business; but from what now became annual, if not more frequent, trips to New York, he returned with his appetite for the Inquiry redoubled. Journeys never tired him, and he thought nothing of arranging interviews for the hour after his arrival on the evening train from Liverpool. He made extra time for himself by reducing to the minimum the necessities of eating and sleeping. After a week-end in the country with his family, he habitually returned on an early train on Monday mornings: 'In the early chills of the morning, greetingless and fireless and breakfastless—I woke to find you gone', his wife lamented. Indeed, he reduced his own life to a point of austerity which provoked her to remind him to eat a little food now and then: 'It is a capital way of avoiding extreme exhaustion.' It is significant that those who recollect him in these days think of him as standing at his high desk in the office eating a piece of fruit in order that no time might be wasted on lunch. Life with his family at Gracedieu provided his only relaxation. Nevertheless, at intervals even that failed to suffice, and his digestion would cease to function through sheer exhaustion. Downing tools with his usual thoroughness, he would set off for a tour abroad, seeking out some village inn where living was of the simplest and human nature at its least self-conscious. A few weeks would prove sufficient. Warmed by the sunshine—he never found even the summer heat of New York too hot for comfort—relaxed by the complete banishment from his conscious mind of any thought of work or worry, he would hasten home again to his wife, to the business and to his beloved Inquiry.

His life thus organized, Booth settled down with enthusiasm to the execution of the undertaking to which he had committed himself. He was perfectly clear in his own mind as to what he wanted to do and how he proposed to do it. In the Papers to the Royal Statistical Society he had emphasized the methods by which he had carried out his investigations rather than the specific results which had emerged, and by so doing had, as it were, erected the skeleton of that statistical framework into which the results of all subsequent surveys could be fitted. This having been successfully accomplished, he now felt able to forge ahead with the full-scale project which had all along been his aim and object, the analysis of the life and labour of the entire population of London. His intention at this stage was to stick closely to the lines of his two preliminary studies; it was only subsequently that, in the interests of speed, he decided to concentrate exclusively on how the people lived and to reserve for a later date and a separate study the question of how and where they worked.

The general plan of the inquiry, as applying to the whole of London [he had told the Royal Statistical Society in his First Paper], is to divide the entire population by districts and by groups of trades, each answering to a similar division in the census; and then to deal with each district by a local inquiry, and with each group of trades by a trade inquiry. The principal object of the district inquiry would be to show the conditions under which people live, but it would also give their employments; the principal object of the trade inquiry would be to show the conditions under which the people work, but it would indirectly deal with their manner of life. The double method would provide a check upon the results of each, and much light be thrown upon one inquiry by the other.[1]

The information sought was to be of a similarly dual character so that statistics might be verified by those 'fruits of personal observation' for which there had been little room in the earlier studies. There he had had to restrict himself to the bare bones of the statistical framework.

[1] First Paper, p. 326.

Now he was free to attempt the task to which he had long looked forward, of clothing that skeleton with living flesh so that the impersonal facts might become endowed with the vitality of real life.

The task was obviously of a dimension far beyond his own powers, even when aided by Argyle, and Booth accordingly recruited the services of the group of seven people whose names duly appeared under his own on the title page of Volume One of the new publication.[1] It was, of course, the essence of his whole concept of social investigation that, given the statistical framework, the greater the number of people who contributed and the more various their source of information, the better.[2] On what footing those who rallied to Booth's support at this juncture did so, is not known, but the point is immaterial since it is plainly apparent that what bound them so closely to him was their personal loyalty rather than any contract of service. The team consisted mainly of young men and women, several of whom were later to achieve positions of considerable distinction. Amongst them Beatrice Potter was perhaps the most remarkable, both by virtue of her sex and status, and because of the brilliance of her intellect, and the studies she undertook of the Docks, the tailoring trade and the Jewish community, attracted considerable attention. As in the business, Booth picked his assistants on grounds of character and ability. His faith in the importance of education led him to favour university graduates, but he was characteristically indifferent to questions of social origin: Llewellyn Smith, for example, had worked his own way to Oxford, having kept himself from an early age.

Of this team, Booth was very much 'the chief'. His attitude to the administration of the Inquiry was essentially that of the head of a large and complex business who was accustomed to bear responsibility, to issue orders, and to take risks. He assumed that his own function in this organization was to co-ordinate and direct the labours of others, who, having been trained to work on a common pattern, were capable

[1] Three members of the team, Stephen Fox, H. Llewellyn-Smith, and Ernest Aves, were residents at Toynbee Hall, and had probably encountered Booth when his street map was displayed there. David Schloss was a member of the Royal Statistical Society and a leader of the Jewish community in London, and Clara Collett was one of the first women to graduate in arts at the University of London.

[2] His optimism in this regard tended to diminish with experience and a subsequent letter of Mrs. Booth's gives a rueful account of a meeting with a group of earnest women whose eagerness to undertake inquiries was not matched by any idea as to what they might inquire into. To their argument that surely all information was worth something she made the mental reply, 'Worth a rotten apple', though she remained outwardly polite.

of independent work, and yet were none of them indispensable. He was an admirable editor in that he could and did delegate responsibility to his assistants on the basis of an honest recognition of his own limitations. 'I could not myself do a long course of reading of the authorities on any subject to save my life, but I must not undervalue the result to those who can', he told Beatrice. 'I think such work should be done by deputy as much as possible, or at least strictly divided.' Nevertheless, though he accepted the final responsibility for the administration of the Inquiry, Booth did not allow this to deter him from playing an active part in every branch of its operations. 'Spent the morning with C. Booth at the West India Docks', Beatrice recorded in February 1887, and again, 'Dined with Charles . . . and took the tram down the Commercial Road to 42, Brunswick Road, where we had an appointment with Stephen Sim, Secretary to the Stevedores Association. . . .'[1] As in the business, he insisted on making himself thoroughly conversant with every aspect of the work, actively supervising the organization of the small secretariat of paid workers, and advising and assisting each of his collaborators in the collection of material for their special subjects.

However accurate and comprehensive might be the description of technical detail, however vivid the picture of what was happening at the dock gates and in the sweated workshops, I was always confronted by Charles Booth's sceptical glance and critical questions: 'How many individuals are affected by the conditions you describe: are they increasing or diminishing in number?' 'What proportion do they bear to those working and living under worse or better conditions?' 'Does this so-called sweating system play any considerable part in the industrial organization of the four million inhabitants of London?' Thus, though I never acquired the statistical instrument because I had not the requisite arithmetic, I became aware that every conclusion derived from observation or experiment had to be qualified as well as verified by the relevant statistics.[2]

The fact that, when Beatrice came to write her autobiography, she entitled the first volume *My Apprenticeship* denotes the importance she attached to her experiences as Booth's 'industrious apprentice'. Her account conveys admirably the sweep of the enthusiasm with which he set to work and the sense of high adventure with which he carried his collaborators along with him. He 'delighted in upsetting generally accepted views', she tells us, but was at the same time 'singularly appreciative of any suggestions, however irrelevant or far-fetched these

[1] Passfield.   [2] *My Apprenticeship*, p. 339.

might seem, from fellow-workers and subordinates. . . . Indeed if he had a bias as an investigator, it was in favour of the unlikely and unpopular explanation of a given series of facts.'[1] Those who worked for him were made to realize that in the evolution of the craft of social investigator, he was as willing to learn from them as he expected them to be from him.

Booth undertook a major share in the arduous task of observing and describing the conditions under which the people lived. Though the misery and squalor necessarily encountered on these expeditions sometimes depressed him, nothing ever blunted the eagerness of the curiosity with which he regarded the life of the East End. Absorbed, he walked its streets and alleys, delighting in the vigour and drama of the London scene, and relishing to the full the infinite variety of its character even whilst he was recording in minute detail all that he observed.

Each district has its character—its peculiar flavour. One seems to be conscious of it in the streets. It may be in the faces of the people, or in what they
carry—perhaps a reflection is thrown in this way from the prevailing trades
—or it may lie in the sounds one hears, or in the character of the buildings. . . .
The other districts have each some charm or other—a brightness not ex-
tinguished by, and even appertaining to, poverty and toil, to vice, and even to
crime—a clash of contest, man against man, and men against fate—the absorbing interest of a battlefield—a rush of human life as fascinating to watch as the
current of a river to which life is so often likened. . . . The feeling that I have
just described—this excitement of life which can accept murder as a dramatic
incident, and drunkenness as the buffoonery of the stage—is especially characteristic of Whitechapel. And looked at in this way, what a drama it is![2]

During the winter of 1888-9, in addition to countless journeys of exploration into the East End, Booth also took lodgings in the houses of at least three families typical of his classes C, D, and E, sharing the life of those who lived on or about his 'poverty line' with a gusto which moved his wife to wonder.[3]

I think it rests him more in some ways than even Gracedieu's quiet and beauty.
At any rate it is plainly a second string to one's bow looked on as a holiday

---

[1] Ibid., pp. 220, 346.   [2] *Poverty* i, p. 66.

[3] It is perhaps no coincidence that about this time Beatrice came to the conclusion that neither direct observation nor even the most informal of interviews were in themselves enough. She must realize for herself 'what it felt like to "wait at the gates" for work', she reported to Charles, and with his approval set herself to 'learn how to sweat' in order that she might gain experience of the working life of a tailoring hand. (*My Apprenticeship*, p. 297.)

relaxation,—as one would not have expected beforehand. He likes the life and the people and the evening roaming—and the food! which he says agrees with him in kind and time of taking better than that of our class.

Others had of course done this before: Beatrice Potter had already stayed incognito with her working-class relations in a Lancashire mill town,[1] and those of his assistants who lived in Toynbee Hall had at least a working acquaintance with the realities of life amongst the poor. Nevertheless, one cannot help but admire the audacity with which Booth picked his lodging entirely at random, simply by reason of the fact that in a street whose life he wished to experience, a card in the window of a house announced a vacancy within. The quality of his accommodation may be judged by the fact that he paid something like four shillings a week for it, a sum which included attendance. The descriptive notes published by his wife in her *Memoir* conjure up a striking picture of the ease with which this wealthy stranger was able to slip into the ways of the various households in which he stayed, eating with genuine pleasure the coarse porridge and thick bread and butter set before him, enjoying the run of the house, and in the evenings sitting comfortably by the kitchen fire to write up his diary till the return of the family brought supper, the passing round of the common mug of beer, and general conversation.[2] It is plainly apparent that he genuinely preferred many of the customs and habits of his East End hosts to those of his own social circle and that his experience revived the old half-envious regard for the poor of his young manhood. The only criticism he ever made referred to the 'penalty of fleas' which he endured in a house cluttered with rubbish.

I may have been exceptionally fortunate, and three families are not many, but I can only speak as I have found: wholesome, pleasant family life, very simple food, very regular habits, healthy bodies and healthy minds; affectionate relations of husbands and wives, mothers and sons, of elders with children, of friend with friend—all these things I found, and amongst those I lodged with I saw little to mar a very agreeable picture, fairly representative of Class E and applicable to some at least of Classes C and D.[3]

Though he did not reveal his identity to the people with whom he thus came into contact, Booth made absolutely no attempt to disguise himself. 'If you want to conceal yourself, you must be yourself' was his policy, and the unquestioning ease with which his fellow lodgers accepted the fact that he went out to his place of work as they did to

[1] *My Apprenticeship*, p. 151.   [2] *Memoir*, pp. 105 et seq.   [3] *Poverty* i, p. 158.

theirs is proof of its validity.[1] 'My object which I trust was a fair one, was never suspected, my position never questioned. The people with whom I lived became, and are still, my friends.'[2]

Much of what Booth recorded on these journeys of exploration lies unused in his notebooks, but enough of it was included in the published works to 'add life and warmth to the columns of figures which, taken by themselves, are somewhat colourless and cold', just as he had hoped.[3] Booth was a born field worker. The photographic eye which his water colours reveal him to have possessed, observed with accuracy every last detail of the scene before him; and in preparing his notes for publication, he made no effort to censor or fiddle the evidence, to sift the shocking or the unpalatable. The frozen garbage in the gutter, the overflowing bucket in the common closet, the penny toy clutched in the hand of a child, the bird in a cage or the plant in a pot on the sill, were reported in faithful detail as part and parcel of an unemotional record of the inhabitants and their way of life. His account made horrific reading at the time just because of this complete lack of sensationalism. Carefully, noncommittally, it was all written down with only here and there a dry turn of phrase which revealed the personality of the editor: for example, he could not find it in his heart to condemn the factory girl who spent all her savings in one abandoned fling. But these were only incidental comments and the cumulative effect of these detailed descriptions was one of the most scrupulous detachment.

The nearest he came to a personal intrusion into the scenes he described was when he made some reference to the work of those who sought to uplift the poor, and even then his point was implied rather than stated.

The mother works hard for her children and attends every mothers' meeting she can, as well as every mission hall if possible. This brings her soup three or four times a week and sometimes a loaf of bread, and so the poor woman keeps her little room, and the children with bread. At Christmas she may contrive to get two or three Christmas dinners from different places.[4]

The sincerity of the regard in which he held not only these special

---

[1] The Matthews, a working class family with whom he frequently stayed when in Liverpool, only discovered his identity when he later invited them to act as caretakers at Gracedieu, his inquiries on behalf of his wife as to how much coal a kitchener should normally burn in a week conveying nothing to them of the difference between the two establishments.

[2] *Poverty* i, p. 158.   [3] Ibid., p. 156.   [4] Ibid., ii, p. 54.

friends but the working classes generally, shines out through all the descriptive notes he wrote about them: his characteristic interest in and appreciation of the point of view of others, infused his detachment with affection and understanding. He wrote with feeling of the 'silent want' with which the respectable poor endured ill-fortune, and with understanding of the appeal to certain types of humanity of the freedom of living from hand to mouth: 'The life has its attractions in spite of its hardships.'[1] He was thus able to offset the happy hours in the lives of the poor against the miseries and misfortunes and to conclude in all sincerity that though 'Their lives are an unending struggle and lack comfort. . . . I do not know that they lack happiness.' To which he added a revealing footnote: 'An analysis of the elements of happiness would hardly be in place here but it may be remarked that neither poverty nor wealth have much part in it. The main conditions of human happiness I believe to be work and affection and he who works for those he loves fulfils these conditions most easily.'[2]

Booth had set himself to produce the finished book within a year of the presentation of his Second Paper to the Royal Statistical Society in May 1888. Social tension was mounting: nothing seemed more important than to get his account of the actual facts of the situation into the hands of the public regardless of the faults and omissions which such haste must necessitate. 'Drink is treated incidentally, but deserved a prominent place. On the "Housing of the Poor" nothing is said. Early marriages, prostitution, education, religion are barely touched upon, and yet each has a side especially connected with a more or less poor and altogether working-class population.'[3] The book was divided into three parts. The first, for which he made himself wholly responsible, consisted of the two earlier Papers, 'reprinted with alterations and additions' which greatly increased their length. Thus the descriptions of the various classes and neighbourhoods were considerably extended by the inclusion of Booth's own notes and of actual pages from the investigators' notebooks which detailed, family by family, and room by room, all the information collected concerning the condition of the overcrowded population. The data on more general aspects of the problem of poverty were also amplified into chapters. One of these, on 'Institutions', foreshadowed the Religious Influences Series, in that it contained a review of the 'influences' to which the people were subjected, varying from hospitals to clubs and

[1] First Paper, p. 329.   [2] *Poverty* i, p. 131.   [3] First Edition i, p. 591.

missions, and from public houses to Board Schools and religion. This was followed by a chapter on 'Poverty', based on the first two Papers, but it also included fresh material comprising an analysis of the expenditures of thrifty families, carried out in order to make his definition of poverty more precise.[1] All of this appeared as Part One under the heading of 'The Classes'. Part Two, 'The Trades', consisted of studies of the trades peculiar to the East End prepared by his collaborators, to which Booth contributed an introductory review of the industrial position in the area as a whole. Three articles on special subjects, Sweating,[2] The Influx of Population and The Jewish Community, made up Part Three; Booth made himself responsible for the first of these, as well as for the 'Point of View' with which the book concluded.

With such a programme Booth had no time to develop a writer's craftsmanship; he did not, indeed, aspire to literary distinction. His wife did what she could, but despite her efforts, the book tended to be repetitive and diffuse, and the tables of statistics were insufficiently digested. Even so, the general effect was overwhelming. The stark fact of the unexpectedly high proportion of the population living in poverty had already received wide publicity after the presentation of his Papers, but the mass and the evident veracity of the detailed evidence with which it was now supported gave it a fresh and startling power to shock which affected even Booth himself.

It may with some show of reason be regarded as not so very bad that a tenth of the population should be regarded as very poor, in a district so confessedly poverty-stricken as East London; but when we count up the 100,000 individuals, the 20,000 families, who lead so pinched a life among the population described, and remember that there are in addition double that number who, if not actually pressed by want, yet have nothing to spare, we shrink aghast from the picture.[3]

At the beginning of his work Booth stated that he had 'no preconceived ideas, no theory to work up to, no pet scheme into agreement with which the facts collected were to be twisted or to which they would have to be squared'.[4] As a direct consequence of his encounters with the poor as individuals, and of the high regard in

[1] See Appendix IV.

[2] The appointment of the House of Lords Select Committee on Sweating in 1888 has been attributed to the publication of Booth's work (Mary Agnes Hamilton, *Sidney and Beatrice Webb*, Sampson Low, Marston & Co., 1932, p. 95).

[3] *Poverty* i, p. 177.   [4] Ibid., p. 165.

which he held them he emerged as a convinced defender of the people against those who would do them good and were prepared to destroy their way of living because of its imperfections. Nothing that he had discovered caused him to retreat from the conviction which he had expressed in his earlier Papers, that the poor and the working class constituted quite distinct groups, and that the crux of the problem of poverty lay in the removal of the burden of the helpless and hopeless of his Class B from about the necks of the true labouring classes. If anything, this opinion was strengthened by the increased regard with which he came to view those whose way of life could be described in terms of simplicity rather than want, and of whom he now declared that they were his clients, to whom especially he dedicated his book.[1]

> I perhaps build too much on my slight experience, but I see nothing im-
> probable in the general view that the simple natural lives of working-class
> people tend to their own and their children's happiness more than the artificial
> complicated existence of the rich. Let it not be supposed, however, that on this
> I propose to base any argument against the desire of this class to better its
> position. Very far from it.[2]

Boldly he reiterated his belief that the State must assume responsibi-
lity for the 'helpless and hopeless'; elaborating the suggestion tentatively indicated in his second Paper,[3] he outlined a scheme for their com-
pulsory removal to some such institution as an industrial colony. With characteristic integrity, he grasped the nettle of the implications of this declaration. Certainly this was socialism but it was socialism of a definable and restricted character. The principle implied in the Poor Law, that responsibility for those who could not achieve the minimum of civilized living must be assumed by the community as a whole, was already generally accepted. All that he suggested was an extension of its application. 'Our Individualism fails because our Socialism is incomplete', he argued, and on this proceeded to develop the doctrine of 'limited socialism' to which he had already referred in his two Papers.

> In taking charge of the lives of the incapable, State Socialism finds its proper
> work, and by doing it completely, would relieve us of a serious danger. The
> Individualist doctrine breaks down as things are, and is invaded on every side
> by Socialistic innovations, but its hardy doctrines would have a far better
> chance in a society purged of those who cannot stand alone. Thorough
> interference on the part of the State with the lives of a small fraction of the

---

[1] *Poverty* i, p. 177.   [2] Ibid., p. 160.   [3] See above, p. 96.

population would tend to make it possible, ultimately, to dispense with any Socialistic interference in the lives of all the rest.[1]

Volume One of *Life and Labour of the People of London* was published in April 1889. The reception accorded to it belied the modest description of its contents with which Booth had concluded his Paper to the Royal Statistical Society the previous year. Fragmentary and inadequate the book might appear to one whose comprehensive intention had been to cover the whole of London, but to the general public its significance was immediate and immense, and the first edition was quickly exhausted. Only Booth knew that in spite of this fact the sales did not entirely cover the cost of production.[2] Its appearance was greeted with 'wondering admiration'. Every type of newspaper— daily and weekly, serious or sensational, at home and abroad—carried reviews and articles which provoked readers to a brisk correspondence. The mere fact that such an investigation had proved possible, coupled with the distressing revelations that had resulted from it, produced general agreement that this was the most important contribution so far made to the study of the great new problem of the urban poor. Booth and his fellow workers were declared to merit the deepest public gratitude: reviewers loudly proclaimed that no one interested in social problems could afford to miss this book. Beatrice Potter was specially commended for her brilliant contributions, and Booth was credited with 'a faculty for taking pains beyond even the fabled capacities of genius'.[3] The book was variously claimed to be the first blue-book ever published to have made the statistical method readable, and to have provided chapter and verse for each note of anguish in *The Bitter Cry of Outcast London*. It was appraised, indeed, as the one practical outcome of all the gush that had recently been poured out.

So ran the chorus of praise as review after review appeared. Nothing could be more eloquent of the force of the impact which Booth's exploration of the principles and practice of social investigation made upon the thinking of his times. Only a few were critical. The *Athenaeum*, for example, remarked coldly that 'The book is entirely without literary merit but contains information useful for philanthropists. It has a curious map of East London. . . . There is no attempt

[1] *Poverty* i, p. 167.

[2] In a letter to Macmillan and Co., who published all his subsequent work, he wrote at a later date: 'Personally I am content if the price covers cost. I do not think a profit can be expected.'

[3] *Daily News*, 16 April 1889.

to make the book readable, nor is it provided with an index, so that its perusal is a work of solid labour.'[1] The Charity Organization Society veiled its flat opposition to his concept of limited socialism in polite expressions of appreciation. 'It would be especially ungracious to quarrel with Mr. Booth for his single excursion into the pleasant dreamland of world-making. He has fairly earned the relaxation, and the modesty with which his scheme of sanctified pauperism is submitted disarms criticism.'[2]

Such criticisms were irrelevant to the point Booth had wished to make. What mattered was that the tool which had taken such long years to perfect had been put to the test and had proved its worth. Quite apart from the value of the specific results achieved, he had succeeded in demonstrating that human society could be analysed and described by means of a combination of statistics and observation. More particularly it would now be possible to provide an accurate and factual basis upon which the politician and the philanthropist could base their proposals for reform.

The divergence between these two points of view, between relative and absolute, is in itself enough to cause the whole difference between pessimism and optimism. To judge rightly we need to bear both in mind, never to forget the numbers when thinking of the percentages, nor the percentages when thinking of the numbers. This last is difficult to those whose daily experience or whose imagination brings vividly before them the trials and sorrows of individual lives. They refuse to set off and balance the happy hours of the same class, or even of the same people, against these miseries; much less can they consent to bring the lot of other classes into the account, add up the opposing figures, and contentedly carry forward a credit balance. In the arithmetic of woe they can only add or multiply, they cannot subtract or divide. In intensity of feeling such as this, and not in statistics, lies the power to move the world. But by statistics, must this power be guided if it would move the world aright.[3]

No wonder Booth was eager to get to work on the next instalment of his great plan. ' "The Book" a great success and C.B. delighted', wrote Beatrice in her diary while on a visit to the Booths at Gracedieu on 21 April. 'Leaders in all the principal papers; and C.B. quite the head of the statistical tree.'[4]

The astonished admiration with which the book was received would have spurred any man on to further endeavours, but the fact that Volume One was so labelled proves that Booth needed no such

[1] 27 April 1889.   [2] *The Charity Organization Society Review*, May 1889.
[3] *Poverty* i, p. 178.   [4] Passfield.

incentive and had every intention of continuing the task which he had begun. Indeed, before the reviewers had finished commenting on this first book, he was already at work on its successor, setting about it so unostentatiously that there is hardly any reference to what he was doing even in his private correspondence. Booth's plans for the continuation of his work were, however, hampered by the inadequacy of the support accorded to them. Together with five friends, whose names are not known, he formed a working committee to tackle the description of Central London on the lines of his own inquiry into the East End, and under his inspiration Graham Balfour[1] undertook a similar investigation of Battersea, but apart from these two, none of the parallel inquiries for which he had hoped showed signs of materializing. Forced to accept the fact that he would have to trim his sails if he was to achieve his original intention of surveying the whole of London's population, he therefore decided to use the street as his basic unit instead of the individual family. In consequence, it became necessary to drop for the time being all direct reference to the employment of the people and to concentrate on their condition. In making this decision, he was influenced by the fact that he had in mind another scheme for the more thorough investigation of industrial conditions to which he proposed to return in due course. He was strongly attracted to this—'my beloved trades inquiry' he called it—but, methodical as always, he determined to finish off the classification of the condition of the people of London before he allowed himself to pursue any fresh interest. The hope which he had originally expressed that the two sides of his inquiry, into life and into labour, would illuminate each other, was accordingly deferred, permanently, as it turned out.

There is no evidence to suggest that Booth ever questioned the wisdom of this decision or considered the possibility that what was required might not be more facts but a reconsideration of the implications of those already in his possession: being acutely aware that the facts he had so far collected made the problem plain enough but threw little light on its solution, he apparently concluded that this must be due to some deficiency in the quality of his information. Nevertheless, it is significant that it was at this juncture that Beatrice Potter decided that her active participation in the work of the Inquiry must cease. Booth had invited her to undertake a more thorough study of women's

---

[1] Presumably the Dr. T. Graham Balfour who took the chair at the meetings of the Royal Statistical Society at which Booth's First and Second Papers were presented.

work, but this she refused on the grounds that she preferred to examine the Co-operative Movement as providing a possible alternative to the capitalist system. Her autobiography makes it clear that this decision was the direct outcome of her experiences as an investigator. The complexity of the problems she had encountered had convinced her that they were beyond solution by individual effort and could only be dealt with by collective action, which she assumed must automatically involve a departure from the principles of individualism.[1] Booth's only reference to the conflict to which this difference of opinion gave rise occurred in the 'Point of View' with which Volume One concluded. Referring to the fact that the book is sometimes inconsistent and seems to speak with an uncertain voice, he wrote, 'The unanimity of thought and expression in the book . . . is much more noticeable than are any divergences.'[2] Beatrice's diary records the dismay with which she came to realize the personal implications of the difference of opinion which lay between them:

My friendship or rather my companionship with Charlie is for the time dropped—our common work is ended. His brave vigorous life with its varied interests and unselfconscious and disinterested pursuit of them will always be an encouraging thought, his thoughtful kindness and true affection will always be one of the comforting memories of my life.[3]

So they went their separate ways, and in due course Beatrice's engagement to Sidney Webb confirmed the growing sense of difference between them, emphasizing as it did her socialist tendencies as opposed to the Booths' growing conservatism. The secrecy which surrounded this engagement was 'evidently supremely distasteful to them', and when she suggested that they should therefore ignore it, Mrs. Booth heartily concurred. 'That curious little look of veiled determination came over her face, and she said, "You see Charlie and I have *nothing* in common with Mr. Webb. Charlie would never go to him for help, and he would never go to Charlie, so that it would not be natural for them to see each other. When you are married it will be different." '[4]

Although from time to time the cousins met again in succeeding years, the old triangular partnership had been damaged beyond repair.

[1] *My Apprenticeship*, p. 350. Discussing this, Beatrice stresses the point that it was no coincidence that the two most distinguished members of the staff of the Inquiry (Aves and Llewellyn Smith) were later 'influentially associated with perhaps the two biggest experiments in public administration and public control in the interest of the manual workers that the century had yet seen' (ibid., p. 255).

[2] *First Edition* i, p. 591.   [3] Passfield.   [4] Ibid.

'A shadow has crept between us and has deepened into darkness', was Beatrice's regretful comment. However, when she came to write her reminiscences, she was able to look beyond that darkness to the light of the days which preceded it, and her description of the work she did with and for Booth constitutes one of the most interesting parts of her autobiography, as well as a tribute of no mean order to the man and his work.[1]

The task to which Booth next set himself was of awe-inspiring dimensions, his proposal being no less than to classify 'every single street, and court, and block of buildings' in the entire Metropolitan area. First, the total number of people in each street would have to be estimated in proportion to the number of children living there, then the means and position of the parents of these children must be ascertained, and finally, the street would have to be allocated to the appropriate 'Class', as defined in the earlier analysis. For his information he proposed to rely as before on the School Board Visitors. At this stage, no attempt was made to classify or analyse. 'Those who gave the information did not know what use would be made of it, nor were they asked to decide in what class each family should be placed. The accounts of each street and its inhabitants were noted with running pen, and the result is a very vivid picture, honestly drawn, and I believe true.'[2] Booth was, of course, well aware of the cogency of the criticism that, however experienced and reliable these men might be, basically the information they offered as to the condition of the people was a matter of opinion rather than fact. Accordingly, the classification of the streets on the basis of these interviews was subjected to a most meticulous revision. Booth and his secretaries inspected the streets themselves to see whether the classification agreed with outward appearances, whilst the School Board Visitors were invited to scrutinize the lists.

After this it was referred to the parish relieving officers for each Union, and to the agents of the Charity Organization Society throughout London. The police were also referred to with regard to the streets marked black. Finally, I have consulted the clergy and their district visitors as to most of the poorer parts, obtaining from them, by the way, interesting details of typical streets.[3]

Only after this was each street given its final classification, and duly marked 'in the shade and colours of its prevailing social character' on a specially prepared map of London. Sixteen feet by thirteen in size,

[1] *My Apprenticeship.* Chapter 5, *et passim.*   [2] *Poverty* ii, p. 230.   [3] Ibid., p. 17.

this was drawn to the scale of 25 inches to the mile. On it the streets were marked in eight colours varying from black through blue to red and yellow. Elasticity was given to the system by combining the colours, a dark blue background being striped with lines of black, for example, to indicate a street in which not only 'great poverty' but also 'vice' prevailed.[1] Considerable though the task of accumulating and analysing all the evidence proved to be, this was by no means all. In accordance with what had become his custom, this information was implemented by short studies of subjects of peculiar interest which were undertaken as special commissions by individuals amongst Booth's colleagues. These were concerned mainly with problems of poverty. They included an independent inquiry into the conditions of life in the blocks of model dwellings then being built by the Peabody and similar Trusts, and commonly urged as the panacea for all social ills. As usual, his findings in this miniature investigation were carefully classified, and supported by the 'fruits of personal observation', which this time included an article by Octavia Hill deploring the influence of the conditions obtaining in such blocks of dwellings on the character of the inhabitants. Again, by way of verifying the reliability of the observation of the School Board Visitors, he instituted a separate investigation for the purpose of 'looking at the same facts through the eyes of the teachers',[2] his informants on this occasion being invited to fill up forms issued to them for the purpose instead of being personally interviewed.

In assembling this mass of material, Booth did not hesitate to make use of the assistance of the group of friends, acquaintances and employees who had been attracted into his service,[3] but the task of editing he once more accepted as his own. Night after night he toiled away after his day's work was over, each evening's stint being submitted to his wife for her approval and correction before either of them thought of calling a halt. As before, he found himself with far more information than he could use. The flow of population from the country into London, and the contrary movement outwards towards the suburbs, were only two out of the many topics on which he had

[1] See above, p. 94. See also Appendix II.

[2] *Poverty* iii, pp. 195-306. The opportunity was taken of surveying the provision of education in London for children of the poorer classes, and the extent to which it met their needs.

[3] The Table of Contents in the volume as finally published specifically mentions twelve collaborators.

acquired much knowledge, but to which he felt unable to do justice either from lack of space or insufficiency of evidence. In view of later developments, it is of particular interest that another line which he had pursued but not completed concerned 'the influences at work to make or mend the condition of things indicated by the map'.[1]

The book finally appeared in 1891 as Volume Two of the First Edition of the Inquiry, two years after the publication of the first volume. It was accompanied by a separate appendix in the form of a folder containing additional statistical tables and what became known as the 'Poverty Map', reduced in scale and cut up into sections. This time the title was reversed to read *Labour and Life of the People, London, Continued*, life before labour having been claimed to be the copyright of Samuel Smiles,[2] though in all the subsequent editions Booth reverted to the original order. In spite of all his care, the book remained something of a hotchpotch, consisting in part of the individual studies of Central London and Battersea already mentioned and in part of the description of the whole of London, street by street, together with the special chapters relating to each of these sections. By far the greater bulk of the book consisted of the detailed descriptions of individual streets with which he supported his system of classification. These ran into many pages, a mass of evidence reproduced just as it had been recorded in the first instance. Thus he introduced a group of 'black' streets by saying:

> I propose to take the reader from end to end of each of these streets and some adjoining courts, and to tell the story, house by house, as I have received it from the City missionaries, who, one for 11 and the other for 29 years, have made it their business to visit here, carrying the Gospel with impartiality to willing and unwilling ears.[3]

The results were even more distressing to the middle and upper classes than those that had emerged from the earlier inquiries. In his first Papers, Booth had estimated that about 25 per cent. of the people of London as a whole, lived in poverty, this being based on the assumption that poverty would be proportionate to density of population. He was surprised to discover that this was nearly 6 per cent. too low, the figures for the individual classes being as follows:[4]

[1] *Poverty* ii, p. 17.

[2] *Life and Labour*, or *Characterization of Men of Industry, Culture and Genius*, by Samuel Smiles, was published in 1887.

[3] *Poverty* ii, p. 46. See also Appendix II, where a specimen page is reproduced.

[4] Ibid., p. 21.

		%	%
A (lowest)		·9	
B (very poor)		7·5	In poverty, 30·7
C and D (poor)		22·3	
E and F (working class, comfortable) . .		51·5	In comfort, 69·3
G and H (middle class and above) . .		17·8	

Moreover, the highest percentage of poverty in London was not to be found in its most crowded districts but in an area in Southwark between Blackfriars and London Bridge, where it was nearly 68 per cent.[1] In addition, high percentages were also found in West London, as in Maida Vale and Notting Hill, where upwards of half the population were classified as living in poverty. These areas lay alongside the residential districts of the middle classes, who thus were suddenly awakened to the realization that the familiar exhortation that 'the poor are always with us' was all too literally true.

In the light of these figures, Booth could only conclude that the gloomy thoughts to which his earlier work had given rise must remain unchanged.[2] It was this fact which moved *The Times* to describe *Labour and Life* as 'the grimmest book of our generation', and accounted for the widespread interest with which its appearance was greeted. Once more astonishment was expressed that any one man, even aided by so expert a team, should have been able to devise and to implement a scheme for analysing factually the social condition of so motley a mass of human beings as the population of Central London. Once more dismay was registered at the extent of poverty which that analysis revealed, and once more Booth was cordially thanked for the service he had rendered to all those who were concerned with the deplorable problem of the chronic poor. This time even *The Pall Mall Gazette* could find little to criticize. 'If he could only get himself and his young men and women to write better English we should not know where to find a fault.'[3]

Public tributes to Booth's labours came fast and from afar. Papers to the Royal Statistical Society became almost an annual event, and he served an active term of office as its President (1892-4) during which he was awarded the Society's Guy Medal for his statistical work, and led a delegation to the President of the Board of Trade to press for

[1] *Poverty* ii, p. 31.   [2] First Edition ii, p. 592.

[3] Incidentally, reviewers found it necessary to explain that the Editor was 'Mr. Booth, not the General', the latter having published his book *In Darkest England* in the previous year. *Pall Mall Gazette*, 31 July 1891.

the establishment of a permanent statistical organization and the taking of a quinquennial Census.[1] His support was sought by the organizers of all manner of campaigns and conferences. He served as Vice-President of the Economic Section of the British Association. He was an obvious choice for membership of the Royal Commission on the Aged Poor in 1892,[2] on which occasion his wife wrote drily that she was thrilled to hear of his having a Despatch Box with his name on it in gold letters, and being invited to bask in the smiles of Royalty: 'You are at last a member of "Society" with a very big S— which is defined to be the whole body of persons personally known to the Prince of Wales.' He himself was probably more gratified by a 'command' to visit Florence Nightingale, doubtless in connexion with the scheme for the alleviation of poverty in India on which she was then engaged.

Many a man would have been content to rest on the laurels thus justly and hardly won. Not so Booth, to whom this preliminary exploration of the jungle of poverty served merely to inflame the always acute sense of unease with regard to the poor which had originally inspired his work. In spite of all his labours, the answer to the 'problem of all problems' still eluded him. As he put it in the brief 'Outline of Further Work' with which he concluded his survey of poverty:

At an early stage in my work, when asked by one from whom I sought information—'What is the good of it all?'—I had to admit that I walked in faith. This attitude had changed but little when I reached the end of the first volume. . . . The conclusion of a second volume leaves my position unchanged. An extension of the area of the inquiry from East London to the whole of London has enlarged the wilderness of figures, but has not done much to make the path more clear.[3]

To make the path more clear: there lay the problem. Though the lack of concrete results emerging from his investigations disappointed him, he was convinced that his personal contribution to its solution lay in carrying on with his investigations. 'To action I have never pretended, and any claim on abstract thought I abandon as a childish delusion, so nothing is left for me but investigation', he once assured Beatrice.[4] What form should these further investigations take? His results had satisfied him that the social problems of his day could not

---

[1] He had already served on a committee set up to advise the Registrar-General on arrangements for the 1891 Census.

[2] See also Chapter VIII.   [3] First Edition ii, p. 591.   [4] Passfield.

be understood, or remedied, in terms of poverty alone. Poverty, in fact, was only one aspect of a complex situation which, he recognized, also required an analysis of earnings, and an examination of the 'moral questions' which he had thus far omitted from his work. These were subjects which he had long looked forward to studying. The hope that in so doing he might find the answer to the problems left unsolved by the Poverty Inquiry increased the enthusiasm with which he now fell to work upon them.

6

The Labour of the People

WHEN he had finished the Poverty Inquiry, a multitude of possibilities for continuing his researches presented themselves to Booth, and it was therefore difficult for him to decide how best to deploy the resources at his disposal. The project nearest to his heart was almost certainly the extension of his survey to cover the 'labour' of the people of London: the orderly filling-in of the vacant spaces of his 'gigantic statistical framework' possessed for him a charm which almost rivalled that of the business in his affections. The way having already been prepared by the studies included in the first two volumes, he regarded this as a straightforward task on which he proposed to start forthwith.

Further exploration of the problems which his investigations into the 'life' of the people had revealed, presented greater difficulties. His inquiries so far had made it plain that Class B was 'the crux of the situation', but had not made it any 'more easy to see how it should be dealt with'. However, two lines of advance seemed promising. The first concerned the revision of the Poor Law, a subject on which he had already touched, and to which he had promised to return when he could secure the basic information without which practical discussion could not start.[1] Beyond that he glimpsed a second entrancing vista, again one which he had previously begun to explore, but which now seemed doubly attractive in view of the opposition aroused by his advocacy of even a 'limited socialism' in the breasts of those who staunchly supported the principles of the Charity Organization Society.

Before attempting to decide what further or other action should be pursued,

---

[1] First Edition ii, p. 592.

we need to take stock of all that is being done now, so as to trace the effects of the agencies actually at work upon the existing state of things; to compare the principles by which they are guided, one with another, and the condition of districts left to themselves on account of the lack or lapse of such agencies, with that of others in which religious or philanthropic enthusiasm is active; and so gather into one focus a mass of varied experience. This I shall try to do.[1]

There is also reason to believe that he considered the possibility of extending his inquiries to the provinces:[2] a letter written in 1892 suggests that when he took up lodgings in the Scotland Road area in Liverpool, his purpose in doing so might have been to study conditions of employment at first hand.

Here the house is now quite full and more than full—but 2 are going today. We have a carpenter and a coppersmith, a barman and a pawnbroker's assistant besides the Matthews and myself, the Kings (man wife and child) who leave today. King is a worker in iron. So we have a considerable variety of occupation. The Matthews had to sleep in the kitchen on Wednesday night on the sofa and in the arm chair but last night the coppersmith was working all night lining a brewers vat with copper to be ready for today and so (Box and Cox like) his bed was available, he kindly consenting. These men and I all take our meals in the kitchen, but they are half an hour or so before me at each time. The Matthews have their meals mostly down at the shop or at odd times. With the house full and the shop they are busy from 5 or 6 a.m. to midnight every day. It is all interesting to watch and share as one's daily life. Makes a variety like.

The tone of this letter points the way in which his thoughts were moving, and makes it evident that his interest at this stage lay in the study of the problems of industry rather than in the relief of destitution or the analysis of religious and philanthropic influences. This is borne out by his Presidential Address to the Royal Statistical Society in 1892.[3] Characteristically refusing to follow the tradition that the President should regard the occasion of his inauguration as an opportunity to review the present position of the Society and to forecast its future, Booth chose to present a paper on 'London's Dockside Labour'. He took as his starting point the remarkable change which he felt had come over the situation since he first described it in 1887.[4]

[1] First Edition i, p. 592.

[2] 'At last accounts, Mr. Booth was in a lodging in Liverpool, at an address unknown to his friends, making preliminary observations for a full study of the poverty of Liverpool.' R. A. Woods, *English Social Movements*, Swan Sonnenschein & Co., 1895, p. 216.

[3] *Journal of the Royal Statistical Society*, 1892, pp. 521-57.   [4] *Poverty* iv, p. 12.

In 1887, when I was considering dock employment as a principal East End industry, I found the position to be very hopeless as well as very unsatisfactory. The employers were content, and the men, though far from content, were entirely unorganized. The dock managers accepted the crowd and struggle at the dock gates as an inevitable phenomenon, which happened to fit in well with the conditions of their trade. They could always be sure of labour and though its quality might be bad, its pay was correspondingly low. The character of the men matched well with the character of the work and its remuneration. All alike were low and irregular. The vicious circle was complete. How should it be broken?

In 1892 all this is changed. The unions, founded under the greatest difficulties in 1888, have had a wonderful career; and if some mistakes have been made, and some hopes disappointed, there yet remains a solid foundation on which much may be built, and an inspiring record.[1]

This far-reaching change seemed to demonstrate the possibility of effecting improvements in the standard of living by other means than those advocated by the socialists: what had been achieved by voluntary action on the part of employers and employed in one industry could surely be emulated by others? The argument lent renewed conviction to the belief that the life of the people must be studied in relation to their work, and it was in the specific hope that the answer to the unsolved problems revealed by his study of poverty lay in this relationship that Booth therefore organized his next venture. 'I am trying to connect the social classification of the workers throughout with the terms upon which they work', he told the Royal Statistical Society when, in accordance with his usual practice, he presented a report on the progress of his inquiries in 1893.[2]

The objectives of the new survey were made clear in the introduction to the Industry Series, where he wrote:

The first Inquiry had been an attempt to describe the inhabitants of London, especially the poorer part of them, and their social conditions, as they lived, street by street, family by family, in their homes. The aim of the other method [on which the Industry Series was to be based] was to review the people as they work, trade by trade, in their factories, warehouses or shops, or pursue their avocations in the streets or on the railways, in the markets or on the quays; to consider their relations to those whom they serve, whether employer or customer, and the remuneration they receive; and finally, to examine the bearing which the money earned has on the life they lead.[3]

[1] *Journal of the Royal Statistical Society*, 1892, p. 522.
[2] Ibid., 1893, pp. 557-93.   [3] Second Edition ix, p. 159.

In extending his investigations to the sphere of industry, Booth's first concern was to discover some common measure which would render possible comparisons between one trade and another, and between the results thus obtained with those derived from the poverty inquiry. In the Poverty Series, his system of classification had necessarily been dictated by the nature of the records of the School Board Visitors; as his critics pointed out and as he readily acknowledged, this amounted in effect to no more than a matter of opinion. He was now able to utilize statistical data recorded for the first time in the Census in 1891, largely at his own instigation. As a member of the committee set up to advise the Registrar-General, he had urged the inclusion in the enumeration of 'some simple facts by which the position and manner of life of each family could be measured'.[1] Acting on this advice, the Registrar-General had instructed his officers to record the number of rooms occupied by each householder living in four rooms or less, and the number of servants employed in households of five rooms or more. Booth went to considerable personal trouble to see that this instruction was carried out efficiently.

> To meet the difficulty of novelty, and to make sure that the enumerator's work was carefully and intelligently performed, at any rate in London . . . I personally saw all the Registrars more than once, and discussed the subject with them, pointed out the object to be attained, and the important uses that could be made of the material to be collected; and my appeal was very heartily responded to both by them and by the enumerators.[2]

He was able to use the material thus provided to create a new 'statistical instrument', the overcrowding index, which he regarded with the greatest delight and enthusiasm; he was always a lover of inventions. Admitting to the Royal Statistical Society the possibility that he exaggerated its value—a doubt which events proved to be well founded—he nevertheless declared that:

> It seems to me to render possible comparisons of great social interest and to open up a large field of inquiry into the actual structure of society. The facts which I have used to classify the inhabitants of London could be applied to any city—to Paris or Moscow, New York or Melbourne, Calcutta or Hong Kong; and for the matter of that would have served equally well in ancient Rome or Babylon.[3]

The measurement of 'position and manner of life' was intended to

---

[1] *Industry* i, p. 16.   [2] Ibid., p. 12.

[3] *Journal of the Royal Statistical Society*, 1893, p. 590. See also *Industry* i, p. 16.

supplement rather than to supplant the methods of the inquiry which had just been completed. As before, the investigation was to be based on a combination of intensive and extensive researches, and statistics and verbal descriptions were to be blended together:

> Without a full comprehension of unexpressed details, general statements are always lifeless, and often misleading; without some trustworthy generalization—some ground plan of classification, by which, as in the drawers of a mineralogist's cabinet, details can be classified and seen in their proper place—elaboration is partly thrown away.[1]

Each trade or group of trades was to be described on an identical plan so that information regarding conditions of employment, rates of pay and the standard of living of those engaged in it, might be comparable with that concerning any other trade. In this way, and by this variety of approach, Booth hoped to be able to present so complete an account of the industrial scene in London that every man in all its millions should be able to find his own circumstances described in it, even if he were a pauper and had no occupation or lived at ease as a rich man. 'There is no life that is led in London which may not serve as an illustration of this book—no individual who may not find his place in its schedules.'[2]

The precise plan of his campaign is outlined with characteristic clarity in a letter written to Ernest Aves in February 1892 when the preliminary exploration had been completed and the time was ripe for detailed operations to begin:

> You were so good as to say you would perhaps give me some aid over my 'London Industries' and we are now in a position to divide up the work. So if you think it will suit you, will you come to a conference at my office?
> The plan roughly speaking is as follows:
> We have divided the whole population into groups—100 groups in all, according to occupations, and for each group in each district we expect to be able to give from the Census or through the kindness of the Registrar-General:
>
> (1) Numbers employed—by sexes and ages.
> (2) Numbers of Heads of families and of those apparently dependent.
> (3) Birth place (in or out of London) for Heads of families.
> (4) Social position of Heads of families as shown by number of rooms occupied or of servants kept.
>
> To this we shall add (and to a great extent have got already):

---

[1] *Journal of the Royal Statistical Society*, 1893, p. 591.   [2] Second Edition ix, p. 161.

(5) The facts as to trade organization; and concurrently shall study,
(6) System of work.
(7) Remuneration—hours and seasons.
(8) Character of labour
        i.e. Male or female
           Young or old
           Skilled or unskilled, etc.

All of which is to be got from three sources:

        (*a*) Trades Unions (part done).
        (*b*) Masters.
        (*c*) Individual workmen.

And from the individual workmen we wish if we can to get as vivid pictures as possible of their working life as these alone will make the book readable.

Each group of trades will be made the subject of a report with appendix of actual notes and from these reports and notes I shall write the book. I cannot leave the writing in several hands because of the need of obtaining unity and preserving proportion.

If you will undertake one or two allied groups I shall be very grateful.

I am writing also to Mr. Fox who has volunteered to help and am proposing a meeting for Monday morning next 11 o'clock if that will suit you and him.

It is especially interesting that this letter should have opened with an invitation to Ernest Aves to collaborate in the Inquiry, for he was quickly to take Beatrice Potter's place as Booth's most intimate colleague and the one who shared more of the responsibility for the enterprise than any other. Aves first met Booth when he came to Toynbee Hall from Cambridge. Their collaboration began in the course of the Poverty Inquiry, for which he wrote a paper on 'The Furniture Trade': he remained with him as his co-editor and deputy until the entire Inquiry had been completed. The sheer bulk of his contribution would in itself constitute a claim to fame, for he was responsible for the lion's share of the Industry Series, and played a major part in the conduct of that on Religious Influences. Her husband was the more enthusiastic of the two, Aves the more judicial, wrote Mrs. Booth, in her memoir:

Aves had a natural gift of fairmindedness beyond any that I have ever met... a thing all the more remarkable as his mind was by no means indifferent. He held definite views, he was suggestive, even audacious in suggestion, and could argue convincingly in support of his opinion.[1]

[1] *Memoir*, p. 131.

To which comment Mrs. Barnett's description adds a caustic note:

Ernest Aves . . . the 'Pater', so wise, deep-voiced, judicial, so steadfastly dutiful and strong in his slowness, so wholly loveable and generally so tiresomely right.[1]

The brief account given by Booth in the Industry Series conveys little of the intensive activity which now ensued, but the quantities which survive of notes of interviews, of questionnaires, and of letters, convey some impression of the dimensions of the undertaking on which he embarked. The work was again divided up between the members of the team of secretaries and investigators who, one can only presume, were employed and paid by Booth. Individuals from amongst his acquaintances were commissioned to prepare special studies of particular trades, and complex machinery for the extraction and analysis of information from knowledgeable persons was rapidly evolved. Questionnaires were devised which were to be filled in with black or red ink respectively, if the information given related to slack or busy periods. Lists of firms and of trade and labour organizations, to which the questionnaires might be sent, were compiled from the Factory Inspectors' notebooks, directories, and similar sources.

As regards employers in each trade, the plan adopted has been to approach as many as possible by circular asking from each an exact account of those employed, whether men, women or boys, and the wages paid to each in an average, or better still, in a maximum and minimum week. This appeal brought in every case a fair proportion of replies. Those firms who were willing to give us further assistance were then personally waited upon and consulted as to other points of interest; for instance, as to usual hours and overtime; regularity and irregularity; seasons, methods of training, etc. Nothing could exceed the kindness with which our troublesome quest has in most cases been met.[2] Factories have been opened to us, wages books have been shown, and

[1] *Canon Barnett*, Murray, 1918, Vol. 2, p. 21. Aves eventually made a name for himself as Government Commissioner on Wages Boards. He also served the Government of New Zealand as Industrial Conciliation and Arbitration Adviser.

[2] A revealing letter is that from the proprietor of Simmons' Export Perambulator Manufactory, who wrote on notepaper edged with line drawings of perambulators with Ovoid Springs, and the Paragon Child's Cart, to say at some length that 'though we have very little time and have to work very hard to keep this business afloat, I would certainly have the time expended to work up the figures you require if I thought that any useful purpose for the advantage of the poor or the increase of the peace and happiness of the country generally, could accrue from the publishing of the figures you desire to issue. Do not those statistics tend to foster discontent among the poor, and instead of directing them to exercise the discipline, industry, and thrift by which their condition might be bettered, rather suggest that while such multitudes are poor, and so few are rich, the many might plunder the rich. . . .'

particular and elaborate returns have been specially prepared for us setting forth in the most accurate way the hours worked as well as the pay received in busy and slack weeks, and the exact terms of piece and time employment.

Nor have the trades union officials been less ready to join in helping me to understand the relative positions of employer and employed in the trades with which they are connected.[1]

The reception accorded to his request for information was on the whole kindly. Some refused, more or less bluntly telling him to mind his own business, but more were only too eager to help. Infinite pains were taken to follow up any possible inaccuracy or misunderstanding, to pursue any offer of information, and to acknowledge with gratitude any services rendered. For example, as soon as the work on each group of trades was completed, it was submitted for verification to whatever associations of employers or employees were concerned. It is obvious from the correspondence that has survived that the investigators threw themselves heart and soul into their work; their interest in the information they sought was genuine and active. Thus there are references to a search for pictures of Byzantine jewellery on behalf of a small craftsman in silverwork, and to the effects on a tiny group of striking workmen of a visit from one of the investigators. One would give a great deal to know more about this side of the Inquiry.

Booth had looked forward to playing an active part in the collection of the material for the Inquiry, and he did in fact collect some of the information on which his chapters on the docks and on shopkeeping were based.[2] Unfortunately, his plans were seriously curtailed by the encroaching demands of his investigations into the administration of the Poor Law. These demands were, he found, hard to resist, so acute was his sense of obligation in any matter concerning poverty.[3] The full story of the long years of work that he undertook on behalf of the aged poor is told in a subsequent chapter. Here it can only be remarked that it involved him in the execution of a full-scale inquiry into the extent of pauperism, with particular reference to the problems of old age, which was conducted concurrently with the investigation of London's industries, and provided the material for two books and a series of papers and pamphlets. He also played an active part as a

---

[1] *Industry* i, p. 27. Branch Secretaries of the Unions were apparently recompensed for the time they devoted to being interviewed at rates varying from 1s. to 4s. per hour.

[2] See, for example, his first-hand account of the working of a small general shop, *Industry* iii, p. 251.

[3] A letter to his wife reveals that they were at this time planning, for reasons of moral principle, 'a diminished expenditure on luxury and a simpler form of household'.

member of the Royal Commission on the Aged Poor from 1892-5, attending its meetings regularly and undertaking visits to institutions all over the country on its behalf. All this was, of course, in addition to his normal and busy life as a businessman, which took him across the Atlantic at least once in every year to deal with the American end of the firm's affairs. There is no doubt that even his unrivalled capacity for keeping several pots boiling simultaneously was taxed to its uttermost and it was not until after the publication of *The Aged Poor* in 1894,[1] that he saw any prospect of being able to give to the Industry Series the attention which he felt it merited. However, he found himself frustrated once more.

My other job, my beloved trades of London for which I was jealous has been neglected a good deal because of the interloping pauper and now just when I was hoping to get on a little faster I am drawn back to the business [he told Professor Marshall]. My partner who very kindly undertook all the work last year up to this spring has been ill since Easter and is now away and will be away for some time; so the responsibility falls again on me. I must say however that it does me good, I come back to it as to a sort of mother nature and look forward keenly to my visit to New York in June or in July.

The claims of all these other interests notwithstanding, the Inquiry into Industry made steady if slow progress. The two volumes of the Poverty Series having been sold out immediately they were published, Booth had not been able to resist the temptation afforded by the need for reprinting them, to embark on a wholly new edition which would enable him to present as a single unit all of his findings up to date. The first four volumes of this second edition were issued in 1892 and 1893. They consisted of the material of the original two 'rearranged in a more popular form but not otherwise altered', though the title was qualified by the addition of the words *in London,* 'such being the actual limitation of the subject matter'.[2] A halt to publication was then called whilst the material on industry was collected and written up, this last being a process in which both Booth and his wife played a major part. Progress was yet further delayed whilst the Report on the 1891 Census was awaited, but eventually, as and when each was completed, he presented to his public four volumes of material relating to the various trades. 'Twins it will be at first and another to follow

[1] See below, Chapter VIII.

[2] Booth offered to purchasers an opportunity to exchange, free of charge, the two volumes of the First Edition in their possession for the equivalent four volumes of the new edition.

before the year is out', he wrote in 1895: in fact, the third and fourth volumes appeared the following year.

Apart from a general introduction in which he discussed his methods of classification, these volumes consisted entirely of detailed studies of the individual trades or groups of trades. Each was prepared on a common pattern. The first, that of the Building Trades, written by Ernest Aves, provides a typical example.[1] This includes an individual enumeration by age and sex of those employed and an enumeration by families, based on material collected in the course of the 1891 Census and apparently made available to Booth by the Registrar-General. The social condition of those employed is discussed and the over-crowding index applied. Changes between 1861 and 1891 are noted. The general organization of the London building trade is dealt with at length, and the process of building a house is described in detail. Particulars of the individual professions (Architects, Engineers, Builders, &c.) involved in building are given, together with similar particulars of all the individual trades involved (Foremen, Labourers, Masons, Bricklayers, Contractors, Plumbers, &c.). Conditions of employment are discussed and labour relations examined. The description ends with a brief analysis of 'abuses' connected with the building trades, and an account of the health and social conditions of those employed in it.[2] This outline was repeated in the account given of all the other trades of London in the ensuing four volumes.

To anyone who is interested in the processes of trade and manu-facture, particularly in what has now come to be termed 'industrial relations' and 'human relations in industry', the intrinsic attractiveness of the various studies is high. One finds oneself reading on, one's immediate purposes forgotten, entering into the lives of all concerned with pleasure and sympathy, one's interest captured. The picture painted was of a predominantly competitive economy; its general tone was optimistic. The small firm was the typical enterprise, though a tendency towards the creation of larger units was noted, and sur-prisingly large numbers of people were found to be working on their own account. The lives of the artisan and labourer, the small shop-keeper so typical of the poorer parts of London, the assistants in the large shops, the 'respectable' clerk, the civil servant, the professional and business man, all were described with accuracy and understanding. The recruitment of labour from the country and by immigration, the functions of trade unions, technical and other education, each in turn

[1] *Industry* i, pp. 31-172.   [2] Ibid.

was dealt with in relation to the trades concerned. Credit for improvements in the standard of living was attributed to the growth of industry and commerce under capitalist leadership, but defects and abuses were unflinchingly pointed out.[1]

The public proved unappreciative, however. 'The industrial volumes fell somewhat flat', writes Mary Booth. 'The subjects treated are intricate, and the line taken did not exactly please anybody, or repay them for the reading of difficult and closely reasoned pages, devoid of the stir and the anecdotal character of some of the rest.'[2] The appearance of volume after volume tended to become a matter of routine: a 'new Booth' became a familiar item in his publisher's lists each season, and in his own life. There is no sign that his appetite flagged, but certainly that of the public did, as he was well aware. As each appeared, it was greeted with respect rather than enthusiasm. Though the series was recognized as a remarkable demonstration of the practical possibility of making a survey of the industrial scene, there could be no denial of the fact that these detailed descriptions of individual industries lacked the obvious relevance to the topical problem of poverty which had attracted attention to the earlier investigation. Nor could it be denied that the demands made upon Booth by his other interests, and chiefly, of course, his devotion to the cause of the aged poor, had left their mark upon the vitality of the finished work. In particular, very little of the evidence of individual workmen on which he had relied 'to make the book readable' had been collected, and such human interest as was included lacked the dramatic quality which had enlivened the pages of the Poverty Series.

The preparation of the descriptive accounts of London's industries was a routine editorial job, arduous and exacting though entirely to his liking. The task to which he turned on its completion in 1896, that of collating all these individual contributions into a coherent whole, proved much more difficult. Booth proposed to devote the first part of his ninth and final volume to a comparative review of the conditions obtaining within the various groups of trades as described in the preceding four volumes. This would, he hoped, provide the basis for a discussion of industry in general and so make possible an analysis of the relations between industry and poverty. It was an intention which

---

[1] For instance, the hostility of workers in the building industry to the system of subcontracting was found to be 'indiscriminating', but it was added that 'the instinct of the men has been sound'; the justice of their position had been recognized by 'most public authorities'. Ibid., p. 153.

[2] *Memoir*, p. 27.

proved to be extraordinarily difficult to execute, however. He had relied on the 'common measure' of overcrowding to enable him to compare one trade with another, and to relate conditions in industry in general with social conditions. In practice, it provided him with a check on the estimates of poverty he had made in the First Series, which he considered most gratifyingly vindicated his faith in the reliability of the School Board Visitors: 'The similarity is even startling', he commented.[1] But its application as a means of appraising the significance of the information relating to employment proved disappointing:

> The test of 'rooms occupied' is unequal in its application, and rates of rental have to be considered. With trades which are carried on in the inner as well as the outer rings of London this difficulty does not exist. But when one employment is concentrated in crowded, high-rented neighbourhoods, while another is to be found entirely in the outskirts, some allowance will be necessary on the one hand for the crowded who are not poor, and on the other for those who are poor but not crowded.[2]

The difficulties created by the unreliability of this system of classification were increased by the fact that while he had been absorbed in other affairs, his assistants had tended to concentrate on finding out the facts about industry rather than on collecting material which would make it possible to relate the degree of poverty to the type of occupation. Consequently when he came to review the industrial studies already published with a view to preparing an account of the condition of the people which could be compared with that contained in the Poverty Series, the relevant information was not available. The descriptions of the various groups of trades compiled by Aves and his colleagues were often brilliant and always valuable, but they were essentially economic studies. They shed no direct light on such socio-economic questions as the relation between unemployment and poverty, a subject which would certainly have roused widespread public interest. Nor was there material in them which would enable him to draw general conclusions as to the bearing which the money earned had on the social life of the working classes. Such information as he had himself collected regarding conditions of life, for example, from individual dockers, had accordingly to be jettisoned, to the detriment of the finished work. It would be eminently unjust, of course, to imply that any blame for this can be attached to his staff or to Aves in particular, all of whom carried out

---

[1] *Industry* i, p. 10.   [2] Ibid., p. 20.

his instructions with unsurpassed loyalty and devotion. On the contrary, it was the essence of his faith that facts must be gathered impartially, without reference to preconceived ideas or *a priori* theories: only after the information had been acquired would he allow himself to examine the validity of the hypothesis to which it related.

Booth seems, indeed, to have failed to understand that information about conditions of employment could not necessarily be assimilated with data relating to social conditions, and subjected to analysis as part of a more complex whole. The imperfections of the overcrowding index denied him any common measure of comparison between social and economic conditions, and his own preconceptions deprived him of the unifying influence of a firmly constructed hypothesis or theory. He was therefore compelled to abandon his original intention and to fall back upon a straightforward description of industrial conditions. This he did with considerable gusto, and his partiality for his subject was undisguised. Indeed, one cannot help but conclude that his enthusiasm ran away with him, so that he lost sight of that 'long view', constant reference to which was, he once assured his wife, the only sure safeguard against losing one's way amidst the trivialities of daily life. His intention had been to examine industry with a view to throwing light on the vexed question of the cause of poverty: what emerged was a testament of his faith in capitalist enterprise. The concluding volume constituted, in effect, a self-portrait of the Economic Man in terms of what he saw and how he saw it in the world about him. The steadfastness of his faith in competitive individualism extended over every page: his personal enjoyment of that way of life enthused every opinion he expressed. This was life as he himself had lived it. He loved its 'pleasures, risks and excitements'. He had found his own salvation in fighting his way through its dangers and uncertainties, and he was convinced that it was for the common good that others should do the same.

Nevertheless, although the major premise of the work was the rightness of the individualist way of life, Booth was too honest a craftsman to indulge in special pleading, or to attempt to conceal what was unpleasing in the system he described. The picture he painted of the darker side of Victorian industry was indeed a most depressing one. Irregularity of work and unemployment were continual menaces to working-class welfare. 'The helplessness of the worker, whether unionist or non-unionist, shows itself not so much in rates of wages as in irregularity, or actual lack of employment.' The poverty in

London found to be due to low wages was 'less in volume as well as less acute than that which is consequent on some form of lack of work'. Nor was it only the workmen who were thus reduced to helplessness: reviewing the sweated industries, then the subject of anxious public concern, Booth concluded that the sweater himself was as much at the mercy of forces beyond his control as was the worker in his employ. He made no attempt to disguise the seriousness of the defects which his investigations thus revealed. They were, he admitted, inherent in the capitalist system, the necessary reverse of a medal on the other side of which much good could be found. 'Heightened competition and great irregularity of work' seemed to be 'necessarily involved' in the opening-up of world-wide markets, 'bringing with them serious evils'. Competition dealt out 'stern justice' to the less efficient, 'whatever the cause of their inefficiency may be'. The periodic stress of bad times was a necessary stimulus to increased endeavour even though it was also the cause of much misery.[1]

These were serious defects, and Booth was conscious of the urgency of the need for their reform. 'As our starting point', runs the opening sentence of his chapter on Industrial Remedies, 'we recognize and admit the anomalous combination of poverty and industry. This it is that cries for remedy.' To him as to many of his contemporaries there seemed no reason why, since so much progress had already been achieved in such a comparatively short time, the evils of poverty and want could not be wholly eliminated by an even greater production of goods and services: 'Where there is industry there ought to be no poverty.' The issue as he saw it was whether this could be achieved by capitalism or whether the nation would have to turn in one degree or another to socialism to remedy the ills that had become only too plainly apparent. This he regarded as a problem of paramount importance. 'The question then is—Can the central action of the State or the interference of local government, either increase the total volume of enterprise or beneficially regulate its flow?' His diagnosis of the industrial system and his suggested treatment of industrial ills accordingly took the form of a discussion of remedies in terms of socialism versus individualism. Socialism was, of course, suspect in the highest degree to him, and he made this abundantly clear; it appeared to him that it 'boldly offers a solution' to the industrial and social problems arising out of lack of work, 'and to this owes its influence over the minds and hearts of men. But the ideal it holds out has no solidity of

[1] *Industry* v, pp. 72, 80, 280, 314.

structure and no firm basis.' State enterprise might be relied on in some circumstances to build railways and rebuild cities but, in the long run, the lot of the unemployed would not be improved by public works undertaken merely to give them work, for 'the incapable would refuse to submit to the discipline which alone would give any value either industrial or educational to their work.'[1]

Apart from this repudiation of the criticisms of capitalism, Booth had little to say about the reform of the industrial system in general. Fundamentally, his analysis of the industrial organization of London was hopeful; whatever shortcomings he found in it did not detract from his conviction that capitalist enterprise had greatly increased the nation's wealth, and that still greater achievements lay ahead, provided that incentives to individual effort were left to operate with unimpaired effect. Nevertheless, though his faith in the capitalist system remained unshaken, he recognized that things could not be left as they were. Such suggestions for reform as he put forward were firmly founded on the belief that the solution to the problem of 'the anomalous combination of poverty and industry' lay in enabling the individual to act more freely and more intelligently for himself, rather than in subjecting him to restrictive controls such as socialism implied. He therefore began by restating his faith in education as a beneficent influence 'of the first importance'. He considered, furthermore, that a wide field presented itself 'for remedial action . . . in the enforcement of special provisions for the preservation of health and safety'. His only proposal which could be translated without further discussion and inquiry into the language of legislation and administration, was his recommendation, repeated from the Poverty Series, that landlords should have imposed on them a larger share of responsibility for the use and maintenance of factories and workshops, 'not only in the matter of registration, but as regards all provisions of the law'.[2]

Booth was frankly pessimistic as to the possibility of improving the lot of the working man under capitalist enterprise by trade-union action. In so far as such activities consisted of collective efforts to strengthen the bargaining position of the individual member, he held that 'trade unionism is to be regarded rather as representing an

---

[1] Ibid., pp. 293, 315, 316, 318.

[2] Ibid., pp. 295-382. These proposals were worked out in some detail, and provoked Sidney Webb's comment that they would have 'delighted the heart of Jeremy Bentham'. *Problems of Modern Industry*, Longmans Green & Co., 1898, p. 109.

expanded form of individualism, rather than any thorough collectivism'. As such, it had its uses, 'in reducing the hours of labour, and in
checking the abuse of overtime; moreover, by giving expression to
common aspirations they breathe life and spirit into the hearts of the
men'. Nevertheless, their scope was limited. He believed that rates of
wages were determined 'at bottom' by general conditions, such as
custom and the standard of life, depending on 'subtle forms of competition which no combination can control or evade'. Moreover, his
inquiries had revealed that trade unionism was practically limited to
two out of the eight 'sections' into which he had classified the working
population of London. Summing up the Industry Series, he stated
somewhat dogmatically that the trade unions could 'exercise no
control' 'on the cause of a fluctuating demand for labour; they might
help an individual member to find work, and in doing so they were
performing a useful function'. But if they sought to restrict the use of
improved methods of production, they would merely hasten or even
create, 'a tendency towards the substitution of one product for another',
and the result might be 'to weaken rather than strengthen the trade
whose position it is sought to defend'.[1]

The whole gist of the Industry Series was thus to emphasize the
fundamental importance of individual enterprise. In Booth's opinion,
nothing could be gained by individuals otherwise than in return for
something which they had previously given. It was 'the industrial
activity of capable men' which created 'opportunities for all the
world',[2] and if their enterprise was frustrated, universal ruin would be
the inevitable consequence. This steadfast opposition to the idea that
something could be given for nothing, without corrupting the
recipient or undermining the energies of the person from whom it had
to be taken, makes the concluding argument of the Industry Series
an essentially moral one. Booth's last thoughts at the end of the Series,
indeed, left the economic plane altogether:

> For the purpose of these concluding words I incline to discard trades or
> groups of trades, classes or groups of classes, and think of the whole population
> simply as individuals or as families, each and all fighting for themselves and for
> those who belong to them, the good battle of life.[3]

What did this battle amount to? As Aves had pointed out, a stage
had been reached:

> beyond the recognition of the need to live. The modern world is ready, not
> only to see the necessity of life, but of a life worth living. . . . Almost every

---

[1] *Industry* v, pp. 80-1, 150, 159, 305-6.   [2] Ibid., p. 310.   [3] Ibid., p. 336.

social and economic question . . . derives its ultimate practical importance from a more widely spread and more human care for the individual life. . . . John Smith is a 'free' man, and so also is his employer, and it is perhaps the highest social aim to realize, maintain, and develop the freedom of both, in their mutual as well as in all other relationships.[1]

So he came to his final disappointing conclusion: 'It is to other quite as much as to industrial remedies that we must look for the cure or relief of poverty.'[2] Out of all the vast bulk of information that had been accumulated, and from all the long years of patient labour, there had come no positive answer whatsoever to the 'problem of all problems'. Even his courageous proposals for the abolition of Classes A and B were tacitly left out of account: on second thoughts the difficulties of persuading the incapable to submit to discipline appeared insurmountable.

Booth made one last attempt to bring the findings of his two Inquiries into line with each other by preparing a long chapter on Expenditure and Standard of Life. This included a brilliant account of the economic history of a working man's life in which what Rowntree afterwards called the 'alternating periods of want and plenty' are dealt with in a manner which has never been bettered. With that, he decided to rest content. 'I have finished my vol. ix and feel greatly relieved', he told Alfred Marshall in March 1897. 'It will be published at Easter and I shall send you a copy as usual. I think this volume will be of more general interest than has recently been the case and I rather look forward to your criticism. It has occupied most of my time and thoughts for some weeks past.'

Though he never succeeded in shaping the concluding Volume in the Industry Series to his complete satisfaction, Booth always 'considered that he had put into these volumes some of his best and most original work'.[3] He had, for one thing, proved the possibility of making a statistical analysis of the industrial scene. 'What has here been done for London might be much better done—and done for the whole country—at the epoch of any numerical census; and if undertaken, would constitute a social industrial census of very great value.'[4] He hoped, and subsequent events have justified that hope, that his 'imperfect attempt had done something to point the way' to the collection of statistics of this kind by the Board of Trade. He was also in no doubt as to the value of the studies of individual trades, and it

---

[1] Ibid., pp. 199-200. [2] Ibid., p. 318. [3] *Memoir*, p. 27. See also below, p. 219.
[4] *Industry* v, p. 65.

gave him special pleasure when this fact was acknowledged by the inclusion of the Series as a textbook in the Economics Course at Cambridge.[1] Nevertheless, he found himself forced to admit that so far as the analysis of the cause and cure of poverty was concerned, the outcome of his investigations into industry was almost entirely negative. Nothing had emerged which could equal the value of his concept of the Poverty Line, nor was the picture which he had drawn one which 'told a story' in terms of practical suggestions for action. He had, indeed, anticipated criticism on this score in the closing pages of the concluding volume, where he defended his lack of results by reiterating his claim that he had never intended to do more than explore the possibility of collecting accurate information about human affairs.

What I have endeavoured to present to my readers is a picture of a way of looking at things, rather than a doctrine or argument. I have been glad to see that my book furnished weapons and ammunition for absolutely opposed schools, and can even make shift to stifle my annoyance when it is occasionally quoted in support of doctrines which I abhor.[2]

To the critic who asked 'What is the use of it all?' he once again made the defensive reply that his investigations were not yet complete and that the drawing of conclusions must await the collection of still more information:

I shall still attempt no answer. I trust in the efficacy and utility of the scientific method in throwing light upon social questions, and the work on which I am engaged is not yet finished. In spite of the length to which it has attained, I have to ask once more the patience of my readers.[3]

At first sight, this plea appears to contradict the somewhat dogmatic assertion, made in the Introduction to the final volume of the Industry Series, that 'the design originally laid down and expressed in the title of the book' had been completed. However, as he went on to explain, what remained to be done was 'of a different character, being to estimate the forces for good or evil that are acting upon the conditions of the population before we can arrive at that balancing of hopes and fears that will form our final judgement'.[4]

We have to consider what the State or private enterprise does or might do in London for the young and for the old, for the morally weak and for the sick,

---

[1] *Memoir*, p. 27.   [2] *Industry* v, p. 337.   [3] Ibid., p. 338.   [4] Ibid., p. x.

as well as for the unemployed; and what religion and philanthropy are doing or might do to form public opinion, to supplement or modify the influences of legislation, and to disseminate wholesome views of human life; or what other action, public or private, may assist in eradicating the causes or softening the hardships of poverty.[1]

Thus, after ten years of labour, the ultimate problem of motivation was encountered by Booth as a major issue in the Inquiry. At once his mind seized on the question as to how the 'life worth living' could be attained as the result of the influence of those who devoted their lives explicitly to the promotion of good, and the combating of evil. To these questions Booth turned his attention in the Third Series, devoted to Religious Influences.

The Industry Inquiry, in fact, had opened up many more issues than it had settled.

[1] Ibid., p. 318.

7

The Religion of the People

THE last volume of the Industry Series appeared in March 1897. Within a month, Booth was writing to the leaders of the various denominations asking them to co-operate in his proposed examination of the efficacy of the religious and social influences at work upon the lives of the people in London.

The speed with which he set to work reveals the enthusiasm with which he regarded the subject of his new inquiry. This was only qualified in small measure by the sense of unease with which he regarded the negative conclusions which were all that he had been able to extract from the Industry Inquiry. 'I have at times doubted whether the prolongation of this work has had at any time any other basis than an inability on my part to come to a conclusion', runs the first sentence of the Third Series. 'I have asked myself whether I should indeed have anything more to tell my readers than had already been told them in previous volumes.'[1] This can be interpreted as evidence of nothing more than a passing feeling of despondency, however, for deep in Booth's mind there was an enduring determination to understand the problems of man's destinies, as reflected in his religious life, which could not be gainsaid. Religious ceremonial and the practices of public worship had held an absorbing interest for him for a considerable part of his life. For instance, his wife's memoir records his serio-comic concern that in a household in which he was staying in New York in 1878, 'piety does not pervade the atmosphere'; a text was displayed, but 'I was absolutely almost shocked at no blessing being asked before tea'.[2] In another letter written in 1880, there is an account of 'a religious watering place' near New York owned by the Methodist Church; his uninhibited description of the strange scenes

---

[1] *Religious Influences* i, p. 3.   [2] *Memoir*, pp. 53–5.

he observed is in astonishingly similar vein to the pictures he was to draw twenty-five years later of religious practices in London.[1]

This habitual interest in religion provided both the spur which urged Booth on to start the Religious Influences Inquiry, and the staying power which enabled him to complete it. The immediate objective of the Inquiry, however, was to provide a basis for the final conclusion which was so eminently lacking in the Industry Series and whose absence had provoked criticism. It was only too obvious to him that the results of the social analysis he had so far carried out were still incomplete. Introducing the new Series he explained that although his previous results had satisfied him that poverty, crowding, and low wages were connected with each other, so that better wages would lead to better housing, and improved cleanliness and order to better wages, and so on, he did not feel inclined to end his work at this stage:

The task which I had originally proposed to myself was done. Yet I did not feel satisfied to leave it so, for just as life day by day is conditioned by the character of the home, the opportunities of education or recreation and the chance of employment, so there are other social influences which form part of the very structure of life, and some account of them is necessary to complete the picture of things as they are.[2]

Among these influences, he went on, 'Religion claims the chief part, and the investigation of organized religious effort in all its forms has taken the first and largest place in the additional inquiry of which I now give the results.' 'But', he concluded,

I have besides tried to appreciate other organized social and philanthropic influences, and also those that come under the heads of local Government and Police, and in connexion therewith have sought information on Housing and Health, on Drink, Prostitution and Crime, on Marriage and on Thrift; and though questions as to the extent and degree of Poverty do not enter directly, they will come constantly under consideration.[3]

This leaves little room for doubt that when Booth began the inquiries on which the Religious Influences Series was ultimately based, he had no intention of restricting them to religious institutions. He had, in fact, always been interested in the whole complex problem

---

[1] Ibid., p. 63.   [2] *Religious Influences* i, p. 4.

[3] Ibid., pp. 4-5. An earlier draft includes the sentence: 'The object I have in view is to describe the people and the conditions in which they live, in the light of the efforts that are being made after improvement; and the agencies at work, in the light of the success or failure of these attempts.'

of social influences and motivation even though he had hitherto concentrated on industrial organization as the primary influence shaping
the lives of the masses of the people. The Poverty Series, for instance,
included a section entitled 'Institutions' which dealt with influences
of this more general kind.[1] None of his subsequent references to his
intention to resume these investigations suggest that he had it in mind
to limit himself to religion. The purpose of the third stage in his
Inquiry, as foreshadowed in the concluding chapter of the Industry
Series, was stated to be the examination of the effectiveness of 'social
action', and in particular, the appraisal of the effects of the 'agencies
and influences' on the life of the people of London.[2]

Just how he proposed to do this is not clear, however. A curious
diagram has survived amongst his papers which suggests that he considered ways and means of analysing the 'use of leisure' by the individual under two heads: 'inside interests', which comprised time
spent on sleep, meals, and reading, and 'outside interests', which
included church attendance amongst such other miscellaneous and
disparate activities as street-lounging and visits to public houses and
theatres. Though Booth's scheme for a systematic investigation of
interests of these kinds was never proceeded with, a large amount of
information relating to them was collected in the course of the final
stage of the Inquiry, and it can only have been when it was drawing to
a close that the decision was taken to devote the bulk of the new
volumes in the Third Series to religious influences. At the outset, and
no doubt as a matter of principle, Booth does not appear to have
attempted any definition of what was to be included or excluded, and
it was apparently a combination of the sheer weight of the numbers
of organizations devoted to religious objects that led to the eventual
decision to concentrate on religion.

He had, of course, no desire to set himself up as a critic of religious
truth. His declared purpose had always been to restrict himself to the
description of things as they were, and not as they might become or
ought to be, and he saw no reason for departing from this principle
at this juncture:

My concern in the matter of religion is solely with the extent to which

---

[1] *Poverty* i, pp. 24 et seq. The active part he played in connexion with the housing
problems of Central London similarly suggests that he was interested in the effects of
housing on social behaviour; it was on the basis of information which he collected on
this subject that he became convinced of the need for better means of suburban transport
to provide access to the new housing estates (see below pp. 169 et seq.).

[2] *Industry* v, p. 339.

people accept the doctrine, and share in the work of the religious bodies, and with the effect produced, or apparently produced, in their lives.[1]

This had proved a comparatively straightforward task in his previous investigations, but he was well aware that his new field of inquiry would necessitate a fresh method of approach. The lack of any existing source of data such as he had found in the records of the Relieving Officers and the School Board Visitors, the intangible nature of the subject to be examined, and the impossibility of applying to it any kind of statistical yardstick, such as income or the number of rooms occupied,[2] all meant that far greater reliance would have to be placed on personal observations and individual impressions. His plan of campaign demonstrated that these considerations were plainly evident to him. Until he entered on the final phase of his work, it had been possible for him to conduct all his inquiries from his central office in Adelphi Terrace. An entirely different plan was now evolved. In the belief that the dangers of having to rely so extensively on personal impressions could only be surmounted by the most scrupulous examination of each piece of evidence that was collected, he decided that he and his assistants must personally verify the accuracy of every item of information supplied to them. Accordingly, the usual procedure of preparing lists of names and addresses, and the devising of 'forms of schedule' (suitably adapted in this instance to accommodate denominational differences), were based on an intensive campaign of inquiry in each locality in turn, carried out personally rather than by agents:

Our plan of action may be likened to a voyage of discovery. We have removed our camp from centre to centre all over London, remaining for weeks or even months in each spot in order to see as well as hear all we could.[3]

With his staff by now reduced to a compact team of five,[4] Booth endeavoured to interview, and with comparatively few exceptions did in fact interview, all the responsible heads of every religious and social agency in London. He believed that no work of any importance failed to find a place in their notebooks: only the Jewish community was excluded on the reasonable ground that their activities had already been the subject of a full report by Beatrice Potter.[5] Every possible

[1] *Religious Influences* i, p. 2.
[2] Booth's views on the significance of statistics of church attendance are discussed below, p. 154.
[3] *Religious Influences* i, p. 7.   [4] Aves, Argyle, Arkell, Duckworth, and Howard.
[5] See above, p. 107.

care was taken to verify and cross-check the accuracy of the evidence obtained from these interviews. It was supplemented by a mass of publications, such as parish magazines and annual reports, good, bad, and indifferent alike, frequently accompanied by syllabuses of classes and clubs, pamphlets urging the value of this or that movement for reform, leaflets setting out aims and ambitions, and letters containing offers of further information without limit.

To counter balance the effect of any tendency on the part of our informants to magnify their office, we have trusted mainly to the insight gained by a long series of such interviews, but have been guided also by what we have seen when we have ourselves visited the churches and institutions in question. We have also been able in most cases to compare what men say of themselves with what others say of them.[1]

The interest in religion which had so often taken Booth into churches when abroad now developed unchecked; what before had seemed like idle curiosity now had a genuine scientific purpose. Sunday after Sunday was spent in visiting the immense variety of places of worship which constituted such a feature of London life at the end of the nineteenth century, and there can be no doubt that the majority of the reports on religious services were prepared by him in person. Every sort and size of agency which endeavoured to improve the moral welfare of the people received his interested attention. Sometimes accompanied by one or other of his family, but more often alone, he went from church to chapel, mission hall to open air meeting, staying long enough in each to get the feel of it, and then moving on to the next, on occasion returning later in the day to attend a second service in order to verify or correct an impression:

I had a wonderful day amongst the Poplar churches seeing them at all hours [he wrote to his wife in January 1899]. It is the only way to do it so far away as Blackwall, and I ended, curiously, with an Old Age Pension meeting to hear Lansbury on the Social Democratic Federation's view. I was wanting to meet him so went there after the Churches were finished and finally did not get home till half past eleven and I think it was 1.30 before I was in bed. I did not say a word at the meeting, only claiming acquaintance when it was over.

His impressions were recorded while they were still fresh in his memory, as soon as he reached home each night, however late the hour. As in the case of his earlier work on poverty, they reveal him to have

[1] *Religious Influences* i, p. 7.

been a natural reporter who could write, quickly and accurately, a detailed account of whatever scenes he had just observed: it was, of course, this same photographic eye for detail which stamped everything he did with its particular character. No deliberate attempt was made at this stage to evaluate what he saw, though there was occasionally an asperity about his comments which startled those who only knew him as an amiable friend and host:

At another church I attended a men's meeting on Sunday afternoon. When I arrived at 3.15 there were about thirty men present, but many of them were obviously members of the committee. The orchestra began to play at 3.25, and by the time it had finished the piece, there were, including the orchestra and the members of the committee, just seventy-five people present, and no more came. Of these, about half, I should think, were working men, and the rest middle-class 'top hat' people. While the orchestra was playing, a bright little man, evidently the minister, went about the church talking to the men and shaking hands. He came to me, shook hands, and said, 'How are you, my friend?' At the end of the overture, which was secular, we sang a hymn. There was then a prayer, which was followed by a solo very poorly sung by a lady. The minister then spoke. He began by thanking God (amidst applause) for the result of the London County Council election, and then delivered an address on Christianity and Health. It contained a good deal about health and very little about Christianity, and was full of extreme socialistic radicalism. There was no indication that he had thought at all how to carry out the number of gigantic schemes he advocated for improving the health of the people, but the sentiments won a good deal of applause. After the address, which was delivered in a high, monotonous, 'open-air' voice, we sang a song of triumph over the downfall of the tyrant, with evident application to the recent election. It is impossible to believe that any man's spiritual nature is touched by this sort of thing, and certainly no great numbers are attracted by it.[1]

Yet though intellectually he strove to remain detached, he was at the same time happy to confess that he enjoyed participating in the life he observed, and was always willing to accept the fact that his mere presence amidst any group necessarily involved him in a relationship with its members.[2] As was his usual custom, he made no effort to disguise himself on these visits, his natural modesty of demeanour serving to render him acceptable to whatever congregation he chose

[1] Ibid., i, p. 226.

[2] For example, one of his daughters recollects her father's amusement when, at a Salvation Army meeting, an elderly woman withstood all attempts to persuade her to accept salvation. 'I think she derived moral support from our presence' was his dry comment.

to visit. His interest in the services he attended was transparent and genuine: as in his anonymous visits to working-class homes, the redeeming feature of what has since been stigmatized by the ugly epithet of 'snooping' was the evident sincerity of his desire to comprehend.

Year by year with unflagging interest, he continued his pilgrimage round the churches and chapels of London. Year by year, he and his staff laboured on through their schedule of interviews, which eventually reached a total of approximately 1,800. Year by year, information continued to pour in from all sorts of people with all sorts of ideas as to how the condition of the people might be improved, though often with very little notion of the relative merit of their own particular contribution. Turning over the mass of papers and notebooks which still survive, the variety and complexity of the material at Booth's disposal is strikingly apparent. Every type of reformist agency, from the People's Refreshment House Association to the Metropolitan Gardens Association and the 'Darkest England' Social Scheme organized by the Salvation Army for the provision of City workshops for the unemployed: every brand of religious endeavour, from wealthy City churches to the meanest of Nonconformist missions or the most intense of revival meetings: the organizers of these and of many others, seem to have been eager to grasp the opportunity of a sympathetic hearing. Many wrote letters in addition to filling in the schedules, some on the official stationery of a parish church or an established social agency, others on sheets torn from a penny notebook or cheap writing pad by some obscure doer-of-good.

Slowly and methodically the notebooks were filled up and the literature sorted and filed. Gradually the great map of London, which was later to be exhibited at the Paris Exhibition, was spotted over with the little symbols whose purpose was to convey 'an impression of the ubiquitous and manifold character of the three most important social influences':[1] scarlet for places of worship, black for houses licensed to sell intoxicating drinks, and a 'lovely blue' for the schools of the Board in whose endeavours Booth placed such faith.[2]

By the end of 1900, the collection of material was nearly finished, and Booth began to prepare himself for the arduous task of writing it up for publication. 'I am steadily drawing in as to business work', he wrote in March of that year, 'and hope to get a good spell at Easter pretty free. I look forward to doing a lot at the old book before the

---

[1] *Final*, p. 119. The map was published in the *Final Volume*.   [2] *Poverty* i, p. 129.

end of this year.' He was under no illusions as to the complexity of
the task ahead. 'It will be awfully difficult to get really right,' he told
his wife, 'to say enough and not too much—to speak truth without
hurting many good people's feelings terribly—and somehow or other
to produce the right effect—but we will do our best, you and I—and
you and I are a match for anything when we are put to it.' From
October of that year onwards, he devoted practically the whole of his
time to writing, working sometimes in the large plainly furnished room
in Adelphi Terrace which looked across the Thames to a good slice
of that workaday South London which was the subject of so many
volumes, but later concentrating all the boxes of material in his room
at Gracedieu, where they remained until his death.

Booth made himself personally responsible for the first draft of the
book. In doing so, he said, 'I think my idea was to strike certain main
notes early—ideas coming to the front at once, as they did in fact, and
then being slowly worked out and widened and modified and absolutely assured as we proceed.'[1] His plan was to produce as rapidly as
possible what he regarded simply as a working outline. 'As I go on
I am very conscious of the extent to which later chapters affect the
earlier ones; but I always knew it would be so, and have therefore
pressed on and left a great deal for the work of revision.' A letter to
Aves describes the system on which he worked:

The boxes as I am using them have been cleared of everything except the
interview books and the original draft reports. This leaves the books easy of
access for reference. The boxes are ranged in order each containing the books
that belong to it, which is the best order to keep for ready references. The
abstracts etc. are ranged on sundry window ledges and shelves in the same
order and finally the bundles of materials are spread out on tables. I believe you
will find it quite essential to observe and maintain some such order, but it
takes up a lot of room.

On this occasion the whole business of writing up his material was
found to be an especially difficult and tormenting experience, and the
surviving drafts of chapters in the Third Series show what a struggle
it was for Booth to express himself to his own satisfaction. He normally
turned to his wife for assistance, she being the more facile with words,
but one of the young men then in process of becoming his sons-in-law
remembers the pride with which he sought to assist him on the rare
occasions when he discussed with him some sentence which 'would not

[1] *Memoir*, p. 36.

go'. His manuscript is typical of him; he wrote on large sheets of paper breadthwise, to permit of exceptionally wide margins in which corrections and additions might be entered, the lines of clear, round writing running evenly across page after page. He worked in pencil in the first instance, and the number of erasures demonstrate his difficulty in finding words or phrases which exactly expressed his meaning, though the finished page is clear and easy to read. He used the first printer's proof as a working draft, inserting and deleting freely, chopping pages up with scissors in order to paste their contents together in a better order, pinning in new material on odd scraps of notepaper, scribbling memoranda inside 'balloons' for his own or his secretaries' attention.

This preliminary draft having been approved by Mrs. Booth almost page by page as it was written, the manuscript was then circulated for criticism to the several members of the team, together with the material on which it was based, in numbered box files. 'Pray knock it about as much as possible', was Booth's instruction to Aves on one of these occasions. 'Nothing in it is sacred except the truth, and that has to be said in the best way and at the right time.' Each of his assistants worked independently, so that in due course Booth was presented with no less than six critical versions on the basis of which he then began an intensive revision, often amounting to a complete re-write. 'The North West, like the North, has all to be re-written' was a typical cry as the months went by. It was indeed a most meticulous and pains-taking process, and the fact that only a single error of any significance was subsequently revealed is a tribute to the care expended on it.[1]

Meanwhile, the revision and rearrangement of the contents of the earlier Series on Poverty and Industry were being undertaken in prepara-tion for republication along with the religious influences material in the definitive edition of the Inquiry on which Booth had set his heart. The process of revision was carried out with a thoroughness which would have constituted it a whole-time occupation for any other man:

[1] It will interest those responsible for social researches today to learn that Booth had to face a libel suit on only one occasion. This arose out of a misunderstanding concerning the ownership of a row of tenements 'with no backs to them'; he assumed that a local property-owner with the same name as the street concerned was the owner of the tene-ments, which was not in fact the case. Booth was threatened with legal proceedings, an injunction being sought to stop publication of the Inquiry. The owner, in his turn, confused Booth with the 'General' Booth who founded the Salvation Army, and supposing him to be too poor to fight, proceeded against the publishers. The suit was, needless to say, vigorously defended; the application for the injunction failed, and the case was finally settled out of court, a conclusion which Booth described as 'humiliating'.

Booth had hit on the happy idea of utilizing the experience of members
of the police force as a means of verifying his original classification of
the streets of London,[1] and he and his assistants were accordingly at
this time engaged on what they called 'police walks', covering every
street in the whole of London. His only comment on what must have
been a fascinating experience, and was certainly a considerable achievement, was that:

> In our prolonged walks through London, when engaged on this revision—
> walks to be measured by hundreds, or even thousands, of miles we had . . . the
> company and co-operation of experienced members of the Police force,
> chosen for their local knowledge.[2]

Every spare moment of 1901 was devoted to 'the book'. When the
survey of religious influences had been begun in 1897, Booth estimated
that it would require three more years and three more volumes. In the
event, the collection of the material alone had taken that length of time,
whilst the process of writing threatened to last as long again and to
result in double the number of books. The work of analysing the
material progressed steadily enough, he found, but it 'seemed rather to
develop at the same time'. This was a far more subtle and difficult task
than the statistical analysis of poverty or the factual description of
industry, both in quantity and quality. 'The finishing of the book will
require a great and sustained effort but if we pull together we can do
it', he assured Aves—and incidentally himself.

Though his intention in preparing the Third Series had been to
adhere to his habitual methods, in practice Booth found himself
defeated by the intangible nature of the material with which he had to
deal. His plan had been to analyse his information on the basis of the
various districts into which the metropolis had been divided for the
purposes of collection. The character of each neighbourhood and its
general response to religious influences were first to be described, the
appropriate sections of the coloured street map being inserted at this
point together with sketch maps and tables of statistics relating to the
composition of the population. After this the work of the various
denominations was to be discussed in detail. Notes on such other
'influences' as marriage, the police, and municipal administration were
also to be included, together with extracts from the investigator's notebooks by way of illustration. All this he could and did do with a
frankness of speech such as has seldom been extended to the subject

---

[1] See above, pp. 113 et seq.   [2] *Religious Influences* i, p. 7. See also *Final*, p. 61.

either before or since, and with results which make fascinating reading to this day. They were, however, essentially personal impressions since the lack of any common standard of measurement deprived him of the means of translating them into impersonal and comparable statistics. In consequence, the task of evaluating the influence of the various agencies necessarily became a matter of opinion. Booth had himself foreseen that this would prove to be the case, but he had almost certainly underestimated the extent to which it would add to the difficulty of writing up his results.

These problems notwithstanding, by working as hard and as fast as ever he had done before, the marshalling of the evidence in the first six volumes was completed by the summer of 1902, although he was compelled to leave it to his wife to see the books through the press during the autumn whilst he went to the United States. Even then the revision of the earlier editions lagged so far behind that he was forced to rouse himself from the seasickness which had laid him low 'to revise a lot of Vol. IX (of Industry) which badly needs it. It has got to be got up again for the rearrangement and so it is a good chance to lick its awkwardnesses into shape'.[1] He could no longer afford to take time off from the business for writing. Trade in general was bad, but the particular anxiety of the moment lay in the mounting tension between the Booth Line and its German competitor, which had become so acute as to amount almost to a private war. The drama of this duel was entirely after Booth's own heart: it was, he felt, a pre-eminent example of the adventure and excitement which properly belonged to commercial life.[2] Yet though he found himself 'hard put to it to keep anything like a clear mind' in regard to the progress of the Inquiry, he subsequently declared that these were, perhaps, the happiest years of his life.

Back in England after this interlude, with very little time to spare from the business, he toiled on with the task of summarizing in a seventh and concluding volume, the general impression conveyed by the detailed evidence contained in the preceeding six. 'Your good

[1] Only minor alterations were, in fact, made.
[2] He was in New York in the hot summer of 1902 when the tense last moments in the long fight were reached. Cables flashed between the waiting groups of directors in their several offices in Hamburg, London and New York and it was only after a dramatic last hitch that agreement was finally reached. 'It has been an exciting day', he wrote to his son. 'After your two messages and my replies, as we waited hour after hour, one could not help pacing up and down at times. Then at last the short conclusive satisfactory message came and we metaphorically threw up our hats in the air and shook hands all round.'

words of approval on the parts you have read warm me up and will
make it far easier for me to fight through to a finish', he wrote to his
wife. All attempts to make the main object of the Series anything
other than a study of religious influences were abandoned, and the last
volume became specifically a summary of the evidence relating to the
various religious agencies, with the sole exception of a brief chapter on
Settlements and Polytechnics. The appraisal of such information as had
been acquired on the work of social as distinct from religious agencies
was, Booth assured his readers, held over for inclusion in a Final
Volume which had yet to make its appearance. In a last endeavour to
make plain the basis upon which his summing up of the power of
religious influences was founded, he attempted to draft a statement
embodying the personal point of view on which his valuation finally
depended. It is significant that he found himself unable to complete
this and that no reference to it appears in the final manuscript.

The picture which finally emerged of the religious influences at
work in London was a depressing one, though Booth did not so regard
it himself. He was generous in conceding that the motives of those who
laboured in this field were often of the highest order, but the results
of their work he described in terms of failure with a dispassionate calm
which was often more devastating to his readers than would have been
a cry of lamentation. 'It is just because the effort is so great that the
results are so disappointing' was a typical remark.[1] Though his
explorations of this unknown territory had held him entranced for
years, he had found no evidence to support the claim that organized
religion was in any degree effective as an agency for the improvement
of the condition of the people except, as he drily commented, in so far
as those who did the work themselves benefited from so doing. He
thought that Income Tax and Christianity were practically the
preserve of the same classes: the mass of the people he believed to be
beyond the reach of any denomination.[2]

His analysis led him to the conclusion that the churches had adapted
themselves to the class structure, rather than acted as a force trans-
forming it. Each class had a church which catered for its needs, though

---

[1] *Religious Influences* i, p. 38.

[2] Incidentally, he dismissed his old love, Positivism, with a passing phrase. The detailed
notes on positivist activities supplied by Aves were cut out of the final draft, and replaced
by a comment to the effect that there was no need to do more than mention the existence
of the Positivists, 'whose universal philosophic Church of the future, too soon rent in
twain, has looked in vain for any fresh bursting of the waters which originally carved this
channel out'. (Ibid. p. 147.)

most of the working classes held aloof altogether. The Evangelical Churches which were most hospitable to them, and in which they felt most at home, were also those which strongly emphasized the doctrine that conversion implied a changed way of life, a dedication of oneself to higher living, and the admission of a sense of guilt. However, the ordinary working man did not feel inclined to give up the simple pleasures and sins to which he was accustomed, and so far as guilt was concerned, his political leaders were busy convincing him that he was more sinned against than sinning.

The overriding impression conveyed by the Inquiry was thus that somehow or other the churches had lost contact with the stream of events at the end of the nineteenth century; the doctrines they preached simply did not make sense to the mass of mankind. It could not be argued with any show of reason that this was due to mere apathy, for the response by working men to the appeal of socialist principles provided direct proof that a creed which seemed to be relevant to the problems of their daily lives could stir them to active support. He recorded the opinions of two of his informants that 'it is only as to trade unionism that the working classes are keen', and that whilst there was a power in politics to stir the masses 'what impotence there seemed in the Gospel to do the same'.[1] In the Industry Series he had already discussed the remedies for industrial discontent propounded by the socialists, though his approach was entirely 'academic' in the sense that he was concerned, albeit in a somewhat anxious frame of mind, with their logic rather than their influence. Socialism appeared to him to be a somewhat pernicious creed; that being so, any influence that socialists had was to be deplored. He had not asked himself then, why or how this influence had been acquired, and it is therefore of significance that he returned to the subject of socialism in the Religious Influences series.

The picture he painted of the socialists in 1902-3 was an entirely different one from the very abstract design which he drew in 1897. When he looked at the scene from the industrial standpoint, with his experiences as an employer and merchant in mind, he saw socialism in a sinister light; when looked at from the point of view of the development of higher standards of culture and behaviour, and community life generally in the East End, things appeared to him in a quite different guise. Detached analysis of industrial institutions had led to one set of conclusions; analysis of religious and community life led in a contrary direction. Once more his scrupulous honesty and his sincerity of

---

[1] *Religious Influences* i, p. 182: vii, p. 104.

purpose triumphed over his preconceptions: despite his distrust of socialism which remained undiminished over the years, he was lavish in his praise of the work of socialists as social reformers. Crooks in Poplar and Lansbury in Bow were leaders of a new and powerful movement, whose true significance he was one of the first, if not the first, to appreciate. 'Whatever their mistakes', they 'unquestionably' had 'the gift of honesty'. 'Out of all comparison more energetic than the previous régime, [the new democracy] is certainly not less honest, and seems to be at all points fairly amenable to reason. This, if it be maintained, is to be accounted, without doubt, as a public asset of no small value.' In Bermondsey, again, a change for the better had occurred 'with the advent of a more democratic constituency', according to the opinion of the local clergy. It was a noteworthy fact that the Public Libraries Act had been 'welcomed' in the East End, whereas wealthier districts, such as St. Pancras, Islington, and Marylebone, had refused to make use of the opportunities it offered.[1]

Booth observed that the control of the local government machine had passed in these and other areas to the representatives of the working classes, 'full of zeal for reform and suspicion of the old order and its ways'. The outcome was 'a purer as well as a more energetic administration'. 'No one now fears revolutionary results or thinks that ruin will be the price for experiences of this kind.' In Hackney, as in Poplar and Mile End, working-class control had 'given an impetus to sanitary improvement and public enterprise'. The working classes in these areas were 'without any religious organization of their own, and to them the various religious bodies appealed in vain; but they have their ideas. It is to political action that their hopes turn both for themselves and for the class below'.[2]

In effect, though he did not say so in so many words, his conclusion was that his investigation of organized religion, like that of industry, had proved a blind alley in so far as any solution of the problems of poverty were concerned. He had himself no doubt that one basic cause underlay this universal failure on the part of the churches: without melodrama but equally without any attempt to wrap up the unwelcome truth, he wrote his concluding paragraph:

There is, no doubt, a real difficulty in squaring the teaching we find in many

[1] Ibid., i, p. 193; iv, 161; v, 173.
[2] Ibid., i, pp. 60-1, 105, 165. Booth expressed this opinion even more plainly in his *Final Volume*: 'Democratic local government is at present in the making, but it is one of the points in which I believe our country to be in advance of all others, and if we can keep the lead in this particular, we shall not fail to hold our place in the economy of the world' (*Final*, pp. 213-14).

LCB

passages in the Bible with the practical rules of action now laid down, not by the Charity Organization Society alone, but by all serious thinkers, including the leading representatives of every religious community in London, Jew or Christian, Roman Catholic or Protestant, Established or Nonconformist, Trinitarian or Unitarian. All practically admit the impossibility of acting upon the Gospel precepts, as does the whole of Christendom, with the possible exception of some sects in Russia. But by all the difficulty is evaded rather than met.[1]

So at long last, in 1902 and the spring of 1903, the sixteen volumes of the Third Edition gradually made their appearance, elaborately bound in white vellum, generously stamped with gold, each with a silk ribbon marker, sold at the nominal price of 5s. per volume. So far as Booth's contemporaries were concerned, his plain speech evoked a surprisingly favourable reaction on the part of the churches collectively that was at least as strong as the unfavourable reaction aroused by the criticisms of individuals and individual churches. The work was praised as 'temperate', 'extraordinarily accurate', 'soundly instructive', and 'really true'. His 'absolute fairness' was commented on. There was in the Inquiry, wrote the *Methodist Times*,[2] 'a graphic, carefully drawn portraiture of the sectional religious influences' active in London. There is a singular combination of detachment and living interest. The writer avoids exaggeration, cynicism, and favouritism.' The impression given was that of 'a friend and ally of the religious organizations dealt with'. 'For our part', the reviewer continued, 'we find no fault' with the account of Methodism, despite the sharp criticisms it contains. The leading article printed in the same issue of the newspaper as the review even went so far as to quote Booth's assertion that 'in self-deception the Wesleyans have no equals', adding that 'nothing is further from our thought or would be more foolish than to resent this verdict or to neglect it. It is not an attack in any sense, and we may learn much from the criticism of a fair outsider.' The *Examiner*, a Congregational newspaper, began by giving its readers some of 'this most able and competent observer's home truths', and ended by saying that 'for the work as a whole no praise can be too great'.[3]

In general, the friendliness of the reviews in the religious press was so pronounced that it may be said to provide a magnificent demonstration of the intellectual integrity and spiritual soundness of those by whom and for whom they were written. As one reads them through, one is struck by the extent to which the reviewers appear to have been

---

[1] *Religious Influences* vii, p. 413.   [2] April 1903.   [3] 2 April 1903.

influenced by Booth's honesty of purpose, his unwearied search for
accuracy, and, above all, by the sympathy with which he regarded
their way of life and the values which dominated it. This was, indeed,
his intention, for he endeavoured to maintain in his interviews 'a
sympathetic' rather than 'critical attitude'.[1] 'His spirit is reverent and
sincere', wrote Dr. J. Scott Lidgett on behalf of the Methodist Church.[2]
Preaching in St. Paul's Cathedral as Bishop of Stepney, Dr. Lang
emphasized the 'impartiality' with which the Inquiry had been carried
out, but added that there was 'no lack of sympathy' in it.[3] In this sense,
Booth's genuine interest in the subject-matter of his researches proved
to be a source of strength to him, as it gained a respectful hearing from
an audience that might otherwise have been much more hostile.

In another and a more familiar sense, however, Booth's personal
approach to the work and life of the churches exposed him to attack.
The fact that the whole Religious Influences Series was written in the
first person, and that all the criticisms embodied in it, sharp as they
often were, were presented as his own personal opinions, necessarily
provoked resentment against himself as an individual, and a minority
was stung to bitter retort. 'The book is undoubtedly creating a stir,
and the unfavourable criticism which you foretold gathers force', Aves
wrote to Booth. This was most evident in the Nonconformist press,
but it is a remarkable fact that even there anger was confined to a single
article, and to a number of subsequent contributions inspired by it.

The attack was led by Dr. Robertson Nicoll, a prominent exponent
of Nonconformist doctrine. In a leading article in the *British Weekly*,
attributed by his contemporaries to him, entitled 'Mr. Booth's Pseudo-
Scientific Study', he attempted to demolish the Inquiry by adopting a
line of destructive criticism which appears astonishingly up to date to
the social scientist reading it some fifty years later. For the first time in
the literature of the social sciences, indeed, the value of a piece of
research work was decried on the ground that it was 'unscientific', the
material on which it was based being held to be 'unrepresentative'. Dr.
Nicoll admitted 'that the volumes contained fragments of worth', and
that there was in them 'the evidence of much shrewdness, and an un-
compromising desire for truth'. He also found them 'very readable,
and, in general, plainly written'. But, he added, they were 'ruined by
the total absence of a scientific method. In spite of the tables and statistics and the maps, there is no real contact with the significant facts'.

[1] *Religious Influences* i, pp. 7-8.   [2] *London Quarterly Review*, July 1903.
[3] *Church Family Newspaper*, 26 June 1903.

The material in them consisted, therefore, 'largely of religious gossip served up in a miscellaneous manner'. The results were 'not worthless—far from it—but they are as nearly worthless as any books compiled with the same care and with the same opportunities could be'.[1]

Although intemperate, these criticisms are valid, in so far as they can be directed in one degree or another against most attitude studies that deal with opinions and value-judgements. These involve the making of a distinction between the study of human behaviour, on the one hand, and the analysis of the beliefs and moral codes of mankind, on the other. The first is obviously the concern of the sociologist, because it is scientific in the sense that it can be treated statistically. The second is usually regarded as that of the moral philosopher and theologian, and it is asserted by many if not most social scientists that it can only be treated 'scientifically' in so far as the inquiry is limited to questions of fact that are significant from the social point of view. This line of argument is a difficult one to pursue. What is a 'significant' fact? By what criterion is its 'significance' to be judged? Dr. Nicoll criticized Booth's work on the ground that he had made no attempt to provide statistical evidence of the figures of church-going, and of the money collected by way of voluntary contributions in the London churches: he was particularly critical of his failure to make use of the statistics of church attendance collected by the *British Weekly* in 1886, or of the detailed census being carried out by the *Daily News* at the time when the Religious Influences Series was published. 'It is characteristic of Mr. Booth's slushy methods', he wrote, 'that he makes no reference to either of these enterprises.' But, it must be asked, what exactly would statistics of this kind have contributed to the research? Nicoll's reply was that 'while church-going is not a test of religion, without it religion perishes'. To assert that church attendance is a pre-requisite of spiritual life is open to argument, however; as Booth pointed out, the zealous church-goer is not necessarily a religious man in the deeper meaning of the term, and as he also pointed out, many good (and perhaps religious) people are not church-goers. The truth of Nicoll's proposition was thus by no means self-evident. This does not dispose of the criticisms, however, for he and several other reviewers were also firmly convinced that Booth was entirely in error when he thought (as he was deemed to think) that he could make confident pronouncements 'on the spiritual effects of Christianity'. 'That', they claimed, 'can never be done on scientific principles. Facts may be stated, but

[1] *British Weekly*, 2 April 1903.

beyond this we cannot go.' Booth had attempted to do so in making his trenchant criticisms of the Church and his 'audacity' was, indeed, 'really staggering'.

Unfortunately for such critics, however, when the results of the *Daily News* inquiry appeared, they were commonly accepted as verifying Booth's work. The information contained in a succession of articles was generally in agreement rather than in conflict with what he had written; disagreements were only in matters of detail. Moreover, when all the available evidence was assembled in *The Religious Life of London* in 1904,[1] Booth's work was accepted as a true account of the situation he described, with hardly any criticism or emendation. The immediate outcome was that though some critics resented his exposure of the ineffectiveness of the churches, none failed to pay tribute to the sincerity and integrity of his motives. To quote Canon Barnett, writing from Toynbee Hall to thank Booth for his gift of a presentation copy:

Thank you for such a present to myself, but thank you much more for such a contribution to the needs of London. The value of your gift to London is not only the facts you have provided but in the start you have given to another way of considering the poor. Every charitable person is doing better work because of you, and so the poor have a better chance of escaping the wounds inflicted by blundering kindness.

Few of the appraisals of the Religious Influences Series, however, got to the root of the matter. So far as the problem of the relationships between religion and its social environment was concerned, Booth was at least a generation ahead of his time. As his wife remarked, the truth was that, apart from a few, amongst whom Dr. Hensley Henson (then Rector of St. Margaret's, Westminster) was outstanding, none of its readers seemed really to have mastered the book. Partly because of its sheer size,[2] partly because of what *The Times* called 'its shortcomings in the way of diffuseness and repetition', partly because he appeared merely to be trying to get to grips with the intangible, the significance of Booth's effort passed them by. They looked for concrete proposals, and finding none, turned away disappointed.

[1] Edited by R. Mudie-Smith, Hodder and Stoughton. See pp. 29, 34, 79-80, 204, 286, 332, 337.

[2] Many of the thousand or more recipients of presentation copies openly confessed that they had but dipped into what they hoped shortly to read with the closest attention. These were chiefly clergy who had supplied Booth with information concerning the work of the agencies with which they were associated. For some curious reason each was given the volume relating to a neighbouring area and not to their own, rather to their disappointment.

8

The Welfare of the People

THE Religious Influences Series ended with the promise of a Final Volume. Booth's friends urged him to use this as an opportunity to justify himself, and to make it a statement of faith and clarification of purpose. Thus Professor Marshall, writing from Cambridge to thank him 'for his angelic book: holy and beautiful outside and in', went on to say:

I cannot profess to be a connoisseur of the pictures with which it abounds. But I find myself drawn on to read a good deal, which ever I look in. But most of all do I yearn for the focusing in the last volume. To that you will of course give the very best of yourself. And I look to it as among the most valuable of economics—ethics—spiritual goods—that have ever been vouchsafed to the world.

I heard someone whose words are very weighty and who takes a great interest in your work, a very eminent man and one older than either of us, say, 'Booth gives materials, but he does not build with them enough.' I was interrupted in my reply by a man with a much bigger voice than mine; and the party almost at once broke up. But thinking over it afterwards, I felt that a person who merely read you and did not vibrate in echo to you—*à la* Marconi—might not see how much construction there is latent in all you do. There seems to me quite as much where you do not point directly to action as when you do; sometimes even more; that seems a paradox, but I mean it in all soberness and reverence.

But now in your last volume you must for the sake of all, for knowledge, for progress, for ideals—and I will throw in, though somewhat irrelevantly, for Booth—for the sake of all you must make that volume the best thing you possibly can. The best of the kind that has been done, I know it will be anyhow. But I want it to be even better than that, ever so much.

Booth was well aware of the pertinence of the argument embodied in this letter: it was one which had greeted him at the conclusion of each stage in his inquiries. For the first time it failed to provoke him to his own defence. On previous occasions, when critics had commented on the failure of his evidence to provide a foundation for practical reforms, he had been able to take refuge in the plea that his fact-finding was not yet complete. Each time he had been able to point to some further vista in the jungle of the problem of poverty which must be explored before a final conclusion could be reached. On coming to the end of the Religious Influences Series, however, he seems to have realized that though much yet remained to be done, and though the collection of more information was obviously desirable, in fact the answer to his critics did not lie here. He actually enumerated a list of subjects which still awaited examination,[1] but nevertheless declared himself content to leave them to others to pursue. The interest in social research displayed by the London County Council and the Settlements had, he assured his readers, reconciled him to the incompleteness of his own work. 'At the best speed possible to me, it would have taken three more years, and I suppose three more volumes, to have dealt adequately with the new subjects I mentioned in the concluding volume',[2] he remarked by way of excusing himself from continuing his labours.

Booth volunteered no explanation for his decision. He must, of course, have been tired: his investigations had made vast inroads on his time and energies, and financially had involved the expenditure of approximately £33,000. The demands—and the charms—of the business were a constant distraction. Perhaps he had come to feel that it was the tool of his invention that really mattered, and not the particular results or lack of results, of its immediate application. Or maybe even his 'long patience' wearied of so constant a devotion to the impartial presentation of facts; admittedly the paucity of practical results baffled and disappointed him. Whatever the truth, well before the completion of the Third Series he had made up his mind that he would embark on no further investigations, but would content himself with publishing such information as he had already gathered about social as distinct from religious influences. 'I incline more and more to make less of and depend less upon the "Social Influences" volume', he wrote to Aves in 1902. 'I do not think it will be wise to pin much upon

[1] *Final*, p. 214. These subjects included the habits of the various social classes, local government administration, Friendly and Co-operative Societies, and the whole range of Literature and the Arts, including the press.

[2] Ibid.

it. We won't print any contents in advance, but merely refer to it as a winding up volume—a thin one, I hope.'

In the event, the *Final Volume* contained no more than three chapters. One was devoted to 'Some Comparisons', and consisted chiefly of a discussion of method. A second dealt with the 'Habits of the People', the result being what he himself described as a patchwork. Into a third, entitled 'Notes on Administration', went a miscellany of comment on subjects varying from prostitution to housing. A major share of the space at his disposal was allocated to a 'guide to the labyrinth of previous volumes' in the shape of a detailed abstract of their contents prepared by George Duckworth.

One last word, he told himself, and he would be done. But that last word proved singularly hard to say. 'The final volume is rather a struggle, and I don't suppose it will ever be satisfactory', he wrote regarding what he and his wife came to call 'Starbook', by reason of the fact that, standing apart from the ranks of the volumes in the three Series as it did, it was allotted a star in place of a number on the spine and title page. Though he might regard it merely as an addendum, nevertheless it seemed impossible to escape from the fact that this was the last and final volume of a tremendous sequence, and as such, must inevitably be concerned with fundamental issues.[1] What did it all add up to, this immense description-in-detail?

Vainly he sought to extract from the vast bulk of the material contained in the sixteen volumes of the Inquiry some formula, some generalization, which would reduce to terms of the written word the essence of his researches. His methods were basically sound, whatever the deficiencies of his application of them. Of that much he was satisfied. Moreover, he was as certain as he had ever been that the investigation of the facts was an essential preliminary to the planning of practical action. Nevertheless, the hopes which he had entertained that out of his examination of religious and social influences might emerge some indication of the direction in which progress might be looked for, or some reassurance even as to the future, had come to nothing. Population problems were obviously important, but such

---

[1] In preparing the Poverty Series for publication in the Third Edition in 1902, he had, for example, committed himself to a fuller consideration in the *Final Volume* of his ideas concerning the elimination of Class B (*Poverty* i, p. 171; see also p. 62). His wife's criticism of the finished work suggests that she was aware of his predicament: 'This star volume does give me a sense of muddle and the pressing in of the extraneous: the suggestion of the statesman into the inquiries of a scientific man: and I am not sure whether science or statesmanship gain.'

factors as early marriage and a high birth-rate emerged from his inquiries as a consequence and not a cause of poverty. 'Not in this direction can we look for a solution of the problem of poverty.'[1] Education, administration, religion: he summed up the inadequacies of the contribution made by each of these to the improvement of social conditions, with the remark that 'at least the effort to attain it must be good in stimulating the consciousness and vigour of common life'.[2] The only real hope for the future which he could discern lay in the irrepressible vitality of the individual, typical as it was of the competitive struggle in industry. Evidence of this was provided by the development of the middle class, the advent of which seemed to him the outstanding social fact of the day.

Those who constitute this class are the special product of the push of industry; within their circle religion and education find the greatest response; amongst them all popular movements take their rise, and from them draw their leaders. To them, in proportion as they have ideas, political power will pass.[3]

But this left the problem of poverty untouched. Once more he reiterated his faith in the fundamental soundness of the principles of individualism as a basis for contemporary society. Once more his own integrity forced him to admit that though 'the passion for acquisition and advancement . . . is a strong beast and it pulls our wagon', nevertheless it 'needs the curb'.[4] Once more he reaffirmed the basic principles of his doctrine of 'limited socialism' which he had presented in the earliest stages of his work.

In order to raise permanently the lowest levels of human life many efforts must converge. Success could only be very gradual, and never perhaps complete, but the principle of action is unchangingly the same: to interfere by administrative action and penalties at each point at which life falls below a minimum accepted standard, while offering every opportunity for improvement.[5]

As it finally appeared, the 'Conclusion' with which the volume terminated amounted to no more than sixteen pages. Summarizing the contents of the preceding chapters, he reminded his readers that 'the indication of directions in which advance might be made' had been no part of his original design.[6] Nevertheless, he felt impelled to offer a comment which was perhaps the nearest he ever came to an

[1] *Final*, p. 20.   [2] Ibid., p. 203.   [3] Ibid., p. 204.   [4] Ibid., p. 95.
[5] Ibid., p. 95.   [6] Ibid., p. 205.

expression of regret that the ultimate object of his research had not
been achieved:

> For the treatment of disease, it is first necessary to establish the facts as to its
> character, extent and symptoms. Perhaps the qualities of mind which enable
> a man to make this inquiry are the least of all likely to give him that elevation of
> soul, sympathetic insight, and sublime confidence which must go to the making
> of a great regenerating teacher. I have made no attempt to teach; at the most
> I have ventured on an appeal to those whose part it is. . . . The dry bones that
> lie scattered over the long valley that we have traversed together lie before my
> reader. May some great soul, master of a subtler and nobler alchemy than
> mine, disentangle the confused issues, reconcile the apparent contradictions in
> aim, melt and commingle the various influences for good into one divine
> uniformity of effort, and make these dry bones live, so that the streets of our
> Jerusalem may sing with joy.[1]

On that somewhat self-critical note, in June 1903,[2] 'Mr. Booth's
Inquiry' came to an end.

It was perhaps only Booth's habitual modesty which caused him to
overlook the immense significance of the work which he had already
accomplished in the very different sphere of social policy and administrative practice. The clue to the unravelling of the tangle that
baffled him when he attempted to write his *Final Volume* was, in fact,
already in his own hands. Had he but been able to interpret its relevance,
his intervention in the campaign for old-age pensions, to take but a
single example, could have provided him with all the evidence he
required as to how and to what extent contributions to the solution of
social problems could stem from the analysis of such evidence as he
had assembled in the Inquiry. In order to make this clear, it is
necessary to show how his participation in the campaign led him
to formulate new principles upon which the industrial society of the
twentieth century could be reorganized.

In his Final Volume, Booth relegated the subject of old-age pensions
to a few pages in the section on 'The Organization of Charity',[3] but
his interest in it had, in fact, occupied much of his attention over a
long period. He had first become aware of the problems created by the

---

[1] *Final*, p. 216.

[2] Booth had sailed for Brazil on 1 April, for the opening of the harbour of Manaos a
'thousand miles up the Amazon', whose conception owed so much to his foresight and
planning. The final revision of his manuscript was therefore carried out by his wife and
his secretaries.

[3] *Final*, p. 142.

existence of a pauper class in the course of the collection of material for the Poverty Series in 1889. He reported to Beatrice Potter at an early stage in his inquiries that he 'had found a mine of great wealth in the books of the Stepney Union', and had set George Arkell to work to explore them, together with similar records in Poplar. Analysing his results in 1892, Booth was much struck by the fact that old age emerged as the most frequent single cause of pauperism in both Unions, being much more important than drink and ill-health:[1] some statistics prepared by Sidney Webb in 1890 had already brought home to him the large proportion of old people who ended their lives in the workhouse. This profoundly shocked him. The further he went in examining the subject, his wife tells us, 'the more certain did he become that to a large number of poor old people the removal to the Workhouse was a very great and genuine trouble'.[2] At the same time it occurred to him that if this large class of persons could be removed from within the scope of the Poor Law, it would be relatively easy to abolish out-relief altogether, a reform which his examination of administrative methods had already convinced him was highly desirable.

Examining the various schemes which were then being urged upon the public by Chamberlain and others as remedies for this situation, Booth found himself attracted by the boldness of the proposal for a universal weekly pension of 5s. on reaching the age of sixty-five.[3] Though he realized that the scheme savoured of socialism, it seemed to him that this would, at a single stroke, remove the aged poor from the orbit of the Poor Law and yet enable them to retain the independence which they enjoyed when in receipt of out-relief.

It offers for those who, without being able to earn a living, are still able to clean and cook for themselves, a far more desired and desirable existence. They can still remain members of the society to which they are accustomed, can still confer as well as receive neighbourly favours, mind a baby, sit up with the sick, chop firewood, or weed the garden. They are not cut off from the sympathies of daily existence, and their presence is often a valuable ingredient

[1] His analysis of the causes of pauperism in Stepney was as follows:

Old Age	32·8%
Sickness	26·7%
Drink	12·6%
Lack of work	4·4%
All other causes	23·5%

(*Journal of the Royal Statistical Society*, 1892, p. 609.)

[2] *Memoir*, p. 142.

[3] Beatrice Webb remarks that it was Canon Barnett's advocacy which eventually converted Booth to this proposal (*My Apprenticeship*, p. 208).

in the surrounding life. When the end comes, the presence of well-known faces, the sounds of well-known voices, soothe and succour the last hours.[1]

Once convinced, Booth wasted no time, but promptly presented a paper on 'The Enumeration and Classification of Paupers, and State Pensions for the Aged', to the Royal Statistical Society in November 1891, 'in order to give the idea of a universal pension an airing'.[2] This Paper consisted of the information which he had already collected concerning the Stepney and St. Pancras Unions, and was originally intended to provide an opportunity for 'considering what changes, if any, are desirable in the [Poor] Law or its administration'. However, in addition to demonstrating the need for improved methods of official tabulation of paupers as a basis for better administration of the Poor Law, he seized the opportunity to state the arguments for and against 'some system of deferred annuity' as a means of dealing with the aged pauper. In so doing, he made no attempt to conceal the startling fact that the sum annually involved would be of the order of £17,000,000.

The evening was a memorable one in his life [records Mary Booth]. The paper fell like a bomb-shell, and in the discussion which ensued not a voice was raised in favour of the proposal, and, as time drew on, so many of the eager critics were unable to obtain a hearing that before the meeting broke up it was decided to give a second evening to the discussion of the subject, so as to enable all who wished to speak to do so.

The adjourned meeting took place on the evening of 22 December 1891. 'Very hostile meeting' is the brief record in his wife's journal.

It was a depressing occasion. A thick fog pervaded London and filled the Hall of the School of Mines, where the Statistical Society are permitted to hold their meetings. Through the mist, which hardly allowed the speakers to be visible, voice after voice emerged, and all unfavourable, many whilst courteous almost contemptuous in their repudiation of so wild a project. . . . The project was indeed attacked on every side. It was inadequate, it was impracticable, it was ruinously expensive, and the cost of collection and payment of officials needed would be as great as that of the pensions themselves.[3]

Deeply stirred as he was by the plight of old people who died in poverty, Booth felt that he had no choice but to devote himself to the collection of the facts which must by their sheer veracity convince

[1] *Journal of the Royal Statistical Society*, 1892, p. 633.   [2] Ibid.   [3] *Memoir*, p. 23.

public opinion of the necessity for the reform of the Poor Law in this regard at least. The Poverty Series being now finished and Industry not yet properly begun, he switched certain of his staff and an increasing proportion of his own time and energy, to this new task. Following what was by now his customary plan, he proposed first to reprint in an elaborated form the Paper which he had just completed.[1] For practical reasons, he was compelled to defer his ambition to present a 'general, or even sufficiently representative, examination of London pauperism', and to restrict himself to the two London Unions about which he already had some information, with one rural Union by way of comparison. His method of presenting his material was similar to that adopted in the Poverty Series: statistical tables were combined with verbal descriptions, the impersonal effect of the picture as a whole being offset by the inclusion of individual case histories. There was, however, one important innovation. As in the Paper he had prepared on the subject, the first part consisted simply of factual information concerning the problem of pauperism, its nature, its extent, its causes, and the methods by which it was relieved.[2] The second part, on the other hand, which related specifically to the aged poor, not only stated the facts, but went on to advocate universal pensions as a practical remedy for the problem thus revealed.

His exposition of the case for pensions was both straightforward and deeply sympathetic. He was less happy in his endeavours to vindicate his advocacy of this breach of the individualist principle. His original conception of 'limited socialism' had restricted its application to 'those who cannot stand alone'.[3] Devoting a whole chapter to the subject, he now attempted to take this a stage further by classifying the various causes of pauperism according to whether they should be dealt with by collective action on the part of the State or not. He was certain that drunkards, prostitutes, and criminals ought to be left to suffer 'all the natural consequences of their conduct, short of actually perishing from cold and hunger'.[4] Early marriages and recklessness in the bringing of children into the world were similarly dismissed as causes of pauperism meriting little sympathy. But lack of work presented exceptional difficulties, and he made no effort to discuss it, possibly because he proposed to consider the subject in the

---

[1] *Pauperism, a Picture, and Endowment of Old Age, an Argument*, Macmillan, 1892, Introduction. The one rural Union was that of Ashby-de-la-Zouch, presumably because it covered the neighbourhood of Gracedieu Manor.

[2] Reprinted in *Industry* iv, p. 311.   [3] *Poverty* i, p. 167.   [4] *Pauperism*, p. 51.

course of the Industry Series, or perhaps because its complexity alarmed him. All he would say was that this problem could not be dealt with by collective action: he believed that the reorganization of industry on socialist lines would require such a radical change in human nature as to call for 'a new heaven and a new earth'.[1]

The relief of poverty should, he thought, only be made a public responsibility when 'the inevitable troubles of sickness, old age and death' were encountered. Here the question in his mind was simply that of the means by which they were to be relieved. He was to return to the problems of poverty due to sickness and death in later days when serving on the Royal Commission on the Poor Laws. Meanwhile, he concentrated on the aged poor, about whom he had no doubts. The book concluded with a remarkable passage in which he explained that the purpose of his 'socialistic' scheme was simply and solely to enable working men and women to retain in old age their lifelong independence. It was to the common sense and self-respect of the working classes rather than to the benevolence of the philanthropic that he therefore addressed himself, with results which he certainly did not expect.

It is not in the name of the people, but to the people, that I would speak in advocating the endowment of old age as at once a practical and possible means of giving a surer footing to those who now, trying to stand, too often fall and sometimes sink altogether. I advocate it as bringing with it something of that security necessary to a higher standard of life, a security of position which will stimulate rather than weaken the play of individuality on which progress and prosperity depend.[2]

So keen was public interest in the whole subject of poor law reform that Booth published his results, under the title of *Pauperism, a Picture, and Endowment of Old Age, an Argument*, in 1892 both in book form and as a 6*d.* pamphlet. Once more his proposals roused instant opposition from those who feared that the sole result would be the further demoralization of the poor. Only Chamberlain seemed to regard the idea with any interest: Octavia Hill and C. S. Loch of the Charity Organization Society expressed profound disapproval, Loch remarking acidly that those who suggested reforms ought themselves to be versed in actual administration. The *Charity Organization Society Review* described his proposal as 'the most outrageous and absurd scheme yet promulgated', the President of the Economic

---

[1] *Pauperism*, p. 51. [2] Op. cit., p. 77.

Section of the British Association being quoted as having said in his Address on the subject:

Mr. Booth has made a proposal which, from its comprehensive boldness, has astonished many of his admirers, and which, coming from any other quarter would, I venture to say, have been generally characterised if not as Utopian, at least as affording to our social and political intelligences, in their present imperfect state of development, no food for serious discussion.[1]

Undeterred, Booth set to work to collect yet further and, he hoped, yet more telling evidence on the subject. Though he was by this time wholly convinced as to the desirability of a pensions scheme, loyalty to his ideal of scientific impartiality deterred him from directing his inquiries towards the specific purpose of proving or disproving his case. Instead, he decided to acquire information which would 'make more possible and more profitable a study of the six hundred and forty-eight separate lessons in administration which the conduct of the Poor Law Unions of England and Wales affords',[2] having been much struck by the fact that every Union was allowed what amounted to complete freedom as to the amount and kind of relief they offered to the aged. In order to execute this mammoth undertaking, a small staff was installed in an office consisting of the vacant room in the premises of the Statistical Society in Adelphi Terrace from which all his investigations were henceforth to be conducted. 'Forms of schedule', accompanied by instructions as to how they should be filled in, were sent to the Chairman of each of the 648 Unions asking for information as to the principles and practices they followed in granting assistance to old people. It is a tribute to Booth's growing reputation that as many as 285 returned usable replies. Clergymen in each Union were similarly approached for information about the condition of the aged poor in their parishes: in this case 360 replies were received. Finally, information was sought concerning the care of the aged in 262 villages, ten of which were examined in considerable detail.

Meanwhile, public opinion on the question of the treatment of the aged poor under the existing Poor Law had been roused to such a pitch as to require the appointment of a Royal Commission in 1893. Its members included the Prince of Wales, Joseph Chamberlain, and inevitably Booth, whose position 'at the head of the statistical tree',[3] together with his known interest in the reform of the Poor Law and

---

[1] *Charity Organization Society Review*, September 1892.

[2] *The Aged Poor in England and Wales*, Macmillan, 1894, p. vi.   [3] See above, p. 110.

his advocacy of the principle of pensions for the aged, made him an obvious choice. He was assiduous in attendance whenever business permitted. He also gave evidence to the Commission along the lines of his Paper to the Royal Statistical Society. On this occasion he was cross-questioned in a spirit of some antagonism by his fellow Commissioners, but defended himself with a dry brevity, defeating their attempts to trip him up by laying claim to nothing for which he could not produce evidence, and concluding with a robust denial of the suggestion that only the poor would apply for pensions under a universal scheme. 'I am sure I should; I believe that all ordinary people . . . would take the trouble to claim it', he stoutly declared.[1]

The active interest he took in the subject of the aged poor by no means absorbed the whole of his leisure: hard-pressed though he was, he maintained a close supervision of the preparation of material for the Industry Series, and was in addition actively concerned in the affairs of the Royal Statistical Society, of which he was then President. His wife loyally supported him, plodding diligently through the evidence given at meetings of the Royal Commission which he had been forced to miss, and marking the passages which he ought to read. He refused all invitations to dine or speak; his family saw little of him, and his visits to Gracedieu, though frequent, were invariably fleeting. Perhaps because his life was thus overloaded, when *The Aged Poor* appeared in 1894 it proved to be a singularly dull book, a mass of statistics of which even Mrs. Booth could only claim that it provided ammunition for those who were actively campaigning for old-age pensions. This was certainly true. Booth's analyses made it painfully clear that old age indeed presented a major problem for the working classes, as many as 40-45 per cent. of those over the age of sixty-five having been revealed to be living in poverty. People were poor because they were old, was his summing up of the situation. Beyond this, however, he was not able to go. His inquiries had provided such a mass of detail that even his methodical mind was hardly able to master it: the extraordinary variations in the amount of pauperism amongst the aged as between one Union and another remained as much a mystery as ever,[2] and he bluntly admitted to the members of the Royal Statistical Society that his efforts to define what he meant by 'poverty' in terms of overcrowding had not been wholly successful.[3] No general conclusion

---

[1] *Report of the Royal Commission on the Aged Poor, 1895*, Minutes of Evidence, Q. 11013.

[2] *Journal of the Royal Statistical Society*, 1894, p. 239.

[3] Ibid., 1893, p. 566; see also *Industry* i, p. 10.

emerged from the information he had collected. 'These facts are to a great extent such as elude analysis and defy summary treatment', he remarked.[1] Whether he asked himself why this should have been so is not known, though his unhappy comment in a letter to Professor Marshall is suggestive: 'Never, I should think,' he declared, 'has a book been the occasion of so much bad language on the part of its author—I cursed every minute I gave to it—I could not escape, though I continually tried to do so—the wretched thing was my master, and not I its, at any rate till very near the end.'

Booth excused the lack of firm conclusions in *The Aged Poor* by declaring that he had been hampered in expressing his opinions by his membership of the Royal Commission, to which he felt the task of advocating specific schemes had to be left. This unhappily it failed to achieve, its deliberations ending in ruin in 1895, with not only majority and minority reports but also a plethora of memoranda, cross-comment and reservations by individual members.[2] He abandoned his own intention of submitting a memorandum, in the interests of unanimity, but only succeeded in offending all those who still clung to their differences. Mrs. Booth declared that she had known all along that it was a mistake to get mixed up with the affairs of the Commission. Clearly the whole process of compromise was foreign to his habit of mind, and he had neither the patience nor the inclination to secure acceptance of his own ideas by means of backstairs intrigue. Eventually, after a 'breakdown' which necessitated a period of rest abroad, he signed the Minority Report along with Chamberlain, but it must have been with a profound determination that in future he would stick to his own last as an investigator.

For the next year or so, his commitments in regard to the Industry Series prevented him from implementing his promise to continue the inquiries begun in *The Aged Poor*. However, public opinion had been too deeply stirred on the subject for it to be allowed to drop. It was generally accepted that something must be done in the matter, though no one could agree as to what precise form that something should take.

---

[1] *The Aged Poor*, p. 419.

[2] Lord Aberdare, the Chairman, retreated to South Wales in a state of nervous prostration. 'I believe an hour in that chair where I spent so many weary, troublous hours, would bring back the sense of weakness and impotency which compelled me to leave my work unfinished', he wrote to Booth shortly afterwards. The Prince of Wales withdrew because it was regarded as impolitic for royalty to become embroiled in controversy. Broadhurst submitted a Minority Report which was said to be written by Sydney Webb (Margaret Cole, *Beatrice Webb*, Longmans Green and Co., 1945, p. 95). Chamberlain in a fury wrangled with all the other members.

Committees were set up: proposals of the most varied character were enunciated. What became known as 'Lord Rothschild's Committee',[1] which was appointed in 1896 to do what the Royal Commission on the Aged Poor had failed to do, also failed to agree, excusably so, perhaps, considering that over 100 schemes were submitted for its consideration. In an effort to resolve the deadlock and secure action, Booth published a sequel to his earlier book. This appeared in 1899 under the title of *Old Age Pensions and the Aged Poor*.[2] In it, he first recapitulated the information contained in the previous volume as to the condition of the aged poor and then once again stated the case for a universal pension. This he admitted would involve a 'socialistic transfer' of wealth on a scale which he made no attempt to deny: he was prepared to talk in terms of some £20,000,000 a year, he declared, adding that everything worth having cost money.[3]

After its publication, Booth was invited to address a conference on the subject held at Browning Hall. It is a tribute to the sincerity with which he stated his case that the outcome was a series of meetings in support of a universal pension scheme, organized in seven provincial cities by local working-class organizations, at all of which he was the principal speaker. Though he wearied of the repetition of what was necessarily the same argument, he greatly enjoyed the contacts with organized labour which this tour involved, and the cut and thrust of debate with keen and often sceptical socialists which sometimes followed his speeches.[4] He proved to be a most persuasive speaker, making no attempt to evade difficult issues, but boldly calling the attention of his audience to them in order that he might discuss them freely and frankly. Apparently he scored his points by his lucidity and sincerity, for he was never an orator: 'Gentlemen, I have done. Please ask questions' was the abrupt conclusion of his Birmingham speech.[5] Everywhere he went, he insisted that all he sought was that the principle should be adopted: practical details could be worked out

---

[1] Treasury Committee on Old Age Pensions, 1896-8.

[2] *Old Age Pensions and the Aged Poor, a Proposal*, Macmillan, 1899.

[3] Ibid., pp. 39, 70.   [4] *Memoir*, p. 144.

[5] An obituary notice in the *Journal of the Royal Statistical Society*, 1917, quotes the recollections of G. N. Barnes, M.P., who, expecting 'to find in Charles Booth a man who would touch the heart of some crowded meeting as with a fiery torch, was momentarily disappointed by the quiet demeanour of this spare man of methodical habits of address'. But, Mr. Barnes continued, 'somehow there were many to do Charles Booth's bidding. . . . He had that about him which inspired others to go out and do what he willed they should do. His arguments were irresistible, his disinterestedness transparent, and his simple desire to serve infectious.'

when that had been done, though he had a scheme of his own in mind. 'My proposal is . . . simply that all old people should receive an allowance of 5s. a week after 65, and that the money should be raised year by year by suitable taxation.[1] Booth's intervention in the campaign proved decisive, and it was as a direct consequence of this tour that the National Committee of Organized Labour was formed to consolidate public opinion behind the demand for a universal pension. Success followed slowly. Booth and his associates had to face the almost fanatical opposition of those who, like Octavia Hill, hated and feared the whole concept of a free pension. 'It was terrible to her', Mrs. Booth wrote,

that one in whose judgement she confided, and of whose honesty she was certain, should come forward to destroy—as she feared would be the case—the basis of her life's work; to turn the thoughts of the poor . . . back into the pestilential habit of holding out a beggar's hand for what she could only look upon as a dole. . . . She opposed him with all her force and with all her own originality; yet she never lost confidence in him, nor he in her, and no shadow of estrangement ever marred their constant friendship.[2]

In 1901, the Charity Organization Society, under the leadership of C. S. Loch, made one last attempt to organize opinion against Booth's proposal, and it was only after the Liberal victory of 1906 that the principle of universal pensions for old people was finally accepted. Legislation putting it into practice was not passed until 1909. At the time when Booth was writing the *Final Volume*, the outcome of the campaign was therefore by no means assured, and this must have contributed to his inability to appreciate the significance of his own statement of the case for pensions.

A second venture in which Booth became actively involved, again as a direct result of information assembled in the course of his inquiries, concerned the development of transport services to the suburbs. Answers to questionnaires sent out in connexion with the Industry Series revealed the considerable distances habitually travelled by workmen between their homes and their places of work. Booth was subsequently led to speculate whether 'this permanently useful and healthy force could not be successfully taken advantage of for the solution of the housing difficulties now experienced in London'.[3]

---

[1] Draft letter to an editor.   [2] *Memoir*, p. 149.

[3] Leaflet prepared in connexion with a conference held at Browning Hall Settlement, 1901.

He was convinced that 'any direct attack on the insufficiency, badness
or dearness of the accommodation available for the people' was bound
to fail. Impressed by the possibilities of modern means of transport,[1]
he reached the conclusion that the only permanent cure for the housing
problem lay in the provision of 'improved means of locomotion'
which would facilitate the wider distribution of the population. It
was his opinion that this could only be achieved by means of a joint
Transport Board whose task it would be 'to attempt to reconcile,
and if necessary to override sectional interests of whatever kind
for the benefit of the whole community'. Responsibility for the
large capital expenditure involved would, he believed, have to
be accepted by the local authorities. Booth's argument was, of
course, another example of the 'limited socialism' which he was
willing to accept in order to ensure the freedom of the individual:
he made it plain that on no account should the authorities themselves build houses, this being essentially a matter for private
enterprise.

Subsequent events followed the pattern of his previous work on
behalf of pensions. An opportunity was found for the presentation of
a paper embodying his views at a conference on housing at Browning
Hall Settlement in 1901. A second conference followed at which a
committee was elected to explore the practical implications of Booth's
proposals. Working as they were under Booth's presidency, it was
inevitable that the first step should be to survey the ground. This was
undertaken by George Duckworth and constituted an Inquiry in
miniature. It was based on an eight-foot square map, on which the
means of transport were shown by a graphic method which it was
hoped would 'greatly assist the quick perception of the salient points
of the map'. Tram routes were shown by ribbons of various colours,
railways by lengths of string, electric railways by silk cords, stations
by black-headed pins, and the main centres of traffic by flag indicators.
No provision was made for omnibus routes because this form of locomotion was one which Booth regarded as bound to vanish from the
scene of any modern civilization. As he remarked, 'they certainly have
their uses, but that they should up to now form the principal method
of transit on so many of our main routes is evidence of how far London

[1] The motor car became a legal vehicle in 1896. Booth was an enthusiastic pioneer car
owner: one of his grandsons recollects that the various interchangeable bodies for the
remarkable Ford Convertible were at one time suspended on the walls of the 'motor-
house' at Gracedieu.

has fallen behind in the adoption of methods which other cities have long regarded as essential'.[1]

The publication of Booth's proposals roused considerable attention. As Stead wrote:

> Five weeks before the last County Council elections he announced what he considered the first step in housing reform—a much more drastic step than either party had seriously proposed—won for it the support of both parties, and secured the written adhesion of exactly one half the new Council.[2]

Similarly, the setting up of the Royal Commission on the Means of Locomotion and Transport in London in 1903 seems to have owed much to Booth's influence on public opinion.[3] As in the case of old-age pensions, the logic of the results of his investigations had led him to conclusions which were not only foreign to his own cast of mind but were also far in advance of those generally held, and there must have seemed to his supporters every reason for hoping that his previous success would be repeated. However, ill-health and pressure of business combined to curtail his participation in the movement.[4]

The partnership between impartial investigation and practical reform which Booth initiated on these two occasions was clearly of exceptional value, and its application to the problems of social planning in an industrial society was of the first importance. This, was, indeed, the declared object of his researches. But more than this was involved, for the outcome had been, in each case, to assert a new principle. In the laudatory address presented to him on the occasion of the passing of the Old Age Pensions Act, for example, the National Committee of Organized Labour specifically attributed to him the contention that:

> Old Age Pensions should be a Civil Right, Universal, non-Contributory, and free from all taint of the Poor Law. In the sphere of Principle, Our Victory is complete, and we are proud to acknowledge that Our Victory is Yours. You have supplied the Ideas, the Arguments, the convincing considerations, which have convinced the Nation.

[1] *Improved Means of Locomotion as a first step towards the Cure of Housing Difficulties of London*, 1901; see also *Final*, pp. 179-99.

[2] *Review of Reviews*, April 1903.

[3] See *Report*, 1905, Cd. 2597. Booth gave evidence supporting the necessity for a permanent authority to give continuous attention to all questions of locomotion and transport.

[4] Whether for this reason or not, it is now impossible to tell, but from then onwards, the campaign gradually lost impetus. The Royal Commission duly reported in 1905 on lines similar to those indicated by Booth, but their recommendations were not implemented in his lifetime, and immediate results were meagre.

However, though Booth was gratified by this tribute, the heart of the matter seems to have escaped him; he never showed that he was aware that his efforts had assisted in bringing to birth a revolutionary change in British social thought.

Had he but been able to grasp it, a whole system of welfare was embodied in the results of the work he had done. By his application of the principle of 'limited socialism' to the problems of poverty he had, in fact, arrived at the concept of the 'minimum accepted standard'[1] below which society could not, for its own sake, allow any of its members to sink, which was to become the corner stone of the Welfare State. Similarly, his argument that pensions must be enjoyed as a right of citizenship embodied a new political concept which he ultimately extended to include the right of every man to have 'his chance, or even his chances' for improvement.[2] Yet again, his demand for official intervention in securing adequate conditions in places of employment and elsewhere[3] was one which became embodied in a new conception of the rights of the citizen; it represented a belief that civil rights were as important in the economic sphere as they were in the political and social. These were thoughts in advance of his time, though they were soon to be utilized in the construction of the new society of the twentieth century: added together they would have provided him with ample material for the 'body of doctrine' which he regarded as essential to the foundation of his new Jerusalem.[4] As it was, his interpretation of his results for the purposes of his Final Volume led him to look backward to the world of the Poor Law of 1834 rather than forward to that of the Welfare State that lay ahead.

Unaware of the possibilities which lay to his hand, Booth's only thought was to implement as quickly as might be his decision to bring his researches to an end. Accordingly, no sooner had the book been published in 1903 than the small staff which had so faithfully served

---

[1] *Final*, p. 208.

[2] Ibid. The Village Institute in the neighbourhood of Gracedieu for which he was responsible was designed to offer opportunities for self-improvement to each and every man.

[3] Ibid., p. 209. Other examples were his recommendations that a Licensing Authority should be set up to enforce improved standards in public houses (*Final*, p. 111), and that provision should be made for a compulsory 'green belt' to preserve the amenities of outer London (*Final*, p. 199), this proposal no doubt being inspired by Octavia Hill. His proposal that transport to the suburbs should be a monopoly of municipal authorities has already been discussed (*Final*, pp. 179-90).

[4] Ibid., p. 216.

him during the years of investigation was disbanded.[1] He himself
intended to slip as quietly out of the main stream of social action as
he had originally moved into it, and in the years that were left to him
he proposed to regard the Inquiry and all it stood for as being, literally,
a closed book. It is significant that on his visits to the Liverpool office
of the firm he now stayed in 'reputable lodgings, not the working-class
home of the past'. 'I make no definite plans', he wrote as the end of the
Inquiry drew near, 'but hope that my life will lay itself out much as
you suggest with plenty of Gracedieu and little responsibility—a
looker-on rather than a doer and above all not *undertaking* to do
things. You see I make good resolutions.'

Nevertheless, the achievement of so considerable a feat as the
completion of the Inquiry inevitably brought with it a certain after-
math of activity and the period immediately following its conclusion
was perhaps as busy as any he had ever known. 'Really, your father's
ceaseless and varied activities are astonishing even to me', his wife
declared. 'He goes on adding and adding to his undertakings.' The
closing stages of the Inquiry were marked by increasingly frequent
expressions of public appreciation of what he had accomplished,[2]
but these were inevitably accompanied by further demands upon him
for service of one kind or another, and very much against his inclination he found himself caught up in a variety of undertakings. He was,
for example, appointed a member of a departmental committee set up
in 1903 to inquire into Post Office Wages, whilst the interest which
he had been led to take in fiscal reform as a result of his exploration of
the effect on land values of improved means of communication made
him an obvious choice for membership of the Tariff Commission set
up in 1904 by Chamberlain. Yet though he found these subjects
fascinating, he grudged the demands they made upon his time—'Oh,
Lord, when shall I have leisure?' he groaned—and deeply regretted
the disapproval with which certain of his friends and admirers greeted

[1] The training and experience its members had derived while working under Booth's
direction enabled them to move on to posts of responsibility in which several of them
achieved considerable reputations (e.g. Duckworth became private secretary to Austen
Chamberlain, and Llewellyn-Smith Permanent Secretary of the Board of Trade and
chief economic adviser to the Government. Aves' subsequent career has already been
noted. See above, p. 125.).

[2] These included a Privy Councillorship, a fellowship of the Royal Society and the
conferment of honorary degrees by the Universities of Oxford, Cambridge, and
Liverpool. Discreet approaches were made to discover his preference as between a
knighthood and a Privy Councillorship. Mrs. Booth in his absence had no hesitation in
indicating that his choice would certainly be for the latter.

his unqualified support of Chamberlain's policy. It is indeed apparent that he was out of his element in the new world of social affairs. His long-standing disagreements with Liberal thought became more pronounced: whereas in the early stages of the Inquiry he had found himself alienated from those he respected by what they regarded as an attack upon the foundations of society, now he was constantly involved in controversy because of his staunch declaration of loyalty to individualism and his formal adherence to the Conservative Party. He was, of course, no longer young, and the heavy expenditure of energy in preceding years had inevitably taken their toll, but he himself observed that the things he had to do for the business were all delightful to him, being 'without contention or effort'[1]; only when he returned to the troubled waters of social reform did his 'old enemy colitis' again attack him.

His appointment to the Royal Commission on the Poor Laws in December 1905 proved to be his last major piece of public service: he had earlier that year suffered from a breakdown in health so severe that he termed it the 'Complete Crusher', which had made essential a retreat to Italy. However, the work of the Commission promised to be both profitable and interesting, and at first all went well. 'A pleasant visit to Gracedieu, colloguing in the old way with Charles Booth as to the proper course of the poor law inquiry', recorded Beatrice Webb, who had also been appointed a member.[2] Together they were influential in persuading the Commission to reject the prearranged agenda and itself to organize the collection and presentation of evidence, Booth assuming responsibility for a sub-committee dealing with statistics. Nevertheless, as the discussions proceeded, he found himself increasingly isolated from the rest of his colleagues. He regarded with deep distaste the intrusion of intrigue and passion into what he considered should be a matter for impartial investigation, whilst his preference for handling witnesses as if he were interviewing them for purposes of the Inquiry met with the disapproval of his associates.

---

1 The fact that 'business was bad' meant that for some years after the ending of the Inquiry he had to play a much more active part in the firm's affairs than he had done for some time past, but this was a circumstance in which he delighted and from which he derived unfailing satisfaction. This was the period during which the development of such subsidiary concerns as that for the opening up of the Amazon called for exceptional energy and drive on Booth's part. See John, op. cit., Chapters V and VI; also above, pp. 148, 160.

2 Webb, *Our Partnership*, Longmans Green & Co., 1948, pp. 322 et seq., on which the following account is chiefly based.

More serious was the fundamental difference of opinion which
developed between himself and those of his fellow Commissioners
who were prepared to recommend the break-up of the Poor Law.
This exposed him to bitter criticism from those who ultimately signed
the Minority Report. Conscious though he was of the strength of the
case for special provision for certain categories of the destitute, such as
the aged and the sick, nothing could shake his loyalty to the individualist principles of the 1834 Act. 'Charles Booth opened with an almost
passionate denunciation of the policy of patching', Mrs. Webb records
of a meeting of the Commission in 1906. 'He wanted to go back to the
principles of 1834, start afresh from those principles, and apply them
drastically. This could not be done by the Poor Law Commissioners
of 1835-47. They had enough to do to reduce the 15,000 parishes to
600 Unions and introduce some measure of uniformity. We must at
all hazard get rid of out-relief.'[1] For some time he struggled on, but the
dissension which accompanied the preparation of the report sickened
him. 'The commission's atmosphere is getting very hot, and it will be
hotter before we have done', recorded Mrs. Webb.[2] He finally resigned in 1908 on grounds of ill-health.[3]

Nothing could better demonstrate the extent to which Booth was
now out of touch with contemporary thought: individualism, even
though restrained by 'limited socialism' could not be relied on as the
mainspring of social welfare, unless supplemented by collective action.
He was not alone in his advocacy of strict administration, preferably on
institutional lines,[4] but taken together with his opposition to any
extension of state provision in the form of welfare services (other than
education), it merely served to emphasize his isolation from the main
stream of his times.

Two years later, provoked by the campaign organized by the Webbs
in support of the Minority Report, he made one last return to the fray.
He had submitted his views on the reform of the Poor Law to the
Royal Commission in the shape of a memorandum. This he now

---

[1] Ibid., p. 357.   [2] Ibid., p. 393.

[3] A letter by Octavia Hill remarks that: 'Dear Mr. Booth has resigned his place on the
Commission. There was great sympathy and warmth of feeling shown, and we all signed
a letter to him.' C. Edmund Maurice, *Life of Octavia Hill*, Macmillan, 1913, p. 570.

[4] See the Majority Report of the Commission, 1909, pp. 534 et seq. Even the Webbs
always maintained that the socialist State they envisaged would have to make provision
for 'drastic action' against the idle and recalcitrant. See Sidney and Beatrice Webb,
The Break-up of the Poor Law, Longmans Green & Co., 1909, p. 559; *The Public Organization of the Labour Market*, Longmans Green & Co., 1909, pp. 267, 306, 308; *English Poor
Law Policy*, Longmans Green & Co., 1910, pp. 306-7.

amplified and published in the form of three papers.[1] These constituted a staunch reiteration of the principle he had adopted over
twenty years before when confronted with the results of his earliest
investigations: the poorest classes must be subjected to compulsory
direction in order that the freedom of the rest of society might go
unimpaired. Responsibility for this residue of humanity was the proper
province of the Poor Law which should only come into operation
'when all else fails; when savings are gone; credit exhausted; energy
sapped, and character (too often) lost'.[2] To enable it to do this
effectively, the Poor Law must be strongly organized and strictly
administered: its rule must be such as would 'strengthen physical and
moral fibre, form good habits or break bad ones, and . . . keep under
control those whose unrestrained lives cause injury to others as well as
to themselves'.[3] This Booth believed could only be achieved in
'graded institutions' in which compulsion could be used.

Even for those whose destitution merited compassion rather than
compulsion, he refused to countenance any form of financial support.
He made no attempt to deny the justice of their claims, of which he
was indeed as keenly conscious as he had ever been, but reiterated
dogmatically his belief that they could best be dealt with by other
means. The aged now received pensions; the sick could be catered for
by 'an elastic combination of Poor Law with voluntary institutions';
the relief of the need of the widow, the orphan, and similar persons
called for the improved organization of means to thrift and of charitable effort. It was easy to say that relief could be given in such cases
provided that it was no more than 'adequate' but he was convinced that
the instruction would prove difficult to interpret in practice:

> To give a trifle and leave the applicant to find the rest is denounced as cruel
> and as encouraging begging. But is it any less cruel for the Guardians to give
> nothing. . . . It may, indeed, be held that relief from the parish is poisoned at
> the source. I think it is. . . . But adequate relief with full inquiry, constant
> watching, and frequent revision, unless undertaken with unusual tact and
> sympathy, is an exceptionally poisonous kind of relief, paralysing to individual
> effort after improvement, and a perfect hotbed of deceit. It is therefore only as
> a tendency to restrict the giving of relief in this form that the doctrine of

[1] *Poor Law Reform*, Macmillan, 1910; *Reform of the Poor Law*, 1910; *Comments on
Proposals for the Reform of the Poor Laws*, 1911. These papers were presented to the Central
Poor Law Conference, of which he served as President in 1912.

[2] *Poor Law Reform*, pp. 65-6.

[3] *Poor Law Reform*, p. 79. This was a repetition of views he had expressed in the course
of the Inquiry. See e.g. *Religious Influences* i, p. 108; vii, pp. 303, 411.

'adequacy' can be welcomed. The evil influence of the Poor Law, as well as its safeguard from abuse, lies in the test of destitution.[1]

Booth never again attempted to play any great part in public life. So far as social problems were concerned, his early love, the study of industrial relations, claimed much of his attention but he achieved no more than a pamphlet on the subject of *Industrial Unrest* before war broke out in 1914. Now in his seventies, his thoughts turned more and more to Gracedieu which had become part and parcel of his life and to whose enjoyment he devoted his days. 'Don't imagine that I am dull', he wrote. 'Life at Gracedieu is heavenly. I am having "the time of my life", I think.' Only when an attempt to put into shape his ideas on industrial reconstruction after the war[2] brought him face to face with the issues which had for so long absorbed his attention did he confess to any sense of the old unease.

I think it is with reading and writing I perhaps knock my head most consciously and have to select; the real taboo lies with the 'After the War' problems none of which I dare touch. They are the dogs that bit me and when, if ever, a hair of them becomes curative, the job will be done.

Charles Booth ended his life as he had lived it, with a quiet acceptance of the inevitable. He died on 16 November 1916 at Gracedieu, and was buried in the nearby cemetery of Thringstone Church. It was not until 1920, when the country was freed from the preoccupations of the war that public tribute was paid to his life and work when Sir Austen Chamberlain unveiled a tablet to his memory at a Memorial Service in St. Paul's Cathedral. Possibly the efforts made by his relatives and friends to perpetuate his memory would have pleased him more. At Toynbee Hall, part of the original premises were re-constructed by members of his family to provide married quarters for those of the residents whose wives wished to share their husbands' labours, and renamed Charles Booth House in acknowledgement of his 'great leadership'. At the University of Liverpool, a Charles Booth Chair of Social Science was founded and endowed by the firm of A. Booth & Co., and a Charles Booth Lectureship instituted with the proceeds of the Memorial Fund raised by his friends and admirers.[3] Without doubt, Booth would have approved of this way of continuing

[1] Ibid., p. 35.   [2] *Memoir*, p. 155.

[3] It is a tribute to the quality of the relationship which Booth established with his working-class neighbours in the village of Thringstone that they generously supported this fund.

his attempts to solve the problems he had encountered in the course of the Inquiry, as a permanent memorial to himself and his achievement. Equally certainly, he would have given enthusiastic encouragement to the endeavours of those who have subsequently sought to take up the burden of his work where he left it, and would have received with modesty the tributes of those who have followed in his footsteps and, out of a painful experience, have come to recognize the debt they owe to him.

Part II

EVALUATION

9

The Poverty Series

'I HAVE had no foregone conclusions', Booth told the Royal Statistical Society when he presented his first report in 1887, 'and it is rather to the method here employed, than to the results yet shown, that I pin my faith.'[1] In saying this, he showed that he was aware that his work broke new ground. His primary objective was not to prove that poverty should be regarded as a social evil of great importance, or that the alarmist reports that had recently appeared could be discounted, even though these had been the immediate occasion for the undertaking of his self-imposed task. What he did intend to do was to demonstrate once and for all that the incidence of poverty could be measured with some precision and that a reliable appraisal of its importance could be given, uninfluenced by emotion or doctrine.

For this reason, Booth's Inquiry marked the beginning of a new era in both public administration and social policy. As a man of affairs, he had the courage to ask questions which the more sophisticated regarded as naïve. Who were 'the poor'? What were they like? How many of them were there? This assumed a degree of ignorance that was unique; most of those who busied themselves about the problem of poverty felt so burdened with information and enlightenment that the very idea of asking such questions was an absurdity to them. Administrators and politicians alike already knew all the answers. The poor were poor because natural tendencies led mankind, as Bentham had made clear, to prefer indolence to activity; there was not much that could be done to help them, except prevent sentimental philanthropists who encouraged indolence from continuing to do so. On the other hand, those who were responsible for the charitable work of religious bodies also knew all the answers. The poor would

[1] First Paper, p. 327.

always be with us because of the sinful tendencies of mankind; all would sink into poverty, through vice, but for the constant battle of the churches against sin. The greatness of Booth as an original thinker arises from the fact that he had the courage to challenge such assertions, even though by doing so he exposed himself to the charge that he was justifying idleness and condoning evil. The road along which he advanced required him to distinguish between indolence and immorality and the conditions in which they were apt to flourish. Though he recognized that poverty was closely associated with 'idleness' and 'vice', he attempted to examine it for what it was: a social condition that might arise for a large number of reasons, of which 'idleness' and 'vice' were only two.

The effect of this fresh approach to what had become a stereotyped way of looking at other men's troubles was dramatic and far-reaching. For instance, poverty was perhaps most frequently regarded by Booth's contemporaries as 'caused' by drink, and the Drink Problem was one which bulked so largely in many people's minds as to obscure the more fundamental miseries of the poor altogether. The results of Booth's work put drunkenness in its place as part of the way of life of the very poor; it could no longer be regarded as the 'cause' of the downfall of men and families from a higher to a lower class. He was well aware of the fact that too many people spent too much on drink, but he was the first to point out that drink might be the result rather than the cause of poverty. Men drank because they were poor; they were not necessarily poor because they were drunkards. 'To those who look on drink as the source of all evil', Booth wrote in 1888, 'the position it here holds as accounting for only 14 per cent. of the poverty in the East End may seem altogether insufficient.'[1] The situation was, in fact, reassuring; the picture he drew of the public houses in 1889 was quite an attractive one:

Public houses play a larger part in the lives of the people than clubs or friendly societies, churches, or missions, or perhaps more than all put together, and bad it would be if their action and influence were altogether evil. This is not so, though the bad side is very palpable and continually enforced upon our minds.

[1] 'I would remind them', he added, 'that it is only as a principal cause that it is here considered; as a contributory cause it would no doubt be connected with a much larger proportion' (Second Paper, p. 297). The same conclusion emerged from Booth's investigation into the causes of pauperism in Stepney, conducted after his survey of poverty had been finished. This showed that drink could be regarded as being the reason why 12·6 per cent. of paupers sought relief, as compared with 26·7 per cent. who were sick, and 32·8 per cent. who were old. *Pauperism and the Endowment of Old Age*, p. 3.

A most horrible and true picture may be drawn of the trade in drink, of the wickedness and misery that goes with it. So horrible that one cannot wonder that some eyes are blinded to all else and there is a cry of away with this accursed abomination. There is, however, much more to be said. Anyone who frequents public-houses knows that actual drunkenness is very much the exception. At the worst houses in the worst neighbourhoods, many or perhaps most of those that stand at the bars, whether men or women, are stamped with the effects of drink, and if orderly at the moment, are perhaps at other times mad or incapable under its influence; but at the hundreds of respectable public houses, scattered plentifully all through the district, this is not the case. . . . Go into any of these houses. . . . Behind the bar will be a decent middle-aged woman, something above her customers in class, very neatly dressed, respecting herself and respected by them. The whole scene is comfortable, quiet and orderly.[1]

Booth was thus the first person to attempt to assess the realities of the Evil of Drink. So far as England is concerned, nobody has as yet followed in his footsteps in an effort to pursue the matter to its conclusion. His sympathies were with mankind at large, and they were extended to publican and drunkard alike, as well as to the 'respectable poor'. Public houses were, he concluded, in danger of being 'undermined by the increasing temperance of the people'. 'As public servants, the licensed victuallers are on their trial.'[2] Like Mary Kingsley, who later examined the traffic in gin to the West Coast of Africa,[3] Booth dealt with the problem of drink in a dispassionate, albeit a purposeful way. His general line of argument was to demonstrate that a clear distinction had to be made between the poverty that was the inescapable outcome of low earnings, insufficient to meet basic needs, and that which was due to improvidence or immorality. The two were not necessarily to be connected together through drink, for it was made clear to him beyond any possibility of denial that poverty existed quite apart from the seductions of the drink trade.

Booth's treatment of drink as a predisposing factor in the genesis of poverty is a good illustration of his treatment of the wider problem of why the poor were poor. Clearly the true causes of poverty as a social phenomenon had also to be sought in quite different directions from psychological weaknesses or moral failings. Booth's conclusions were summarized in the following table based on information which he published in 1889:[4]

[1] First Edition i, pp. 113-14.   [2] Ibid., p. 115.
[3] *Travels in West Africa*, Macmillan & Co., 1897, pp. 663-9.
[4] First Edition i, p. 147.

		'Great Poverty' (Classes A and B) %	'Poverty' (Classes C and D) %
1. Loafers		4	—
2. Casual work	Questions of employment	55	68
3. Irregular work, low pay			
4. Small profits			
5. Drink (Husband, or both husband and wife)	Questions of habit . .	14	13
6. Drunken or thriftless wife			
7. Illness or infirmity	Questions of circumstance	27	19
8. Large family			
9. Illness or large family, combined with irregular work			

This table demonstrates very clearly the lines along which Booth had begun to think. The importance of 'questions of employment' as a cause of poverty was his most striking discovery. If 'questions of circumstance' were somewhat overshadowed by them, they were themselves much more important than 'questions of habit' since very many of 'the poor' were reduced to extreme poverty either because they possessed large families, or because they suffered from bad health. These were conditions that our Victorian ancestors would hardly have considered to be blameworthy. They could only be classified as social rather than moral influences in the life of the people.

The detailed evidence which Booth presented in the Poverty Series firmly supported these conclusions. The way of life of those employed in casual work and the sweated trades was submitted to close examination, which revealed no relationship between poverty and immorality. Furthermore, he found that 'widows or deserted women and their families brought a large contingent into the ranks of those suffering from great poverty': such people accounted in Battersea for no less than 45 per cent. of this, whilst in Shoreditch 18 per cent. of the very poor were members of families with female heads. The part played by old age as a cause of poverty was not at first suspected; since the early inquiries were conducted on a household basis, the data collected related only to families with children at school. This ruled out old people living in their own households, or in poor law institutions. The significance of old age emerged, however, when Booth conducted his inquiry between 1889 and 1892 into the causes of pauperism (i.e. into the circumstances of the people relieved by the Poor Law authorities) in Stepney and St. Pancras. This inquiry eventually led to the formulation of his schemes for old-age pensions.[1]

Another equally important factor influencing the material conditions of the working classes also gradually came to light, when it became apparent that families were likely to be in greater need at some times in their lives than at others. Thus when Booth described the condition of the better-off casual workers, he mentioned that the heads of families were 'in a comparatively comfortable position at the start', but that they became 'poorer and poorer as their family increased . . . improving again as their children became able to add their quota to the family income'; in such cases, he added, 'the loss of elder children by marriage is sometimes looked upon with jealous disfavour'.[2]

Booth never seems to have realized the significance of this fact, possibly because he based his calculations for the whole population on that proportion which came within the knowledge of the School Board Officers. Though he recognized that 'the younger man in some employments, and the older man in others, earn less money than those of middle age who are the fathers of the children at school', he believed this to be offset by the fact that 'both are at less expense', and so came to the erroneous conclusion that 'the condition of the bulk will be better than that of the part we are able to test'.[3] The inference which he should have drawn was, of course, that the earnings of almost all casual workers were inadequate for that considerable period of their lives during which they had to care for young children, or for their own parents, or when they grew old themselves. It was thus left to Seebohm Rowntree to draw attention to what he called 'the five alternative periods of want and comparative plenty' by which the life of the labourer was marked,[4] a phenomenon now referred to as the Poverty Cycle.[5] Nevertheless, Booth's description of the relationship between employment, earnings, and needs was well done, and his readers must have been left with a somewhat depressing confirmation of their vague fears that the economic system of the nineteenth century had failed to provide a secure basis for family life, irrespective of the morals of individual men and women.

[1] First Edition i, p. 41; ii, p. 386: see above, Chapter VIII.
[2] Ibid., i, p. 49.   [3] Ibid., i, pp. 4-5.
[4] B. S. Rowntree, *Poverty: A Study of Town Life*, Macmillan & Co., 1901, p. 136.
[5] Booth dealt with this question at greater length, and much more forcefully, in Chapter XIII ('Expenditure and Standard of Life') of Vol. V of the Industry Series.

Turning to method, Booth's most striking innovation was his invention of the Poverty Line, and his exploration of the methods whereby this might be established. His use of the phrases 'above the line of poverty' and 'on the line'[1] have a strangely modern ring about them to the reader familiar with the social surveys of the 1930s. His definition of poverty was perhaps the first operational definition in the social sciences, 'operational' in the sense that it provided the means whereby the truth or falsehood of his provisional hypothesis could be tested experimentally. This hypothesis was, of course, that there was less poverty in London than Hyndman had asserted. In order to test the validity of this, Booth had to define 'poverty' in such a way that significant information could be collected about it:

By the word 'poor' [he wrote], I mean to describe those who have a fairly regular though bare income, such as 18 shillings or 21 shillings per week for a moderate family, and by 'very poor' those who fall below this standard, whether from chronic irregularity of work, sickness, or a large number of young children. I do not here introduce any moral question: whatever the cause, those whose means prove to be barely sufficient, or quite insufficient for decent independent life, are counted as 'poor' or 'very poor' respectively: and as it is not always possible to ascertain the exact income, the classification is also based on the appearance of the home. Cases of large earnings spent in drink are intended to be excluded, as not properly belonging to the poor, but the results of ordinary habits of extravagance in drink in inducing poverty are not considered any more than those of any other forms of want of thrift.[2]

This definition passed a pragmatic test in so far as it was successfully applied in the Poverty Survey, but sharp criticism was encountered when it was first presented to the public. For instance, when Booth read his first Paper to the Royal Statistical Society, Professor Leone Levi attacked his estimate of the number of those in poverty on the ground that 'an income of 18s. or 20s. a week, even with four or five persons in a family, where there was generally more than one person earning something, ought not to leave the recipient in the condition of poverty'. Professor Levi went on to complain that Booth had not discussed the causes of poverty, such as gambling and drink and had not considered the average wages of the community. 'His own impression was that poverty proper in the Tower Hamlets was more frequently produced by vice, extravagance, and waste, or by unfitness for work, the result in many cases of immoral habits, than by real want of employment or low wages. . . . It would be of great value if

1 F'rst Paper, pp. 339, 375. See also Appendix IV.   2 Ibid., p. 328.

Mr. Booth would add as an appendix budgets of the income and expenditure of as large a proportion as possible of the classes with whom he dealt.' As another member made plain in the same discussion, what was called for was more information concerning 'the proportion of the expenditure of the families to the earnings of their heads, and particularly the expenditure in house rent'.[1]

Another weakness in Booth's definition of poverty was that it depended too much on the School Board Visitors' assessments of earnings, on the one hand, and of needs on the other. So far as their knowledge of earnings went, Booth was optimistic; their official duty to inquire into cases when application had been made for remission of school fees enabled them, he thought, 'to obtain exceptionally good information on questions of employment and earnings'.[2] This was questioned during the discussion at the Royal Statistical Society on his first Paper, on the ground that 'these visitors were not always welcome and the answers given to them might be given with an obvious purpose'.

Booth thus found himself confronted with two lines of criticism. Firstly, his conclusions regarding the condition of the people, especially his estimate of the number living in poverty, were attacked on the ground that an income of 20s. to 21s. was enough for the provident; secondly, it was suggested that his reliance on the reports of the School Board Officers had led him to underestimate earnings. So far as the first criticism is concerned, Booth's attitude was finally summed up in a brief passage in the second volume of the first Poverty Series, published in 1891:

On the one hand we may argue that the poor are often really better off than they appear to be, on the ground that when extravagances which keep them in poverty are constant and immediate in their action, the state of things resulting cannot reasonably be called poverty at all. . . . On the other hand, we may as logically, or perhaps more logically, disregard the follies past or present which bring poverty in their train. . . . In this temper we prefer to view and consider these unfortunates only as they actually exist; constantly put to shifts to keep a home together; always struggling and always poor. . . .

[1] First Paper, pp. 394-5. Professor Levi's line of attack was, as Booth pointed out in his second Royal Statistical Society paper, more or less cancelled out by the criticism of 'the evening paper' which doubted if 'Mr. Booth has adequately realised the struggles and privations of even the best paid of those who figure in his tables', adding that the first paper read 'too much like a complacent and bourgeois statement of the situation' (Second Paper, p. 278).

[2] Ibid., pp. 327-8.

According as the one or other of these two points of view is taken, thousands of families may be placed on one or the other side of the doubtful line of demarcation between class and class among the poor.[1]

Booth found no satisfactory answer for this problem; his final decision was to err 'on the safe side', that is, 'in overstating rather than understating the volume of poverty which exists, or existed when the inquiry was made'.[2] What the Victorians called the moral causes of poverty were therefore to a large extent confused by him with what subsequently came to be termed by Rowntree 'primary' poverty, arising out of insufficient means to maintain 'merely physical efficiency'.[3] In consequence, Booth classified a number of people as 'poor', whose poverty was merely a matter of individual opinion, and would therefore have been supposed by Rowntree to have been suffering from 'secondary' poverty.

The second criticism, that he had drawn his poverty line too high, led him to accept Professor Levi's suggestion and to collect household budgets from thirty families: six of these families were chosen to represent 'very poor' families (Class B), ten the 'poor' (Classes C and D) and fourteen those 'above the line of poverty' (Classes E and F). Difficulties immediately began to emerge. In the first place, a phenomenon was encountered which is now familiar to those who collect working-class budgets, for 'in almost all the poorer cases the admitted expenditure' was found to exceed 'the supposed income'. Booth accounted for this by agreeing that the regular earnings might have been underestimated; in addition, credit might have been given to the families concerned, indebtedness evaded, or windfalls received.[4] He presented the information in an endeavour to show more exactly what he meant by 'poverty, want and distress' but the results were not convincing. The incomes of twenty-five of the thirty families were 21s. or over: most of them were well above the 18s. to 21s. per week for a family of moderate size[5] that he had originally chosen as the line

---

[1] First Edition ii, pp. 18–19.   [2] Ibid., p. 20.

[3] Op. cit., p. 296. Although Rowntree made strenuous attempts to provide a reliable means of distinguishing between primary and (in his language) secondary poverty (ibid., pp. 86-7), he finally had to admit in 1941 that the methods he used in 1899 were 'too rough to give reliable results' (*Poverty and Progress*, p. 461). The subsequent tendency has therefore been to concentrate on the measurement of primary poverty by objective tests, and to leave secondary poverty out of account, as involving subjective assessments that have been thought to be too unreliable.

[4] First Edition i, pp. 132-4. See also Appendix IV.

[5] Booth ultimately defined a 'small' family as one consisting of 'about four members'. *Industry* v, p. 14.

of demarcation. Three of the five families with low incomes were in Class B, one in Class D and one (with no children) in Class E. The range of earnings in Classes C and D was from 19s. 10d. to 27s.

It was therefore obvious that the definition was by no means firm; even as a general description it was inaccurate. The poverty line must in fact have been drawn in respect of each individual family by Booth's investigators, depending on their own judgement. Nevertheless, the definition was repeated once again, without comment, in the same volume, though he also made it clear that the impoverished were sometimes classified as 'poor', regardless (one can only assume) of income.

My 'poor' may be described as living under a struggle to obtain the necessaries of life and make both ends meet; while the 'very poor' live in a state of chronic want. It may be their own fault that this is so; that is another question; my first business is with those who, from whatever cause, do live under conditions of poverty or destitution.[1]

The truth appears to be that too much attention has been paid to the figures given by Booth; his estimate was imprecise and was originally intended to be only illustrative.[2] It must not be assumed from this, however, that the definition itself, or the way in which he applied it to individual families, was unreliable. If the particulars given by him for the thirty individual families are examined closely, it will be seen that the amount of the earnings of the head of the household is by no means the sole deciding factor; of equally great importance is the number of dependent children, and the presence or otherwise in the family of a child or children of over school age, who may be deemed to have been earning substantial wages. If Rowntree's standard of needs designed to be applied in York in 1899 when trade was prosperous, is used as a means of drawing a poverty line in London ten years earlier

[1] First Edition i, p. 33.

[2] Many of those who have relied on Booth's work have taken the definition too literally, but it must be admitted that he did much to encourage this. (See *Industry* v, p. 18.) Misconceptions in this regard were shared by Rowntree, though it is only fair to him to say that Booth did nothing to help him to clear up the confusion, since he was left with the impression that Booth's definition did not cover 'secondary' poverty. Professor Bowley was more cautious when he conducted the Home Sample Analysis for the New Survey of London Life and Labour, establishing the 'standard reached' by the persons classified by Booth as 'poor' for purposes of comparison. Even his treatment of the subject is somewhat confusing, however. See *New Survey of London Life and Labour*, Vol. III, pp. 71-2. A more adequate discussion of the standards adopted in the Booth Survey and the New Survey was given by Sir Hubert Llewellyn-Smith in a paper read to the Royal Statistical Society. *Journal*, 1929, pp. 532-3.

at a time of only average prosperity[1] (admittedly a hazardous operation), it is most interesting to observe that the total effect would be to place five of the thirty families above the line, instead of below it, appearing as they do in Classes C and D. Two of these families were, however, said to be suffering from unemployment at the time of the inquiry, which would classify them as 'poor' on Rowntree's standards, whilst it is recorded of another, with a son aged seventeen, that the 'income is greater than the expenditure'. Booth commented that 'the money, I suppose, does not come home';[2] the case was therefore probably one of secondary poverty. It may therefore be concluded that Booth's rough estimate of poverty coincided with remarkable accuracy with the more exact estimates which might have resulted from the use of Rowntree's methods.

When all is said and done, Booth's work on poverty produced firm results, which have stood not only the test of time, but also reappraisal of a keenly critical order. His poverty line remained unaltered until further work had been done by those who followed in his footsteps, particularly Rowntree and Bowley. Writing in 1929, with the experience of both the Booth Survey and the New Survey of London Life and Labour behind him, Sir Hubert Llewellyn-Smith stated the opinion that:

though Charles Booth arrived at his standards without the aid of the modern scientific apparatus of calories and vitamins, he was guided by a sure instinct to conclusions not appreciably different from those which would have resulted from the use of the more objective methods of measurement now in use. I feel that this confirmation should strengthen our confidence in the soundness of his judgement in matters in which we have not always the same means of verification.[3]

So quickly established had Booth's methods and results become, indeed, that when Rowntree presented the results of his own researches in 1901, he did so with somewhat uneasy backward glances towards Booth's Poverty Series:

From the commencement of my inquiry [he wrote], I have had opportunities of consulting with Mr. Booth, and comparing the methods of investigation and standards of poverty adopted. As a result I feel no hesitation in regarding my estimate of the total poverty of York as comparable with Mr. Booth's estimates of the total poverty in London, and in this Mr. Booth

[1] Op. cit., p. 300.   [2] First Edition i, p. 145.
[3] *Journal of the Royal Statistical Society*, 1929, p. 536.

agrees. I did not set out upon my enquiry with the object of proving any pre-conceived theory, but to ascertain actual facts, and . . . I was myself much surprised to obtain [this] result.[1]

On the other hand, Booth regarded Rowntree's work as a con-firmation of his own results. A superficial comparison was, indeed, reassuring. Booth had found that 30·7 per cent. of the population of London were living in poverty; Rowntree's figure for York was 27·84. Booth thought the two figures were comparable, despite his belief, which he pointed out in a letter to Rowntree, that he had not entered 'into questions of economical or wasteful expenditure' in making his estimates.[2] 'In this respect,' he added, 'my classification falls short of yours; but our totals may be correctly compared, and the comparison, as you have shown, is very close.' Unlike Rowntree, Booth was 'not surprised'. 'I have, indeed, long thought that other cities, if similarly tested, would show a percentage of poverty not differing greatly from that existing in London.'[3]

Booth's calculations became accepted more and more unquestion-ingly as the years went by. It was, for example, on his definition of the poverty line that Alfred Marshall relied when he published *Industry and Trade* as long afterwards as 1919.[4] Even in 1925 Sir Cyril Burt made extensive use of the information contained in the Poverty Survey as a means of relating the incidence of juvenile destitution to that of poverty. On comparing his map of juvenile crimes with Booth's map of London poverty he found 'the correspondence between the darker areas upon either sheet' to be 'immediately apparent'. Though Booth's figures were then twenty-five years old, the demolition of the slums and the growth of suburban districts in the intervening period had 'invalidated them less than might be thought'.[5]

[1] Op. cit., pp. 299-300.

[2] Booth's definition of the poverty line seems to have been closer to Rowntree's than he realized. His appreciation of the value of Rowntree's work was a generous one. It had, he thought, 'in the way of illumination added to the value of mine something more than that which springs from mere comparison or confirmation'. *Final*, p. 28.

[3] *Final*, p. 300. Mr. Caradog Jones has commented on this that 'Rowntree's own admission later, that the measurement of secondary poverty was unreliable, cannot but cast doubts on the validity of the comparison'. *Social Surveys*, p. 62.

[4] Second edition, 1919, p. 78.

[5] *The Young Delinquent*, University of London Press, second edition, 1927, pp. 71, 76. Booth's description of the juvenile gangs in Hoxton was also of interest, as the area was 'still notorious' for this. Ibid., p. 469; *Religious Influences* ii, pp. 114-15. In his analysis of conditions obtaining in Greenwich in 1932, Mr. E. Wight Bakke states that 'Charles Booth describes this district . . . in words which are as accurate today as in the time in which he wrote'. *The Unemployed Man*, Popular Edition, Nisbet & Co., 1935, p. 157.

It is on the contribution he made to the successful measurement of poverty that Booth's reputation has been founded. To restrict the appraisal of his work in this way does him an injustice, however, for he was no mere inventor of a research technique. He is rather to be regarded, on the strength of his poverty survey, as a founding father of the empirical tradition as applied to the social sciences. That this claim has not so far achieved universal recognition is to be attributed to the fact that it is easy to misunderstand the true nature and importance of his work. In the first place his attempts to dissociate himself from dogmatic explanations of social behaviour and finely spun philosophical systems have too readily been supposed to demonstrate that he was simply a gatherer of miscellaneous information for its own sake, and that, as he made no attempt to understand its deeper theoretical significance, his work cannot be regarded as a serious contribution to sociology or social theory. This is understandable, but unjust. If in Beatrice Webb's words, the Poverty Survey was 'perhaps the most impressive achievement, and certainly the most picturesque outcome of the whole inquiry',[1] this was because a new method of fact-finding and statistical analysis was established in it, which could be relied on to give results even if they conflicted with the inclinations of those who used them. This placed Booth firmly on the path of scientific inquiry, which ultimately led him to his Fellowship of the Royal Society.

The scientific quality of the Poverty Survey is also demonstrated by the fact that new hypotheses quickly emerged to take the place of the first and most naïve[2] of them, namely, that Hyndman was wrong. The second series of hypotheses embodied the more complicated generalization that poverty could be regarded as a facet of the structure of society, as well as be attributed to the moral failings of individuals. This contention was validated by brilliantly successful statistical work, which provides a classic example of how sociological research should be conducted. It also inaugurated a new epoch in the formulation of social policy. The simple hypothesis with which the Inquiry began was quickly disproved; this led to a more sophisticated generalization which could be based on the evidence rather than refuted by it. A fresh conception of poverty was thus established, which presented it as an evil capable of being remedied by the creation of a new device,

[1] *My Apprenticeship*, p. 239.

[2] The use of this word is not intended to imply any criticism. In all research the simplest hypotheses are often the best. They can be disproved most easily.

in the first instance, that of pensions for the aged poor. The march towards the Welfare State had begun.

It is thus possible to assert, without doubt or difficulty, that Booth's contributions to the social sciences and to social policy were equally important. It is, moreover, by no means a hard task to defend his reputation from the criticism that the scientific qualities of his work suffered from his desire to ameliorate the conditions of the poor, as well as to study them. Admittedly, it was his anxious need for re-assurance as to the condition of the people generally, and his sense of personal responsibility for whatever was amiss with their lives that had given him the desire to undertake the Inquiry, and the determination to complete it successfully. His declared objective was, in his own words, 'to show who and what are this large body of men whose lot may be counted as the lot of humanity in this country, and what are the conditions under which they live',[1] but it proved impossible for him to restrict his work within these limits. Since the inspiration that energized his work arose out of his intense feelings of dissatisfaction concerning the moral foundations of the industrial society of which he was himself so prominent a member, he found that he could not describe without evaluating; his descriptions of things as they were seemed inevitably to become enlarged into proposals as to how they might be improved. Looking forward to the next stage of his work in 1891, he established the cardinal articles of his faith when he asserted that:

If I can accomplish all that I have laid down, so as to show not only where poverty exists in London and in what degree, but also something of its relation to industry and of the manner in which it is affected for good or evil by existing social action of various kinds, I conceive that the knowledge may be of real value, making it more possible than it is now to avoid the wrong and choose the right path onward.[2]

If 'the consideration and the hope of remedies' were never out of his mind[3] it was, therefore, because this was an integral part of his way of thinking and behaving. Even so it is patently absurd to attempt to question the validity of the facts he discovered on the ground that the process was mainly regarded by him as a means to the end of social action. It is much more pertinent to point out that in general his results conflicted with his preconceptions and his desires, and therefore constitute evidence that his work was not governed by wishful thinking

[1] First Edition i, p. 157   [2] Ibid., i, pp. 592-3.   [3] Ibid., i, p. 165.

on his part. It would be as easy as it would be foolish to take this argument too far, however, for it must be recognized that the sense of personal responsibility that created the Inquiry was part of the individualistic way of life to which he was bound by tradition, by conviction, and by his own temperament. The bare assertion that he had 'no preconceived ideas'[1] was obviously erroneous. His objectivity as an inquirer did not set him free from bias, but rather left him at the mercy of presuppositions which affected his work much more than he realized. It must be recognized that the bias thus introduced into his thinking sometimes influenced his interpretations of the facts. This is most apparent in his treatment of the remedies that were suggested from time to time to deal with the worst evils arising out of poverty. Thus, his comments on the Cocoa Rooms which were first started by philanthropic effort as a counterblast to the public house reflect the strength of his suspicion of anything likely to undermine individual responsibility. 'It was not until the work was taken up as a business that any good was done with it.'[2] Similarly, though he agreed that Dr. Barnardo's work in relieving 'child-destitution' was remarkable, he qualified his approval by adding that 'special dangers show themselves'. Barnardo's efforts might begin to be counted on, and if so, they would 'finally stand convicted as the cause of misery'.[3]

Despite these weaknesses, it is none the less true that Booth's individualism was by no means doctrinaire. He was basically an opponent of all that savoured of socialism, but so far at least as the Poverty Series was concerned, he only adhered to the individualist creed as long as its results could be demonstrated to be beneficial. As a common-sense man, he was compelled not only to admit but also to assert that the State had an important role to play in the social order. The Board Schools, for instance, had his unqualified support.

Nowhere more than in the East End of London does the work done by the 'extravagance' of the School Board stand justified. It was necessary to strike the eye and hold the imagination, it was worth much to carry high the flag of education, and this is what has been done. Each school stands up from its playground like a church in God's acre ringing its bell. It may be that another policy should now be followed, that the turn of economy has come; but I am glad that no niggard spirit interfered at the outset. We have full value for all that has been spent.[4]

Poverty of mind could thus be dealt with by the State or by other

1 See above, p. 107.　　2 First Edition i, p. 116.
3 Ibid., i, p. 127.　　4 Ibid., i, p. 130.

kinds of social action, but Booth was very undecided so far as material poverty was concerned. Chance appeared to dictate the circumstances in which individual working-class families lived. 'The position of the class may be secure . . . but that of the individual must be precarious. For the wife and family it will depend on the health, or habits, or character of the man.' Drink, irregular employment, unemployment, the lottery of marriage, child-bearing, all involved uncertainties which made it impossible for even the respectable man to guard against the dangers of the future:

The lot falls partly according to merit and partly according to chance, but whatever the merit or the lack of it, the same number will be thrown out of work. Thus we see that the 'common lot of humanity' even though not much amiss in itself, is cursed by insecurity against which it is not easy for any prudence to guard.[1]

Booth considered, once more, that the State had its part to play here. The Poor Law system was, for him, 'a limited form of Socialism—a Socialistic community (aided from outside) living in the midst of an Individualist nation'. How the Poor Law was to operate was nevertheless a matter of much perplexity to him. He was incapable of cutting through the tangled growth of economic doctrine that inhibited attempts to deal with the insecurities of working-class life, for this would have involved questioning once more the individualist assumptions on which his thinking rested. The lot of mankind was insecurity; some people were immoral or unfortunate enough to sink into grave poverty; once this had happened to them, then something had to be done by the 'professional almoners' employed by the State to look after them. Insufficient attention was being paid to the welfare of the poor to satisfy his conscience, however, and he therefore found himself compelled to advocate an extension of State services. The result was a paradox that has become famous: 'Our individualism fails', he said, 'because our Socialism is incomplete.'[2] This being so, there could only be one conclusion; unpalatable though it was, he accepted it without hesitation.

Some day the individualist community, on which we build our faith, will find itself obliged for its own sake to take charge of the lives of those who from whatever cause, are incapable of independent existence up to the required standard, and will be fully able to do so.[3]

Paradoxes always endanger the clarity of an argument, and their

[1] Ibid., i, p. 161.   [2] Ibid., i, pp. 166, 167.   [3] Ibid., ii, p. 299.

place in a scientific analysis of a complex problem is dubious, to say the least of it. Booth was badly led astray. The hesitation with which he discussed proposals for reform was abandoned; released from the restraints with which he held his individualism in check, he launched out on a scheme for dealing with the very poor which was founded on tradition and belief, rather than on evidence produced by the Inquiry. It was his intention to act as the champion of the labouring classes as a whole; Classes C and D were his clients, and it was 'to their service especially' that he dedicated his work.[1] He had scant sympathy for the poorest classes and no desire to maintain them in their miseries. 'In spite of the little pay they get, I believe that no work is so dear as that which they do.'[2] Class A was to be 'harried out of existence'; there was nothing to be said in their favour, for 'no sooner do they make a street their own than it is ripe for destruction and should be destroyed'.[3] Class B was 'industrially valueless as well as socially pernicious. . . . Its numbers are not so great as to render the expense of dealing with it in some semi-socialistic fashion, in the interest of self-supporting labour, a crushing burden to the community. It is not, in fact, expense which bars the way, but the difficulty of employing any means, or devising any scheme, which would not tend to increase the numbers to be dealt with.' Nevertheless, Booth formulated precise proposals for the extension of the Poor Law to care for Class B *en bloc*. Its members were only to be allowed to live as families in industrial colonies:

planted wherever land and building materials were cheap; being well housed, well fed, and well warmed; and taught, trained, and employed from morning to night. . . . It would be merely that the State, having these people on its hands, obtained whatever value it could out of their work. They would become servants of the State. . . . It would . . . be necessary to set a limit to the current deficiency submitted to by the State, and when the account of any family reached this point to move them on to the poorhouse, where they would live as a family no longer. . . . It is not possible that action of this kind could be rapid. To open a little the portals of the Poor Law or its administration, making within its courts a working guild under suitable discipline; to check charitable gifts, except to those who from age or infirmity are unfit for any work; to insist upon sanitation and to suppress overcrowding; to await and watch the results, ready to push forward as occasion served—this is all that could be done. . . . The good results to be hoped for from such an extension of 'limited Socialism' would be manifold.[4]

[1] First Edition i, p. 597.   [2] Ibid., ii, p. 299.
[3] Ibid., i, pp. 169, 594.   [4] Ibid., i, pp. 167-9.

In essence, Booth's scheme was of the type familiar in the nineteenth century, based on theories about the moral and physical disabilities of 'the poor' which had never been verified by empirical methods. As such its advocacy was a retrograde step on his part towards the doctrinaire, undermining much of the educative work which he had accomplished. He had already shown that 'questions of employment' and 'circumstance' were far more important than 'questions of habit' as causes of poverty, and that widows had to be included in Class B, even though they could only be regarded as unfortunate rather than 'shiftless'.[1] His scheme of reform was, therefore, based on *a priori* reasoning which had little to do with the evidence he had discovered in his researches. It was unfortunate that he jumped to conclusions so early in the execution of the Inquiry. Had he not been subjected to considerable public pressure to produce remedies, he might have been able to wait until he had completed his survey of the organization of London's industries, especially those of the East End, and he would, indeed, have preferred to do so. Even the Special Subjects dealt with in his First Paper had shown the close connexion between poverty and casual employment in the Docks, and in the sweated trades, and this pointed the way which he ultimately followed. The problems associated with unemployment were particularly important. 'Industry', he regretfully concluded, 'will not work without some unemployed margin . . . but the margin in London today seems to be exaggerated in every department, and enormously so in the lowest class of labour.' 'The total figure of the unemployed', he added, 'may be greater than can be faced with complacency, or than the organization of industry ought to require.' Moreover, 'labour deteriorates under casual employment more than its price falls. I believe it to be to the interest of every employer to have as many regularly employed servants as possible, but it is still more to the interest of the community and most of all to that of the employed.'[2] Further consideration might have enabled him to amalgamate these considerations into a set of conclusions firmly based on the findings of the Poverty Survey. As it was, he allowed himself to propound proposals that involved the adopting of a moralistic standpoint which he had been only too ready to deplore in others. In any event, they were obviously quite impracticable, having regard to the political and social climate, let alone the knowledge, experience and skills of social workers, in the age in which he lived.

[1] See above, p. 182.   [2] First Edition i, pp. 151-3; ii, 297-8.

Nevertheless, even when all this has been taken into consideration, it remains true to say that though Booth was influenced by his bias against socialism, and though the development of his work was in consequence adversely affected, this cannot be held to invalidate his achievement to any serious extent. Provided that the facts spoke with sufficient strength and clarity, he was obviously prepared to let them say what they would, even if the outcome went against his personal inclination: his advocacy of pensions for the aged poor is in itself enough to prove the point.[1] Indeed, the main weakness in the Poverty Survey is to be found, not in a distortion of the facts to suit preconceived ideas, but in the converse; for it was his inability to construct a sufficiently elaborate and clearly defined framework of analysis that led him to accumulate vast numbers of facts that, far from 'speaking for themselves', obstructed the development of a better understanding of their significance, rather than facilitated it. It was an excess of impartiality, and not the influence of either moral purpose or psychological bias that in reality obstructed Booth's intentions.

It is, of course, possible to argue that Booth was overwhelmed by the sheer mass of the facts which he accumulated, and that he might have achieved a great deal more if the technique of random sampling had been available to him, to reduce its bulk. He himself spoke of the 'wilderness of figures' with which the extension of the Inquiry to the whole of London had presented him, commenting that it had 'not done much to make the path more clear'.[2] This demonstrates a certain weakness in Booth's analytic powers. He had always asserted that he saw the advancement of knowledge as dependent on a continuing process of action and reaction between induction and deduction,[3] but when he came to attempt to translate this into practice, he found it irreconcilable with the open-mindedness which he so conscientiously cultivated. The result was to prevent him from asking the ever more penetrating questions that keep a programme of research alive and profitable over the years. For if open-mindedness is left unsupported by a framework of analysis or ideas to give it direction and force, it may result in free-ranging speculation rather than in the advancement of knowledge. Whether that is so or not, it must be regretted that Booth was unable to handle the mass of information he so painstakingly collected, so as to stimulate the formulation of a progressively developing series of working hypotheses which would in turn serve as the

[1] See above, pp. 160 et seq.   [2] First Edition ii, p. 592.   [3] See above, p. 77.

means of building a comprehensive explanation of social structure and social change. This might have resulted in the emergence of the general theory, the absence of which from his work has since been regretted by many sociologists. It would, however, be most unfair to expect everything from the work of the pioneer, who is especially vulnerable to criticism of the cheaper sort. In the last analysis, it is the strength of Booth's work which is more apparent than its weaknesses. His descriptions in the Poverty Series of the social life of London are admirable from the literary as well as the scientific point of view. They obviously ring true; they live in their own right. He recognized that the life of neither the individual nor the class can be understood aright if it is impossible for the investigator to 'lay open its memories and understand its hopes'.[1]

The Poverty Series accomplished this task in more than adequate measure; it must thus be regarded as an historical document of the first importance. However, it is not the specific results achieved by Booth in his study of poverty that offer a complete justification for the considerable reputation which it gave him. This is rather to be found in the simple fact that he studied it as he did. First and foremost, as Lord Beveridge has pointed out, the selection of poverty rather than 'the poor' as a subject for investigation, marks a highly significant turning point in the course of British social thought.[2] Booth's problem was not the condition of 'the poor' who would always be with us, but why there were poor people in a relatively rich society. In the asking of this question, and in the discovery of entirely new methods of answering it, true genius lay. Whether Booth thus made an even greater contribution to the social services than his reputation as it stood on the publication of the Poverty Series in 1889-91 would imply, will be discussed in subsequent chapters. But there can be no doubt that it is entirely true to say that the work done by Rowntree and Bowley and their successors in the development of poverty surveys was based on his, and that those surveys must be regarded as an extension—if not in a large measure a repetition—of the original inquiry carried out in the Tower Hamlets.[3] Furthermore, the analysis of the causes of poverty which Booth began led inescapably to the

---

[1] Ibid., ii, pp. 592-3: see also below, pp. 254-6.

[2] *Voluntary Action*, Allen & Unwin, 1948, p. 128.

[3] The opinion is expressed in the *Encyclopaedia of the Social Sciences* that Rowntree's work on *Poverty* is 'significant chiefly because it verifies major conclusions of Booth's study'. Vol. xiv, p. 163.

development of remedies in the form of old-age pensions, unemployment insurance, and the like, and thus eventually to the laying of the
foundations of the Welfare State. This being so, it can only be concluded that few men can have made a deeper or more enduring mark
on their times.

10

The Industry Series

THE appraisal of the contribution which Booth made to the social sciences in the Industry Series is a complex undertaking. There can be no doubt that the subject-matter of the inquiry was of great importance, and that the accuracy of the researches on which the descriptions were based is unquestionable. This has been generally recognized on many occasions. In *The New Survey of London Life and Labour*, for instance, section after section of the description of London's industries as they existed in the 1930s is based on a comparison with Booth's account of their organization in the 1890s; one of them contains, indeed, a striking tribute to the relevant section in the Industry Series:

> The masterly description by Mr. F. D. Schloss of the conditions of the East London boot and shoe trades as they existed in 1887, and Charles Booth's own chapter on 'Sweating', remain the classic authorities for the situation in the London industry forty or more years ago.[1]

Nevertheless, it is hard to give a simple and straightforward evaluation of either Booth's methods or his conclusions. His characteristic approach was the matter-of-fact empiricism of the man of business, who tends to resent the suggestion that he relies in any way on *a priori* theories to guide him. Despite this, he frequently found himself devoting time and energy to the illustration of theories when he presented the results of the Industry Inquiry. In contrast to the argument embodied in the Poverty Inquiry, much of his work amounted to an

[1] Vol. III, *London Industries I*, p. 350. The New Survey was conducted by Sir H. Llewellyn-Smith, one of Booth's own assistants. The description of the furniture-making trade of Bethnal Green contained in the Poverty Series (Vol. IV, pp. 162–7), was found to be 'still apposite' in 1957. Michael Young and Peter Willmott, *Family and Kinship in East London*, Routledge & Kegan Paul, 1957, p. 169.

endeavour to demonstrate the validity of abstractions propounded by economists, of which he had hitherto been suspicious, and for once his work took on a certain flavour of the doctrinaire. The more truly empirical method of approach in the Poverty Inquiry had not exposed him to criticism in this way. In that case, the compelling nature of the facts which he had elicited about poverty had forced him to adopt what was, in effect, a ready-made framework of analysis; the result had established him in the opinion of the world as a great social scientist. This fortunate turn of events did not repeat itself in his industrial inquiry. Facts and theories, he had recognized at the outset of his work, are inseparable: facts are, of themselves, of no value, as many a subsequent social scientist has discovered to his cost. Yet one searches the Industry Series in vain for evidence of a method of presenting them which would have allowed them to 'speak for themselves' as Booth desired, and at the same time have given the work as a whole unity and significance.

What the situation called for was an analysis of the social structure of industries and typical firms, but Booth did not recognize either the necessity or the possibility of this. It may be that he was prevented from doing so by reason of the fact that the system by which he classified the various occupations had a certain measure of the artificial inherent in it. As Beatrice Webb later pointed out, it was correct to speak of the building trade, for instance, as a social entity, but less obviously so to attribute an 'organic' character to such miscellaneous assemblages of occupations as that comprised by the Public Services and Professional Classes, in which doctors, lawyers, teachers, artists and ministers of religion were grouped together with street sweepers, dustmen and waterworks employees.[1] It is, of course, impossible to dissect and discuss the constitution and functions of a class of social institutions if the class itself has not first been clearly and properly established. This Booth failed to do. No coherent and intelligible method of presenting the data was evolved, and in default of this, a sense of failure makes itself felt as one reads through the volumes of the Series.

The scheme he originally laid down for a twofold examination of the problem of poverty thus only became twofold in practice, in the sense that the themes of poverty and industry were developed in the same volumes of the Industry Series. Each was, however, pursued separately instead of being presented in such a way as to provide each

---

[1] *My Apprenticeship*, p. 242.

other with mutual support. If he had persuaded himself to finish with poverty, and had written his Industry Series as an entirely separate work, he could have been briefer and more penetrating. As it was, the themes of the condition of the people and of industrial organization were continually associated, without being effectively interlocked. In consequence, the significance of the Series is to be found in its merits as a description, pure and simple, of industrial organization. Its strength is derived from the excellence of this description, the impact on contemporary theories often being disturbing and the implications sometimes iconoclastic. Its weakness, on the other hand, is attributable to an inability to keep the work on the track which had originally been marked out. This was most striking when Booth discussed the ways in which industry served as the foundation underlying social welfare whilst, at the same time, acting as one of the main factors creating poverty. This analysis was inconclusive, and he himself claimed to have done no more than show 'something' of the relation of poverty to industry.[1] All that could be positively stated was that better understanding of the role of industry in modern society was not enough in itself to resolve the urgent dilemma represented by the existence of poverty in the midst of plenty. The fact that he decided to leave further discussion of social action until he had completed his survey of religious influences is evidence of the intrinsic incompleteness of his examination of the problems of industry.

The point was underlined in the review of the last two volumes in the Industry Series which appeared in the *Economic Journal*. 'Mr. Booth himself... announces', it was said, 'that he has not reached the practical conclusions to which his inquiries may conduce, and hints, not obscurely, that real conclusions may even be outside the limitations of his work.' The discovery of the causal connexions which this would, it was thought, necessitate, must inevitably have been a difficult undertaking. 'By comparison, the work of description to which the previous volumes were consecrated, is at once safer and easier.'[2] The criticism was a fair one, but it would have required immense toil and searching self-criticism for Booth to have taken advantage of it. His chief error had been made and had become irretrievable; the Poverty and Industry Inquiries had been allowed to run in different directions, the first towards a deeper understanding of the nature of poverty as a social phenomenon, the second nowhere in particular. It was futile to suppose that the investigations of social influences, and of 'the application of

[1] *Industry* v, p. 339.   [2] 1897, Vol. VII, p. 387.

remedies', which it was hoped to carry out during the Religious Influences Inquiry, would unite what had in fact become two distinct researches, conducted in different ways and with different objectives. The only way out of this difficulty would have been to rework the industrial data so as to continue the examination of the themes opened up in the Poverty Series. Booth would have had to abandon much of his work if he had done so, or spend several more years in going over the ground again.

To do Booth justice, it must be pointed out that he seems to have been well aware of the fact that a gulf existed between the first and second stages of what he had intended should be an integrated study. As the analysis of the material on industry progressed, he gave many backward glances at the methods he had applied to the analysis of poverty which suggest a growing sense of doubt in his mind. Was his original determination of the poverty line correct? Was it necessary to alter it in the light of the information made available by the application of the measure of crowding? The results obtained from analysis of the material collected on Industry did little to reassure him on these points. Nor did it prove possible to devise a satisfactory means of relating the system of classification used in the two inquiries. In the Poverty Series the double classification between Classes (based on family life) and Sections (based on types of employment) had not been successful; the Classes had tended to overshadow and ultimately to submerge the Sections. In the Industry Series, the double classification between individual employed persons (primarily, an industrial classification) and heads of families (primarily, a social classification) similarly proved to have many difficulties latent in it. This was only too well understood by Booth, for the final volume of the Series as first published in 1897 contains the following passage: 'The family is not altogether a convenient unit for purposes of industrial enquiry. At most only 85 per cent. of the adult males employed in any industry are heads of families, and this proportion . . . sinks in several occupations as low as 60 or 65 per cent. and in one instance to 30 per cent.'[1]

Booth's chief difficulty in presenting the results of the Industry Inquiry arose, therefore, from the fact that the nature of the data he had collected was fundamentally different from that which had been assembled in the Poverty Series. An appraisal of the value of the Industry Series must thus, in large measure, amount to an appraisal

[1] *Industry* ix, p. 160. This sentence was omitted when the Series was republished in 1903.

of the success or failure of the efforts he made to deal with the two sets of facts as a homogeneous body of data. This was an obvious possibility, because they related to the lives of the same people; nevertheless the ways in which facts about poverty (or consumption) could be added to facts about employment (or production) so as to amount to a picture 'in the round' of industrial society as a whole, proved to be singularly elusive. The immediate difficulty confronting him was that no reliable information was available concerning earnings, the result being that it was impossible to compare the relative proportions of workers employed in the different industries who were living in poverty. Booth does not explicitly state this, but the position in which he found himself is none the less obvious:

> Nothing short of particulars which should include the whole working population for every week in the year could give completely correct results, and such details would be unattainable even by a public inquiry.[1]

Approximate estimates of average earnings could be made, but they were unreliable, and the industrial and social aspects of the survey consequently remained disunited. Booth thought he might be able to relate them to each other by including in the Industry Series what was intended to be a common measure of social conditions, the overcrowding index, primarily designed as a means of assessing the social aspects of industrial employment.[2] It is thus significant that the first chapter of the Series was devoted to the seemingly irrelevant task of establishing this measure. For Classes D and below, the number of persons occupying each dwelling, divided by the number of habitable rooms, was used, the overcrowding line being established at the point where there were two or more persons per room. For Classes E and above, the number of servants employed was made the criterion. The results achieved were compared with those presented in the Poverty Series, and it was concluded that 'the total percentages of "crowded"

---

[1] *Industry* v, p. 13. Booth had been allowed to use the wages returns collected by the Board of Trade in 1886-7, but not published. He also obtained particulars by direct inquiry from employers of the '*actual wages earned* in an ordinary week'. His returns were therefore 'actual' in the sense that they allowed for overtime and short time, unlike those of the Board of Trade (*Industry* i, p. 13). But they only gave 'average earnings for an average number' (*Industry* v, p. 13). Even if Booth had obtained the detailed information which he said would make it possible to relate type of employment and poverty, this could only have been done (a) by making an arbitrary definition of the poverty line in terms of income alone, an error which Booth never made, though this has been generally attributed to him, or (b) by relating wages to the needs of the families of each wage earner, which would have been an impossible task before sampling techniques became available. [2] See above, pp. 122, 130.

and "not crowded" agree very nearly with the totals of the previous classification "in poverty" and "in comfort" '.[1]

The comparisons were, of course, crude, as Booth hastened to point out. Nevertheless, the results reassured him. Whilst the First Series had shown that 30·7 per cent. of the population were living 'in poverty', and 69·3 per cent. 'in comfort', the new measure classified 31·5 per cent. as 'crowded', and 68·5 per cent. as 'not crowded'.[2] The division between Classes D and those above also occurred at much the same point when the new classification was applied, since the total number of Classes E, F and G (2,667,000) approximated very closely to the number of persons who lived at a density of one person per room, or who kept servants (2,547,000). Class H (250,000) was paralleled by the new class with three or less persons to each servant (248,000).

This result would be far too good to allow the more sceptical statistician of today to accept it without searching examination. It has already been pointed out that Booth knew that the overcrowding index was more reliable as an indication of poverty in some trades than in others, particularly so far as the types of employment concentrated in densely populated areas was concerned. High wages might thus be consistent with overcrowding in the centre of London:[3] 'Living in close quarters is no certain test of poverty, and accordingly while some districts are more crowded than they are poor, others are plainly more poor than they are crowded.' The assumption that if men 'were not poor they would allow themselves more space', was obviously very shaky indeed. The operation of this theory needed 'the help of a wide average to go safely, for in individual cases a great variety of conditions would be found with an equal degree of crowding'.[4] Assuming that the original estimates of poverty were correct, therefore, the overcrowding figures could only be brought into agreement with them if the errors in some trades and areas were balanced by corresponding errors in others. The fact that this actually happened can only be regarded as a coincidence.

Booth himself admitted that 'we are compelled by our method to treat the desire for sufficient house accommodation as a force acting uniformly or proportionately on all'. Nevertheless, though he knew that 'this is by no means always the case', he was unable to accept the errors that arose for what they were. He devoted so much energy and ingenuity, indeed, to reconciling his overcrowding measure with the

---

[1] *Industry* i, Chapter I.   [2] Ibid., i, pp. 9-10, 13.   [3] See above, p. 130.
[4] *Industry* i, pp. 10, 17; v, 3. See also *Final*, p. 10.

poverty line (defined by the payment of wages under 25s. a week), that he cannot be absolved from the charge of special pleading. This is particularly obvious in individual cases. The measure was reconstructed on the basis of three persons per room when the figures ran astray in the building trades, whilst 'irregularity of employment', an 'improvident way of life' and size of family were adduced to help him out with the coal porters. All these explanations failed in the case of glass and earthenware manufacturers. 'I am inclined in this case', Booth wrote, 'to doubt the correctness of the returns made to us—at any rate I am unable to find any other explanation.' The explanation to which he devoted no attention at all was that his theory that measures of poverty and overcrowding would give the same results had been disproved.[1]

This is much to be regretted, because there can be little doubt that the attempt to unite the Poverty and Industry Inquiries by way of the overcrowding measure deflected Booth's mind from the possibilities of either separating them altogether, or linking them through the analysis of the structure of the industries in which the incidence of poverty was exceptionally high. Criticism of the overcrowding index as a means of measuring variations in industrial structure, on the one hand, and in levels of living on the other, merely emphasizes the existence of the gulf between the Poverty Series and the Industry Series. It was a gulf which Booth was never able to bridge because of the excessive reliance he placed on the index, and the inadequacy of his attempts to supplement it with other analytic devices when its deficiencies made themselves felt.

To the reader in the second half of the twentieth century, familiar with the social services provided by the Welfare State, the possibilities open to Booth are plainly obvious. It will be remembered that he had divided the 'causes of poverty' between three heads: questions of employment, questions of habit, and questions of circumstances.[2] 'Questions of employment', moreover, represented much the most important of the three groups, accounting for 55 per cent. of the cases of

---

[1] Ibid., i, p. 166; iii, p. 488; v, pp. 5, 18, 22, 25, 40. The value for administrative purposes of the overcrowding index per se, as defined by Booth, is not open to question. Much use has been made of it by public health officers and town planners; though a rough and ready indication of slum conditions and the need for more accommodation, it had not been possible to replace it with anything better, for census purposes, sixty years later. See, for instance, D. Caradog Jones and Colin G. Clark, 'Housing in Liverpool', Journal of the Royal Statistical Society, Vol. XCIII, 1930, pp. 501, 22, 26-7.

[2] See above, p. 182.

'great poverty', and 68 per cent. of the cases of 'poverty'. The connexion between poverty and employment had therefore been shown to be a close one, but Booth never followed up this promising line with any degree of enthusiasm or energy, although he made a number of discoveries on which he might well have dwelt at greater length. For instance, he considered that the relation of the Bermondsey jam-making firms to the neighbourhood in which they were placed was 'probably one of mutual reaction'. The employment they offered was chiefly low-class work at low pay, and was largely seasonal: this tended 'to perpetuate the low conditions of home life upon which their supply of cheap labour depends'. Comparable situations were found in Hackney, and in the Isle of Dogs.[1] He similarly rejected the possibilities that his discoveries concerning the connexion between old age and poverty, which were made the basis of an entirely independent inquiry related to his advocacy of old-age pensions,[2] might be amplified and utilized as the main line of analysis of the descriptive material embodied in the Poverty Series. It can only be regarded as evidence of his unwillingness to be diverted from the plan he had originally laid down that none of the work which he carried out on the problem of the poverty of the aged was embodied in the 'Life and Labour' series, with the exception of brief references in the Industry Series and the Final Volume. Its relevance to the problems of industry seems to have escaped his attention. It is true, of course, that he attached great importance to the statistical analysis of the age-distribution of those employed in each of the industries of London. His figures showed the gross numbers of old and young workers employed in each of them, classified so that the relative proportions of the various age groups could be calculated, with the object in mind of making comparisons possible between the rate of expansion or contraction of one industry with another.[3] However this did not lead him on to

---

1 *Religious Influences* iv, p. 120. The Webbs built up a theory of 'parasitic occupations', out of evidence of this kind, culled from the Inquiry. See *Industrial Democracy*, Longmans Green and Co., 1897, Vol. II, p. 757.

2 See above, Chapter VIII.

3 See *The New Survey of London Life and Labour*, Vol. I, *Forty Years of Change*, P. S. King, 1930, p. 320. It must in any event be doubted whether reliable estimates of the rates of expansion and contraction in one industry or another could have been made on the basis of the age-distribution of the workers employed in them. A low proportion of old workers might merely have indicated that they were being dismissed on attaining an age at which they were thought to be unproductive, rather than that the labour-force was increasing. Similarly, a high proportion of juvenile labour (such as van-boys) might be employed because it was the practice prevailing in the industry to dismiss young workers as soon as they were able to demand the wages of adults.

examine the reasons why some industries kept their workers in employment longer than others, or to attempt to discover the extent to which the incidence of poverty due to old age might be diminished if all the ways and means of employing old people were fully exploited. So far as 'questions of employment' were concerned, the problems of retirement were only incidentally mentioned from time to time, as for instance when it was stated that 'in some trades the difficulties of old age are met by a superannuation allowance' paid by the unions. The reference was a casual one, and no great importance was attached to this problem in the concluding volume. Neither did he deal with the problem of blind-alley occupations, to which attention was afterwards directed by the Report of the Royal Commission on the Poor Laws.[1] He seems, in fact, to have missed the true significance of his analysis of age distribution almost completely. He listed the trades which employed 'an exaggerated proportion of boys', and also those which employed 'an excessive proportion of men in the prime of life', but beyond making one or two comments, he pursued the matter no further.[2]

Booth's failure to follow up the connexion between poverty and regularity of employment was equally unfortunate, for he demonstrated conclusively that fluctuations in industrial activity had deplorable social consequences. From the very beginning of his work he understood the importance of unemployment in working-class life only too well.[3] In particular, he stressed the need for further statistical analysis of 'the mass of those who owe their poverty to questions of employment'. Though he thought that 'the unemployed are, as a class, a selection of the unfit, and, on the whole, those most in want are the most unfit', it was nevertheless true that 'the modern system of industry will not work without some unemployed margin'. But the margin in London appeared to him 'to be exaggerated in every department, and enormously so in the lowest class of labour'. Some employers thought that this was in their interest, but this was, he thought, a completely mistaken view, as 'labour deteriorates under casual employment more quickly than its price falls'. Hence the problem of the work-shy and, ultimately the unemployable, who were

[1] 1909, Cd. 4499, pp. 416-20. See also Minority Report, Part II, Chap. IV.

[2] *Industry* v, pp. 45-6, 305. Booth thought that the demand for boys at high wages 'for employments that have no future' was 'a matter for regret', but he considered that 'the fact that there is this demand for young labour facilitates the absorption of wastrel boys into industry'. Ibid., v, p. 297.

[3] *Poverty* i, pp. 149-55. Second Paper, pp. 297-8.

a bad influence in society at large, besides absorbing the charities of both rich and poor, and being 'a constant bother to the State'.

Booth stated his opinion in the first edition of the Poverty Series that 'to inquire into the condition of the people by groups of trades is the only plan that will cover the ground completely, or show the facts at all as regards the *definitely* unemployed, viz. those whose trade should be, and has been regular, who in a time of depression of trade look for work and find none'. However, after he had finished the Industry Inquiry, he found himself compelled to add a footnote to this passage as finally republished, admitting that 'my attempt to do this failed'. All the same, the Industry Series contains a considerable amount of information about the deplorable social consequences of unemployment. As one section of woodworkers suffered from 'much irregularity of employment', for instance, it was 'not to be wondered at that there is also some complaint of irregular habits among the men'.[1] The whole problem was dealt with by Ernest Aves in a special chapter in the final volume. The employment of electrical workers was found to be well paid, but irregular: 'so too', it was said, 'are their habits'. The evidence of an operative brushmaker was quoted verbatim:

> The great curse of a journeyman's life is irregularity of employment. When I thought it likely that I should be thrown out of employment it seemed to paralyse me completely, and I used to sit at home brooding over it until the blow fell. . . . The fear of being turned off is the worst thing in a workingman's life, and more or less acutely it is almost always, in the case of the vast majority, present to his mind.[2]

Furthermore, Booth found himself compelled to record that the pressure of competition also could be regarded as enforcing a division of labour which might be regarded as excessive. For this reason, those who acquired skill and experience in a single highly specialized employment might find themselves unable to change to a new trade when their old one was left behind in the general advance of industrial technology. Booth deplored the use of such expressions as 'the survival of the fittest', 'the weeding out of the incapable', and the 'constant seeking after improvement' which resulted from 'the invigorating influence of periodic stress' in bad times. These were phrases which stood for ideas he regarded as being harder to justify in practice than in theory:

> The sharp differentiation of labour has been noticed as one of the main

[1] *Industry* i, p. 215. [2] Ibid., v, pp. 231-2, 235.

characteristics of the industrial field of London; and so far as many of the more highly organized trades are concerned, it is in consequence becoming less and less open to the out-of-work artisan or mechanic to make excursions into such other employment as might offer in slack times.[1]

Though it is therefore plain that Booth recognized the existence of widespread evils resulting from irregularity of work and lack of employment, unemployment never emerged as a specific social problem in the Industry Series, save as a consequence of defect of character. It was obvious that employers would welcome the opportunity presented by a slack period to weed out 'black sheep'; 'any men inclined to unsteadiness, drunkenness or sedition are then generally got rid of'.[2] Unlike his analysis of the problem of drink, the converse of the argument was never adequately stated, for little attention was paid to the difficulties the good worker had to face which were due to economic fluctuations. It was apparently assumed that markets would steadily expand, and the question as to what would happen if a chronic shortage of jobs developed was put on one side as merely theoretical.

The reason why the general problem of unemployment was not given formal treatment, or even special emphasis, may be more readily understood if it is remembered that, when the ideas underlying the Series were crystallizing in Booth's mind between 1887 and 1890, trade and employment were improving, the trend being more marked in London than in the country as a whole. It has, in fact, been argued with some cogency that the building industry, which was especially important in London's industrial structure, was passing at the time from a period of depression to the 'prolonged prosperity which culminated about 1900', and that it 'unquestionably played a dominant part in pushing unemployment to the back of the London stage'. Even where conditions of employment were badly disorganized, as in the docks industry, 'public attention was caught less by the demoralizing under-employment which it involved, than by the low rates of hourly pay'; the 'dockers' tanner' was the symbol of public concern, rather than the queue waiting for work.[3] Until the limits of the expansion of the economy were more clearly established, investigators such as Booth could hardly have been expected to regard unemployment and under employment as a self-evident social evil.

[1] Ibid., v, pp. 73-4, 256-7.   [2] Ibid., v, p. 238.

[3] (Lord) Beveridge and L. C. Marsh, 'Unemployment and its Treatment', in *The New Survey of London Life and Labour*, Vol. I, pp. 341-2.

On the other hand, much of his argument was based on an acceptance of the Wages Fund Theory, which assumed the existence of a rigid economy, rather than one that was steadily expanding. This being so, unemployment may be regarded as an issue that Booth might have been expected to have faced more squarely.

The general drift of his reasoning, indeed, tended to emphasize the limitations placed by economic 'laws' on man's endeavours to improve his social conditions. The most important lesson to be learnt from what he had to say about London's economic life was that, however well- (or ill-) intentioned individuals might be, the industrial world so encompassed them about that the shaping of their destinies and their influence on the welfare of those dependent on them, was largely outside their own control. The socialists were quick to point their own moral from the facts presented concerning the sweated trades of East London. Sidney and Beatrice Webb, for instance, commented on Booth's analysis of industrial structure in their *History of Trade Unionism*,[1] that 'the "sweater" turned out to be, not an exceptionally cruel capitalist, but himself the helpless product of a widespread degeneration which extended over whole industries'. This passage echoes Booth's own conclusion that:

> The sweating master I have known . . . works hard, making often but little more, and at times somewhat less, than his most skilled and best paid hands. He is seldom on bad terms, and often on very kindly terms with those who work under him.[2]

Of the studies of individual industries, the one to which most attention was directed was that relating to port transport. In the first place this had been entrusted to Beatrice Potter, who had written a somewhat startling account of the conditions of employment of the dock worker. This originally appeared in the *Nineteenth Century* in 1887, and was afterwards reprinted in each successive edition of the Poverty Series. 'The popular imagination', she wrote, 'represents the dock labourer either as an irrecoverable ne'er-do-well, or as a downfallen angel.' What she discovered led her to the conclusion that pity and blame were alike irrelevant; what was needed was a better under-

[1] Longmans & Co., 1897, p. 367. This work was published in the same year that the final volume of the Industry Series appeared, and the Webbs' appraisal of Booth's work was based on the Poverty Series alone. Booth's remark that he 'could make shift to stifle' his 'annoyance' when his work was 'occasionally quoted in support of doctrines which I abhor' will be remembered. See above, p. 136.

[2] *Poverty* iv, p. 338. See also *Industry* v, pp. 118-19.

standing of the conditions that were so deplorable, and effective action to put things right. 'The casual by misfortune tends to become the casual by inclination. The victims of irregular trade, and of employment given without reference to character, are slowly but surely transformed into the sinners of East-end society.' Irregular employment in East End industries amounted to 'a gigantic system of out-door relief', and to the creation of a class of men who 'have a constitutional hatred to regularity and fore-thought, and a need for paltry excitement'. 'Economically they are worthless; and morally worse than worthless, for they drag others who live among them down to their own level. They are parasites eating the life out of the working class, demoralizing and discrediting it. . . . The existence, and I fear the growth, of this leisure class in our great cities, notably in London, is the gravest problem of the future.'[1]

Beatrice Potter considered that what was wrong with the docks industry was that individualism had 'run wild' in it. 'Why', she asked, 'should one suffer the . . . evil of a system of employment which discourages hard and persistent work, and favours the growth of a demoralized and demoralizing class of bad workers and evil livers?' She therefore advocated the introduction of a 'kind of municipal socialism', which would entrust the management of the industry to a public trust representing the interests of management, labour and consumer. 'Permanent hands' worked far better than 'casuals', and the trust would be able, by better organization, to 'dovetail business' so as to make it possible to employ a larger proportion of permanent staffs of workmen.[2]

Booth went over this ground again in 1896 when he wrote the chapter, 'The Docks and Wharves', that appeared in the Industry Series. In doing so, he found himself confronted by a difficult decision: should he incorporate Beatrice Potter's appraisal of the situation and her socialistic remedies, or, if he rejected them, what alternatives could he offer? His solution was to reprint her article, without comment, in the place in the Poverty Series which it had previously occupied, and to write a new account himself for inclusion in the Industry Series. In general, he agreed with her account of the facts, though he silently ignored her recommendations. 'The dock managers', he wrote, had in the past 'accepted the crowd and struggle at the dock gates as an inevitable phenomenon, which happened to fit in well with the conditions of their trade. They could always be sure of sufficient labour,

---

[1] *Poverty* iv, pp. 12, 29, 30-2.   [2] Ibid., iv, p. 34.

and though its quality might be bad, its pay was correspondingly low.'
On the other hand their attitude had changed since the great strike of
1889:[1] 'it is now generally admitted by them that more regular work
makes better labourers, and the better labourers are more satisfactory
servants even at higher pay'. He found that 'both masters and men
desire to see a reduced proportion of very casual work', but whilst
the employers wanted 'to have a body of men on whom they can
rely, as having too much to lose to engage without very grave
cause in a strike', the men 'see in the employment of a permanent
weekly staff a tendency to prevent the free distribution of work,
and to weaken [their] power of combination'. 'While accepting
the practice as inevitable, [they] desire to limit rather than extend its
application.'[2]

The general conclusion was that too many men were employed as
casual workers in the London docks. Discussing this situation in 1892[3]
in his Inaugural Address as President of the Royal Statistical Society,
Booth had made specific proposals for the registration of dock labour
and the establishment of 'call stands', designed to reduce the insecurities
and inefficiencies of dockside employment. Many of his recommendations were subsequently followed, but he omitted them *en
bloc* when the Paper was republished in the Industry Series in 1896.
The reason why he did so is obscure. He had hoped that the limitation
of the numbers of new entrants would reduce the permanent surplus
of labour to manageable proportions, seasonal fluctuations being
dealt with by the institution of a 'supplementary list', and it is surprising that he apparently retracted what he had had to say four years
earlier. Nevertheless, the general tone of his writing still supported
decasualization, an expedient which became known as 'Mr. Booth's
scheme'. The explanation may be that he was influenced partly by the
opposition of the men, and partly by fear for the welfare of the casual
workers who would be denied employment at the docks. In later years
Sir James Sexton stated his opinion in public that the result would be to
'crush the men out', and that decasualization would provoke 'organized

---

[1] Professor G. D. H. Cole attributed much of the public sympathy to which the strikers
owed their success to the influence of the Poverty Series. 'The first results of Charles
Booth's great survey . . . had opportunely just been made public, and no one could
defend the appalling conditions under which the casually employed dockers lived and
worked.' *A Short History of the British Working Class Movement*, The Labour Publishing
Company, 1926, Vol. II, p. 160.

[2] *Industry* iii, pp. 399, 423.

[3] *Journal of the Royal Statistical Society*, 1892, p. 522.

opposition'.[1] If, as Booth himself pointed out, 'dock labourers are granted more permanent employment and higher pay . . . the casual docker is driven to seek a still more precarious livelihood elsewhere'. This process had, he thought, already begun: those casually employed 'must surely decrease in numbers if less and less work is offered them, but the process is a painful one and some of the distress from lack of employment in London, which has been so greatly complained of recently, is probably attributable to this cause'.[2]

This was a pessimistic conclusion, dictated by *a priori* theorizing rather than by empirical researches. The same pessimism and the same lack of objectivity were associated with his views on the problem of sweating, to which he had given special attention in the chapter on this subject which he had also written himself. All the current remedies —protection, state-aided emigration, the exclusion of immigrants, the regulation or suppression of home industry—all these seemed to be either 'impracticable' or 'not less dangerous than the disease'. 'On these points', Booth added, 'I see no safe policy but "laissez faire". The road is long and steep, but it is the only one we can safely follow.' In the last analysis, therefore, he found himself unable to base any practical proposals for an improvement of social welfare on his investigations into industrial structure. He refused to join with Beatrice Potter in her attacks on capitalist enterprise, but it can only be regarded as a tragic weakness in his system of thought that he did not seek a more typically English compromise between unrestrained *laissez faire* and extreme socialism, based on the facts as he recorded them. Something equally positive but more practical than Fabian Socialism was called for, which would make good use of individual initiative rather than organize it out of existence altogether. Booth came very near to supplying this, but his distrust of *a priori* and abstract arguments, particularly those of the political economists of his generation, proved, in the end, to be insufficiently robust to enable him to strike out on a line of his own. He was content to accept the theoretical objections of those, for instance, who argued that the amount of employment available at a given time was fixed, even though these arguments were entirely unsupported by evidence adduced from the Inquiry. 'The pressure that is relieved at one point', by displacing casual workers from the docks,

---

[1] *Transport Workers—Court of Enquiry, Report and Minutes of Evidence*, Vol. I, Cmd. 936, 1920, qs. 84,323, 84,340. For further discussion of this question see *The Dock Worker*, Liverpool University Press, 1954, pp. 1-10.

[2] *Industry* **v**, pp. 304, 416.

he states, 'is apt to become somewhat more severe elsewhere: the advantages that are secured to some are accompanied by a greater struggle for others, and especially for the less competent and more aged.' The reflex effects of remedial action had thus to be watched and guarded against, lest they 'engender a new disease in some unexpected form'.[1] The result was to leave him saddled with a large measure of pessimism as to the alleviation of the poverty that arose out of the functioning or malfunctioning of the economic system as he knew it.

At this point Booth's thinking followed divergent paths. As has already been pointed out, he allowed himself to be deeply influenced by the *a priori* theories of economists, and the Industry Series, as a whole, may therefore be considered in one sense at least to be a gigantic illustration of the doctrines of the Dismal Science that were current at the time. This by no means does him justice, since at the same time, the influences derived from sound empirical inquiry led his thoughts in a quite contrary direction, and resulted in a second and quite unrelated set of conclusions. This conflict of ideas may be more adequately described in terms of the contrast between his treatment of the position of the trade unions in the industrial system, which was almost entirely *a priori*, and his general analysis of the relations between employers and workpeople, which one can only assume was largely based on his own personal experiences, supplemented by the inquiries carried out in the course of the Survey. His examination of the conditions of work that were typical of the system of mechanized production, rapidly spreading throughout industry at the end of the nineteenth century, was similarly based on an empirical foundation. As a direct consequence of this second line of approach, Booth was able to point the way to the development of new methods of industrial organization, which have since been exploited with very valuable results. In so doing, he gave expression to a more optimistic view of human nature than that accepted by the classical economists.

His optimism concerning the direction in which industrial relations and industrial productivity were developing was, indeed, pronounced. He steadfastly shared the Victorian faith in 'progress'. Aves' description of the building industry, for instance, was most reassuring: 'As regards character', he wrote, 'there is testimony to improvement on almost every hand. . . . Temperance, especially among the younger men, is making rapid strides.' In general, 'the standard of life is rising, and in

[1] *Industry* v, p. 304.

some respects is altering fast. We . . . have the general impression of a well-to-do energetic people, and we find this impression borne out by all the facts and every test that can be applied.'[1] All this could be regarded as a genuine improvement in social welfare, for Booth was a fore-runner of the industrial sociologist of today in denying that the improvement of the processes of production was necessarily at the expense of the humanity of the worker. In fact, his view was the exact opposite of this. Poverty was undoubtedly connected with industrial organization; that was a theme to which Booth often returned. But the connexion did not arise through the development of the characteristics that were typical of modern industry, namely, division of labour, the use of machinery, and complexity of organization. These might bring poverty in their train, but only in the short run.

[They] do not lie at the root of the matter. There is nothing that is necessarily hostile to the welfare of the worker in the specialization of labour, or in the use of machinery, or in good book-keeping, or in the substitution of science for rule of thumb. In some directions the workman's responsibility and the importance of his individuality may be curtailed, but they do not cease to exist; they rather take new forms. Although something is lost in the character of the relations between employer and employed under the large system of industry, something also is gained; and it is to be noted that in the effort to secure the economic advantages of both systems, the development of large businesses becomes more and more departmental in character, giving rise to new forms of individuality in management and providing full opportunities for wholesome personal relations not only between the public and those who serve it, but also in effect, if not in name, between employers and employed. We must dig a little deeper to find the connexion that we seek between poverty and modern conditions of employment.[2]

The passage was written by Booth himself. It is a masterly summing up of the trends of his times that were then apparent to few, and have only become generally accepted in very recent years.[3] His appraisal may be contrasted with Aves' more conventional and pessimistic view.

[1] Ibid., i, p. 167; v, pp. 331, 338.   [2] Ibid., v, pp. 70-1.

[3] Booth repeated these views with even more emphasis in 1912. 'The adverse influence of machinery has been exaggerated, and so far as it does exist is largely unnecessary. It may bring about a change of the individual previously employed, and inflict much hardship upon him from loss of the value of his old, practised skill, but a new skill and a new individuality should be evoked. That there is no place for skill or pride in the work of the machine operator is happily not true; but the employer may do much to find and express in the very machine itself these values for the character both of the work and of the man.' *Industrial Unrest and Trade Union Policy*, p. 26.

This was that 'small establishments are more elastic', and better able to exploit a 'closer personal touch between masters and men'; and that the use of machinery had provoked 'some of the most painful problems of modern industrial life', by reason of the dislocation that followed in its application. Again, the relationship between employers and employed 'under the large system' was, Aves thought, 'more impersonal', whilst 'large business corporations tend to have no conscience'. However, no doubt under Booth's influence, he came to see that the argument cut both ways. The small employer 'tends to impose harder conditions on his workers'; it had, moreover, also to be admitted that it was in the trades in which 'the small system chiefly prevails' that the 'sweating' system 'acted with harmful and deteriorating force both on work and worker'.[1] 'A high value of machinery and plant relatively to the cost of labour employed, tends in itself to promote greater regularity of employment, since the loss from its disuse becomes an additional inducement to the owner to secure its continuous service', a consideration that has assumed the greatest importance in British industry today, particularly in large scale manufacturing enterprises such as steel plants.[2] Moreover, and here Aves' writing has a dramatic quality of up-to-dateness about it, subdivision of labour and mechanization had not necessarily reduced pride in work, or aesthetic satisfactions arising out of the performance of completed tasks.

The modern economic end is rarely found in the maintenance of individual independence as regards the processes involved in any particular occupation. Such independence is often simply an indication of wasted energy. Nor does the fact that a man has produced a finished commodity unaided, give any assurance that therefore he will himself derive a greater satisfaction from it, or that the product will possess a greater utility or beauty. The creation and artistic sense of 'this is my work' need not be more stimulating than the sense of a corporate responsibility and claim. There is rarely, save in the highest forms of creative art, any real independence and detachment. On the other hand, genuine pride in work is to be found everywhere.

The great products of modern industry, such as a building, a ship or a locomotive, necessarily involve the co-operation of many hands and minds, and there is not infrequently a feeling of satisfaction in the result as of a corporate achievement and triumph.[3]

[1] *Industry* v, pp. 107, 109-10, 117, 119.

[2] See W. H. Scott, J. A. Banks, *et al.*, *Technical Change and Industrial Relations*, Liverpool University Press, 1956, p. 258.

[3] *Industry* v, pp. 132-3.

The analysis is a penetrating one, and might have been taken much further. Aves did in fact go so far as to point out that conditions of work might be greatly improved when:

the lesson of the elasticity of the power of human response has been fully learnt; when it is realized . . . that, even with machinery, while its speed and capacity remain the same, output may be maintained though hours be diminished. In factories, this 'reserve of personal efficiency' . . . will tell; while in the case of all skilled labour, in which machinery plays no part, the possible effects of this subtle, unknown, and often unexpected expansion of individual power, may be important beyond measure. Few more fatal fallacies have hindered the path of industrial reforms than the superficial assumption, happily dying, that returns can be simply measured in terms of the hours of employment.[1]

The importance of these considerations had been especially evident when Aves examined the conditions prevailing in the building trade. There the stress of competition was frequently excessive. The cost of materials being well established, the margin of profit on them could be safely reduced to a minimum, but, he added, 'the cost of labour is comparatively an unknown quantity, and thus becomes the recognized field in which good management may seek to find its profit'.[2]

The general conclusion to be drawn from Booth's argument, supported as it was by Aves', was therefore that a whole world lay open to be exploited by 'good management', and that the stimulation of 'wholesome personal relations' had as much to contribute to the development of productive efficiency and the increase of wealth and welfare, as had the great advances in industrial technology of the Victorian age. Booth's abhorrence of State Socialism, Syndicalism, and political and restrictive trade unionism never left him. On the other hand, his faith in the possibilities of good management increased rather than diminished. In 1913, when he discussed the whole issue once more in a pamphlet entitled *Industrial Unrest and Trade Union Policy*, it appeared to him that workmen should be encouraged to 'take an interest in their work; . . . if this spirit permeates an entire employ, the employer, at ease about the loyalty with which he will be supported, can bring a fresher and keener mind to the many difficulties which face him and need solution'. These were neglected values, attention to which would benefit both employer and employee. He also called attention to the latent value which lay 'in the

---

[1] Ibid., v, p. 191.   [2] Ibid., i, pp. 161-2.

recognition and encouragement of individuality, with willingness of the individual to be trained and co-operate'. To give 'each person the task he is best fitted for, would seem to be pure gain. But it lies with the employer to assist, to encourage, and to deal justly.'[1]

The final position which Booth established at the end of his work on economic organization and industrial relations was therefore to make clear his conviction that important possibilities for the improvement of the productive efficiency of industrial enterprise still remained to be recognized and exploited by employers, managers and men alike. His greatest interest was in the relationships established between people in the course of their employment and he was confident that nothing in the nature of revolutionary changes was required before these possibilities could be realized. In adopting this attitude of mind, he displayed an optimism which has been justified by subsequent history. The possibility that the industrial sociologist, by studying the structure and functioning of the working community, can assist in the reaping of the harvest which he so clearly foresaw, only began to be seriously exploited fifty years after he pointed it out.

This is, of course, implied rather than directly stated in the Series itself. It could, in fact, never have been made explicit by Booth himself unless his mind had been awakened to the need to concentrate on the more strictly empirical aspects of his work, rather than to justify capitalist enterprise by *a priori* reasoning. As he left the argument, the Series as a whole amounts to no more than an attempt to defend industry against the charge of having created poverty. Too excessive a concentration on the poverty theme had blinded Booth's eyes to the possibility of refuting Socialist or other critics by demonstrating the extent to which capitalist enterprise had raised, rather than lowered, levels of living. Nevertheless, it must be pointed out in fairness to him, that he did recognize that this line of approach could be followed, and did devote himself to the study of the problems involved. His flat denial of the conventional thesis that machine-production destroys human values, and that large organizations are necessarily inhuman, bears striking witness to his independence of mind, and to his instinctive grasp of realities. It illustrates once again the working of his characteristic genius. Even half a century later it is only just beginning to be possible to measure the greatness of his achievement in terms of the circumstances in which he found himself, and to conclude that the analysis of the social problems of industry has been carried far enough

[1] Op. cit., pp. 12, 13, 25, 26.

in the intervening period to supersede his work as a textbook for current use.

Mary Booth tells us that both she and her husband believed that the Industry Series contained some of his best work. Their faith is justifiable in so far as it must be regarded as the first reconnaissance ever made into the field of social economics. It exists to this day as an historical text of the first importance, for not only does it provide an accurate picture of London's industries at a critical time in their development but it also points the way to a method of studying industrial organization whereby theory and fact can be linked together in a mutually supportive relationship. Thanks to Booth, the study of the problems of industry was for the first time based on empirical foundations, and was thus entitled to rank as a social science, properly so called. That so little use was made for so many years of his experience as a pioneer in this promising sphere should not be allowed to obscure the greatness of his contribution to what is still a novel subject.

On the other hand, the indirect, as contrasted with the direct, influence of the Industry Series has been considerable. The outstanding example of this was the work done by Ernest Aves as Chairman of Trade Boards in the years that followed the completion of the Inquiry, until his death. Aves had learnt much from the compiling of the Industry Series concerning the realities of industrial organization, which he had been able to study through the eyes of both employees and trade unionists. His work in industrial conciliation made it possible for him to bring to bear upon the problems of an important section of British Industry the methods of accurate observation and scrupulously honest analysis on which the Industry Series had been based. In this and similar ways, Booth's methods of work and intellectual standards secured an acceptance which extended far beyond the influence exerted by the much neglected volumes of the Industry Series itself. The approach of the social economist, developed jointly by Booth and Aves, made it possible to evolve and to apply such expedients as the minimum wage in the sweated and other trades to which attention had been drawn by Booth. The improvement in the organization of these industries, and the relaxation of the tensions between employers and workers in them, pointed to the possibility of establishing a middle way between capitalism and socialism which deeply influenced the evolution of the British economy in the first half of the twentieth century.[1]

---

[1] A general account of Aves' work as Chairman of Trade Boards is given in the obituary notice which was published in the *Economic Journal* (1917, pp. 293 seqq.).

11

The Religious Influences Series

EW people, even amongst his intimate relations, seem to have been able to understand at all clearly what it was that Booth attempted in the Religious Influences Inquiry. Mary Booth throws no light on this problem in her memoir. Although she deals at length with his business interests, the poverty and industry inquiries, and the old-age pensions campaign, she only mentions the Religious Influences Series by reproducing, without comment, a series of four letters from Booth to Aves, which deal with administrative details. This is all the more surprising in view of Booth's personal treatment of the subject of religious influences. With the exception of some of the illustrative notes, the whole Series is from his own pen. The contrast with the Industry Series is striking: in that case, only a small proportion appeared as his own work, some of the key sections being written by Aves. In drafting the Religious Influences Series, on the other hand, though Booth was greatly helped by his assistants, the final book was essentially his own creation. Unlike the Industry Series, it is written throughout as it starts, in the first person.

The fact is a revealing one, for this third and final inquiry only acquires meaning and purpose if it is borne in mind that Booth's researches were energized as much by his own interest in the principles upon which religion itself is founded, as by his intellectual ambition to record a true picture of the religious way of life. Proof lies—if, in view of his evident enthusiasm, proof be necessary—in his clear consciousness of the dangers of description and of the difficulties of statistical analysis when he encountered the phenomena of religious experience. These would have been of no great importance to him had he regarded the subject of his investigations as being only a third set of social relationships or institutions. Nothing of this was ever explicitly stated, and Booth made no attempt to put into words even the analytical apparatus which gave direction to his inquiries and led him to select some, but not all, of the material he gathered as significant. Neverthelsss, it is impossible to come to any other conclusion than that in embarking on what he called a 'voyage of discovery' through the London area, he was undertaking a search for the realities of human existence which far transcend the experiences of social life.

Booth's ultimate purposes were therefore very different from the simple 'description of things as they are' of his avowed intention; it is not surprising that they were never clear to him and that they have never been properly understood by his readers or critics. To be at one and the same time personally concerned as to the results of one's researches and impartially detached when analysing and interpreting their content would seem to many to involve an irreconcilable contradiction. It is much to Booth's credit that he demonstrated in the Religious Influences Series that the contradiction can be resolved, and in so doing, provided a classic case-study to which those interested in the techniques of social research of the more fundamental kind can refer with profit.

There was thus a basic dualism in Booth's attempt to comprehend the ways in which the motives and behaviour of individuals are influenced by religion, and his work cannot be adequately understood unless he is thought of as pursuing two distinct lines of analysis which, though complementary, led in different directions. The first, the more strictly social and scientific, was the path that has since led to the development of the sociology of religion; the second involved an excursion into territory that has usually been regarded as that belonging to the philosopher and the theologian rather than the social scientist. The first approach was based on the assumption that the institutional structure of each church can be described and appraised from the point of view of its connexions with the structure of the society of which it can be deemed to be a part. The strength of a church as a social institution can be shown, for instance, to be related to the extent to which it fits in, or fails to fit in, to the class structure of the wider community. Booth carried this line of analysis a long way, and with great profit. At the same time, it tended to become confused in his work with the second line of analysis, that directed to the discovery of the extent to which the moral life of a society is influenced by religious teaching properly so called. This involved him in a critical examination of the teaching of individual churches, and in the appraisal of the religious life from its more personal aspects.

The two themes were pursued simultaneously and in such close association that it is impossible at times to disentangle them. Because its logical foundations were thus lacking in clarity, Booth's argument is often obscure. This obscurity was, moreover, accentuated by reason of the fact that the methods whereby the raw material of the third Inquiry was collected were much harder to develop and to apply than had been his experience in the first two. The problems he had already encountered were grave enough. Those he had to overcome when faced with the technical problems involved in the fieldwork of the third Inquiry were even more intimidating. At its outset, he found himself compelled to deal with the difficulties of appraising the effect on human behaviour of a variety of influences which could not be adequately examined by the use of the statistical techniques on which he had relied in the Poverty Inquiry. Nor could they be fully overcome by applying the methods of institutional analysis which had proved so profitable in the Industry Inquiry.

It was for example clear to Booth that it is not possible to understand how an 'influence' operates so as to change the course of human conduct in one way or another, by merely measuring the extent to which a given course of behaviour is followed, and attributing it to the impact of the 'influences' with which it may be associated. In more technical language, correlation must be distinguished from causation. People go to church, for instance, for many reasons, some of which conflict with religious teaching. Conversely, many people who never go to church are deeply influenced by religion. Church attendances and similar statistical measures cannot, therefore, be expected to provide a wholly reliable estimate of the influence of religious bodies on individual conduct.

These difficulties being plainly apparent to him, Booth took the bold step of rejecting statistics of church attendances as evidence on which he could base his investigations. Nevertheless, he printed a brief 'Social Analysis' which set out the relevant statistics he had collected at the beginning of his account of each of the areas he described.[1] All this amounted to a quite impressive array of figures, but the sceptical reader was entitled to ask what, if anything, had been discovered from them. There was much point in this criticism, because the information

[1] These comprised statistics of population changes and density of population, together with totals of the population by age and sex. In addition, the Social Classification according to rooms occupied or servants kept was repeated, despite the fact that Booth had not been wholly satisfied as to its significance when he had used it in the Industry Series. The statistics were given in full in the Appendix to *Religious Influences* vi.

obtained from the interviews was not directly related to the statistical data, and a general impression was given that Booth was merely seeking to avoid the main methodological problems of this phase of his inquiry by making use of statistical mumbo-jumbo. This line of attack was even more penetrating in view of his deliberate rejection of statistics of church attendances as evidence on which he could rely. At the same time, he made full use of institutional analysis, but while this, as will be seen, gave him valuable evidence of both the strength and the weakness of the social structure of the churches, the special characteristics they possessed as religious bodies tended to elude this method of inquiry. His evidence concerning the impact of 'influences' on the general run of social behaviour could only be hearsay, in the sense that it was based on nothing more than the opinions of individuals deemed to possess specially valuable knowledge and experience. It necessarily suffered from all the defects of evidence of that kind, and it had to be tested with the greatest care. How far, he had to ask himself, could genuinely truthful and trustworthy impressions be gained from the interviews which he and his colleagues carried out with the representatives of the religious bodies? He was able to state this problem, rather than to solve it, and this made his position hard to defend.

Booth therefore found himself facing intimidating problems of methodology. Even if the techniques of modern psychological research had been available to him, they would only have been of value in a relatively small part of the field of work which he was now opening up, and he was compelled once more to forge his own tools for use in this third phase of the Inquiry as he went along. His final conclusions were that:

Spiritual influences do not lend themselves readily to statistical treatment, and we have not attempted it. The subject is one in which figures may easily be pressed too far, and if trusted too much are likely to be more than usually dangerous. Our object, rather, has been to obtain truthful and trustworthy impressions, which we might hope to be able to transmit to our readers, of whom, though many would know accurately some parts, few can have surveyed the whole field.[1]

Though the Religious Influences Series was primarily an institutional study, much, if not most, of the information on which it was based was derived from interviews. In this sense, it was also an attitude study, the first of its kind to be carried out on a large scale and with any

---

[1] Ibid., i, p. 7.

pretensions to accuracy anywhere in the world. There can, therefore, be no cause for surprise that its nature was misunderstood at the time; this was only to be expected. Booth's task was to demonstrate that a relationship, positive or negative, existed between the beliefs and behaviour of individuals, on the one hand, and the functioning of a specially selected set of social institutions, on the other. His conceptual tools were clumsy and blunt, however, and his approach to the problem of analysing the structure of the institutions with which he was concerned was more often that of the man of common sense than that of the sociologist. The techniques available to him for the collection and sifting of information were also primitive. Personal judgement came to play a preponderating part in the researches, if for no other reason than because the informants on whose evidence Booth relied could only be selected, and one part or another of their evidence could only be accepted for analysis, in the light of his own preconceptions; it is for this reason, perhaps, that the Inquiry is at its weakest when the influence of religious bodies on the behaviour of individuals, as distinct from society at large, is under consideration.

The position was made even more difficult by reason of the fact that Booth was not only compelled to identify what he deemed to be typical attitudes on the part of the representatives of the various churches; he was also forced (without, it is true, any reluctance on his part), to evaluate their truth or falsehood in accordance with his own moral and religious preconceptions. The distinctive attitudes displayed by the Churches were deemed by him to be 'good' or 'bad' in proportion to the extent to which they inclined to one end or the other of a scale running from the purely rational at one extreme to the crudely emotional at the other, with a blend of the two in the centre. His own inclinations, deriving perhaps from his early upbringing as a Unitarian, were towards reason rather than emotion as the motive force behind religious activity. The influence of the Congregationalists, for example, though 'more social than religious', appeared to him to be 'good and wholesome', and 'being without exaltation, free from the dangers of reaction'. The 'great contribution' of the Quakers to religious life was the adult school, 'a social and democratic organization of the most democratic type'; they set a 'wise example' in refraining from proselytizing; they gave, indeed, 'the simplest, truest and least embellished account we have had of the work of any denomination'.[1]

The more that the churches relied on emotional appeals, the greater

[1] *Religious Influences* vii, pp. 121, 146.

was his condemnation of them; this point of view was most sharply indicated in his disapproval of the work of missions. He expressed doubts whether 'true religious feeling' would be dispensed by the 'spiritual dram-drinking' which he considered to be a fair description of much mission activity. In general, he concluded that missions did more harm than good: 'They do not reach the class aimed at, and are, for the religious, a spiritual debauch.' Conversions among women and children were said sometimes to be 'of exceptionally hysterical character'. Most mission work in one region of London, for instance, bore 'the character of galvanized activity without one spark of vitality'. In Putney, little seemed to remain of the 'great wave of religious sentiment' which Moody had so successfully aroused. The 'empty benches' of the mission halls built to commemorate his endeavours were 'a great contrast to Mr. Moody's crowded tents'. That the rabble-rousing side of missionary endeavour had failed completely was an evident fact.[1]

Nevertheless, Booth found that missions had been established in almost every street in the poorer parts of London; they were 'more numerous than schools or churches, and only less numerous than public-houses'. Their success was, however, absolutely limited and very far from what they set out to achieve, and the mass of the people remained untouched. Those who claimed success were 'self-deceived. Perhaps they wish to be so.' High Church mission work was 'character-ized by enthusiasm and devotion, and by extraordinary energy', but was 'marred by unscrupulousness, and by unwarrantable pretensions which result in bitter sectarian feeling'. Ordinary parish mission work was 'more wholesome', but the 'favourite delusion' in this case was that 'the people themselves take an interest in the work, whereas they take hardly any at all'. 'Some self-deception', indeed appeared to be necessary to sustain any kind of missionary enthusiasm. The 'pulpit antics' of the founder of the Church Army, again, shocked him deeply; some people might not be driven away by them, but he doubted whether 'they are in truth attracted by dialogues suggestive of Ethiopian minstrels, or appreciate the punctuation of the services by the free use of the trombone which the rector keeps ever handy. He undervalues his people.'[2]

[1] Ibid., vii, pp. 153, 215, 275, 319.

[2] Ibid., iii, p. 24; vii, pp. 270, 274-5, 279-80. In one street, the bad conditions which obtained did not seem to be improving, even though it was 'over-run with Missions' (ibid., i, p. 51).

The conclusion was that the churches were wasting their time in attempting to attract the working classes and 'the poor' to their services by the offer of charitable aid, by making use of emotional language, and in general, by embarking on a series of endeavours so marred by what he regarded as claptrap, hysteria, bribery, and dishonesty that he was moved to vigorous protest. He recognized that individual priests and ministers often did good work[1] in appealing to the masses, but these were exceptions to the general rule. In the main, the tone of his comments was highly critical. A straightforward attempt on the part of a Salvation Army officer, for instance, to intimidate an individual with the threat of hell-fire appeared to him to be a 'most awful exhibition of theological savagery'.[2]

Booth's attitude of moral evaluation is equally evident in his respect for what he considered to be the truly religious element in the work of the churches. His attempt to give expression to this involved him in endless difficulties. It was obvious that the several churches functioned as associations which brought people together, and thus influenced their conduct by providing them with a special kind of social tie. Nevertheless, it was equally obvious that religious influences could not be adequately dealt with as a particular kind of social influence. Booth recognized that the daily concerns of the churches touched on the ultimate mysteries of human existence, and his discussion and criticism of their work was therefore coloured by an assumption that it could only be regarded as 'religious' if it was conducted with a direct relevance to, and with due reverence for, first and last things.

If the Religious Influences Series is examined with care, it will be found that one of the chief foundations on which the argument rests is this contrast between the 'religious' on the one hand, and the 'social' on the other. The religious element in human experience is assumed to exist in its own right, and to be clearly distinguishable from superstition. It was a necessary part of the evaluation of the work of individual Churches to assert that 'the true spirit of religion' could be discovered to be present or absent in the life of a religious body, apart from the doctrine or ceremonial through which it might be expressed, and that 'spiritual destitution' might prevail, despite, for instance, the religious activities of missions. Small wonder, then, that Booth assumed that his meaning was clear when he remarked that 'no feeling

---

[1] See, for instance, *Religious Influences* i, pp. 38-9, 143-5, 223; ii, pp. 31, 35; v, pp. 121, 153, 222; vi, pp. 7-8; vii, pp. 30-2, 41, 56, 393.

[2] Ibid., iii, p. 184.

of sacredness' attached to a Baptist chapel, for 'its way is not that of being a house of God', or that on entering Wren's churches 'one thinks of man and duty rather than of God and faith', or when he expressed the hope that a better use might be found for City churches which would still be 'in accord with true religion'.[1]

These are trenchant passages, but the theme embodied in them recurs throughout the seven volumes of the Series. Booth feared especially that the popularizing of religion by mass appeal would bring with it 'the danger of loss of reverence, the danger that the things of religion may cease to be sacred'. Writing of the work of an East End church, he deplored the extent to which 'religion, to gain strength, is lowered to superstition'. For him, the basic element in religion was personal and transcendental, rather than social and material. 'Religion', he said, 'depends on inborn characteristics of the individual soul.' His comments on the social work of the Unitarian Churches, for instance, were particularly apposite. 'It will, perhaps be said that they lacked the "one thing needful"—that which Mary had and Martha had not.'[2]

A double standard of evaluation was therefore applied in the course of the Inquiry to the work of the churches. How far did their work embody a genuine belief in and worship of God? How far did they succeed as social institutions? While insisting on the distinction between the religious and the social when he asked these questions, Booth avoided the mistake so frequently made in recent years of establishing a false dichotomy between the spiritual and the material. He very properly assumed that two kinds of questions had to be asked about the work of religious bodies, but he was not misled by this into thinking that equally clear-cut answers must necessarily be expected, the theologian speaking solely of things religious and the social scientist restricting himself to social aspects. Though he did not say so in so many words, he set out, in fact, to demonstrate that these two aspects of life interlock. For instance, his well-known conclusion that the strength and success of the Congregational Church were derived from its social structure rather than its religious teaching, was accompanied by a statement that 'such work may be thought to fail if the saving of souls by the preaching of Christ be the ultimate aim, but it is undoubtedly a wholesome and lasting influence for good'. A 'friendly human atmosphere' might prevail in these Churches, but 'religious

[1] Ibid., ii, p. 227; iii, pp. 50, 57; vii, p. 202.

[2] Ibid., ii, p. 36; iv, p. 147; vii, pp. 145, 432.

sentiment' was lacking. Belief in Christ was interpreted in them 'not primarily as that which involves faith in the great sacrifice of a risen Saviour, but rather as the acceptance of an ideal affecting human life and relationships, which may be described as "Christian humanism"'. These passages are paralleled by Booth's summing up of his views concerning the Wesleyans: 'there is', he wrote, 'something hollow, unsatisfactory, and unreal about Wesleyanism as a religious influence which I find it difficult to put into words. . . . The enthusiasm and overwrought emotions of the Wesleyans produce a false atmosphere of exaggerated language'; 'in self-deception', he added, 'they have no equals'.[1]

The weakness of Booth's position in making such statements about the work of religious bodies arose from the fact that they were, and could only be, based on a system of values which ultimately stemmed from his own spiritual life. In venturing to make these evaluations, he went beyond matters of fact, which could be argued; the results sometimes (but by no means always), failed to carry conviction, and occasionally aroused intense hostility. On the whole, therefore, his attempt to analyse the religious element in the relationship between church and people may be said to have been unsuccessful in so far as his methods were sometimes those of a moral philosopher rather than a social scientist. It was only an undoubted success in so far as what he said carried with it general assent: for this reason it can be regarded as having made a contribution to the technique of social research.

Booth's appraisal of the strength of the social structure of the churches, and of its relationship with that of the wider society containing them, is of greater immediate interest to the sociologist, though not of greater intrinsic importance. It is, so far as the general reader was concerned, much more straightforward; at the time it appeared, it was more readily understood, and it commanded more general agreement. His much discussed account of the missions, for instance, indicated that their main value lay in bringing people together in relatively small groups; their influence was therefore more social than religious. But his evaluation of their religious and moral influence overshadowed his analysis of their social structure. His description of the organization of the Congregational Church in North London is a good example of his treatment of a church as a social institution; it may be regarded as his best appraisal of an attempt to make religion a living force within the lives of individuals by encouraging social co-operation, both formal

[1] *Religious Influences* i, pp. 122-4; vii, pp. 119, 135-6. See above, p. 152.

and informal, between them.[1] The description ends on the theme of the lack of 'religious sentiment'. The same theme is repeated in a different key in the account given of the charitable work of the religious bodies. The social appeal of the churches to the external world included in Booth's day an elaborate and expensive array of social welfare activities or services, such as clubwork for men, women and children, and relief services of many kinds, ranging from soup kitchens to weekly doles. These activities often loomed very large indeed in the life of individual churches and missions, but the story he told of work of this kind was one of almost unrelieved shame. It still makes bleak and depressing reading, even when it is remembered that his critical attitude must have owed something to his individualistic presuppositions.

> The admixture of Gospel and giving produces an atmosphere of meanness and hypocrisy, and brings discredit on both charity and religion. . . . Those who have qualms as to the wisdom of what they do, are nevertheless tempted to lay the flattering unction to their souls, and argue that kindness in itself is good, and that benefit must necessarily flow from its manifestation.[2]

Research into the charitable activities of the churches thus led to two conclusions. In the first place, these activities had been shown to conflict with Christian morals; this was one of the reasons why Booth was led to doubt and even to disbelieve that the Christian religion could be made the basis of a viable way of life in his own society. Secondly, he discovered that an important effect of charitable work had been to incorporate the churches in the class system. His analysis of the connexions between class structure and religious organization is, indeed, quite masterly; it is so fully documented and so comprehensive and conclusive in its results that it is hard to do his work justice by giving a brief summary of his findings and conclusions. A few points may, however, be emphasized. In general, he found a close correspondence between class structure and the social organization of the churches. The Church of England, for instance, had 'an easy task' (up to a certain point) with 'the rich and fashionable'. The great bulk of the people of rank and station belonged to this Church, and their relations with it were 'easy and confident. They are not only steady supporters, but, for the most part, truly and warmly attached members. The part played by religion in their lives is as a rule by no means large, but it is constant.

---

[1] Ibid., i, pp. 119-24, 177-80, 324-33. 'By "Congregationalist" is implied a peculiar use of social life in connexion with religious work and congregational unity' (p. 130).

[2] Ibid., vii, p. 278.

The professional classes, including newcomers who have risen in the social scale, join the Established Church', but there were signs that 'this unsatisfactory form of conventional development' was coming to an end. Those belonging to the minor professions, and businessmen, were more likely to join the nonconformist churches; those of them who could be regarded as belonging to the 'new middle classes' formed the bulk of most religious assemblages.[1] In mixed parishes containing both rich and poor, the poor 'cannot be induced to come to church'; though mission halls 'of their own' were built, they still did not attend, and failure was more usual than success in such parishes.

Booth considered that he had shown that denominational allegiance, class and the distribution of wealth were all connected phenomena:

> Where the streets [on the map] are red, we find a vigorous middle-class religious development combined with active social life. Where the streets are pink, there is, as regards religion, a comparative blank. Where the colour is blue we have the missions, and step by step, as it deepens to black, the more hopeless becomes the task. From these broad conclusions there is no escape.[2]

The general thesis can be summed up in the statement that both the amount of participation in religious life and the kind of religious life that attracted adherents were determined by class: 'When we sum the matter up, we shall find that each religious method finds its place in London according to local conditions as to social status.'[3]

> In studying the influence of religion we have seen how limited are the possibilities it presents, and how closely everywhere it follows the lines of class, similar conditions of life yielding similar results whatever the particular sect or whatever the special dogma preached may be.[4]

These ideas are elaborated in the accounts of the attitudes of different classes towards the several churches, based on what some might consider today to be somewhat superficial fieldwork. They have, for all that, a convincing ring of truth about them. Among the middle classes it was found that 'there are social advantages' that attract towards church membership, and 'a social feeling that almost compels a man to put himself in connexion with some Christian community', but 'with the working classes the feeling is all the other way. . . . What the classes above seek in religion is its support, what the working man fights shy of is its discipline.' For Booth, the 'peculiar character of . . .

---

[1] *Religious Influences* vii, pp. 394-9.   [2] Ibid., i, p. 149.

[3] Ibid., iv, p. 85.   [4] Ibid., iii, pp. 177-8.

happy, successful middle-class religious development' was associated with 'the combination of "attractions" with religion', symbolized by 'a *missa cantata* followed by a seven-minute sermon'.[1]

The working-class attitude to religion was more complicated. In general, there was 'no feeling against religion'; sympathy was on the side of religion rather than of agnosticism. 'Doctrinal indifference' was, indeed, quite compatible with personal loyalty. Religious subjects formed the most popular topic of working-class discussion; 'neither intelligence nor interest was lacking, but neither interest nor intelligence leads to public worship'. Both religion and education were regarded 'as things of childhood, not to extend beyond the age of thirteen'. The class affiliations of religious bodies were also important in shaping the attitudes of working men, who were, quite understandably, said to 'feel very strongly about pious employers who sweat their work-people'. 'Those who are recognized as being religious are often profoundly distrusted.' Working men 'expect a religious man to make his life square with his opinions'. Visits to the pub, betting, and so on, were looked on by them as inconsistent with religious professions, and they were 'unwilling to accept a restraint that would deprive them of their everyday pleasures'.[2]

The churches have come to be regarded as the resorts of the well-to-do, and of those who are willing to accept the charity and patronage of people better off than themselves. It is felt that the tone of the services, especially in the Church of England, is opposed to the idea of advancement; inculcating rather contentment with, and the necessity for the doing of duty in that station of life to which it has pleased God to call a man. The spirit of sacrifice, inculcated in theory, is not observed among, or believed to be practised by, the members of these churches in any particular degree, and this inconsistency is very critically and seriously judged.[3]

This penetrating summing up of working-class attitudes may be regarded as completing the account given of them. All the intrinsic interest and fundamental weaknesses of attitude studies are clearly apparent in it. What Booth had to say when he extended his analysis of the social problems of the churches to include an account of the influences on religious life of the increasing urbanism of his age was, on the other hand, firmly based on fact, rather than on shifting opinion. His conclusions are well documented, and amount to a substantial

[1] Ibid., i, pp. 89, 90, 129.

[2] Ibid., i, pp. 87-9, 181, 183; ii, p. 128; v, p. 169; vii, pp. 35-6, 428, 431.

[3] Ibid., vii, pp. 426-7.

contribution to urban sociology. The institutional structure of the churches, he pointed out, had developed in previous generations in a predominantly rural environment, which had had profound effects on their organization. This had, for instance, established the parochial basis of the Church of England, and her continued strength was attributable to the fact that it had been possible to transplant this essentially rural institution into an urban setting, to a certain extent, at least. Methodism, again, was 'at bottom a country organization', in which a federal bond united a number of small village groups, both receiving and giving assistance, 'prepared to conduct the service of God themselves, but recognizing the need for an educated ministry. To provide this want they combine, and all the rest follows naturally.' Conditions were entirely different in a large town. Where the need was thought to arise, a new church was built 'which may be attached to an old circuit, or a new circuit may be formed'. However, the work lacked foundations; and the minister attached to a church for three years, according to Wesleyan practice, found himself confronted with a 'heart-breaking' task. 'It is, indeed, astonishing that any man can work with a good heart under such conditions.'[1]

The primary characteristic that made the traditional methods of church work difficult to apply in urban areas was the fact recorded at the end of the final volume of the Series, that:

London surroundings bring little or no pressure to bear in the direction of conventional church-going. Even men who have been churchwardens in the country feel . . . no obligation to attend church here, and the ordinary resident knows that, in this respect, his conduct, so far as non-attendance goes, is for the most part free from observation, and, if observed, from comment. Among the working classes the pressure exerted is apt to be on the opposite side, such as in the 'ragging' of the workshop, or the sneers of neighbours who connect religious observance with cupboard love. But in a general way, London life secures for all men the maximum freedom of conduct. Even animals find it their best hiding-place. To ask no questions is commonly regarded as the highest form of neighbourliness.[2]

The lack of response to the appeal of the churches was, however, not merely to be attributed to the changes in the pattern of social life that took place when people left the villages for the towns. In a new parish which was established in the suburbs that were part of the 'mushroom growth' round London, there was a notable 'lack of traditions, cohesion, and patriotism'; in other words, the trouble was

---

[1] *Religious Influences* vii, pp. 130-1.   [2] Ibid., vii, pp. 428-9.

connected with the lack of traditional values as well as relationships.
The churches found it difficult even to adjust themselves to the new
values and opportunities for new kinds of social life which were coming to exist, let alone take advantage of them. 'The great mass of men
have more leisure, but the time freed goes in . . . other directions',
such as trade unions, friendly and co-operative societies, and politics;
these, 'with newspapers and even books, are filling, in the mental life
of the average working man, a larger space than in the past, and with
some may be taking a place which might have been otherwise occupied
by religious interests'. This 'may probably be asserted much more
confidently of pleasure, amusement, hospitality, and sport'. This was
particularly evident in prosperous areas such as Woolwich, where the
demands of the Boer War had led to a period of full employment in
the Arsenal and Dockyards. There seemed to be little expectation,
therefore, that a rise in economic prosperity would lead to a religious
revival amongst the working classes.[1]

When Booth came to write the concluding volume of the Religious
Influences Series, he therefore found himself faced with the task of
summarizing two sets of evidence, one related to the personal experience of religion and the other to the church as a social institution.
This fact eluded him, however, and his final summing up failed to
relate the one to the other. All he could offer was a set of random
opinions on points whose importance he sensed but was unable to
analyse. Thus he remarked that formal religious effort only attracted
a relatively few individuals; it did not produce Christians in the mass.
Churches were established by different kinds of men, rather than the
reverse; above all, 'it is respectability that causes people to go to
church far more than it is church-going that makes them respectable'.
Religion was 'the crown rather than the cause' of such qualities as a
capacity for hard work, abstemiousness and self-denial. He made the
point repeatedly that those who hold aloof from religion may be
'most excellent, reputable, sober, and industrious people'. Many of
those Booth admired most were untouched by religion, and though
he recorded 'the great main fact, to which we have endless testimony',
that 'Christian people are nearly all temperate and thrifty, and the
better in every way for being so', they were a small minority, and,
moreover, one which exhibited what he charitably called the defects
of their qualities. He left his contemporaries to answer for themselves
the problem which was posed by the evident decline in the relative

[1] Ibid., iii, p. 189; v, 121-3; vii, p. 425.

importance of religious life. What would happen if Christian influence, exercised through the churches, disappeared altogether? Then, as now, no answers were forthcoming, and Booth left highly troubled minds behind him.[1] In turn, the impact on the organization of the churches of the prevailing social structure and social norms could readily be established, but the influence of the churches on individual behaviour appeared to be slight, and eluded his methods of research.

Nevertheless, it was 'at bottom . . . with the individual soul' that religion had to do. 'Religion', Booth stated, 'is not simply a moral code of life, rather is it a devotional expression; religion is also an impulse and a persistent attitude, an intimate possession of the soul, perhaps not understood even by the individual, and very difficult of interpretation by others.' Moreover, religion could not be regarded as a mere taking 'to good works as an anodyne in order to escape the worry of doubt', because, as he pointed out when discussing the affairs of the Congregational Church, 'when we are told . . . that "my young people are safely over the period of doubt", it only means that they, and their pastor too, have so far escaped it'.[2] Because this distinction between the two aspects of his subject was never explicitly made in the Inquiry, the reader is frequently left in doubt as to whether Booth was dealing with the religious or the social aspect of the Church. What, it might be asked, was the precise significance of the finding that the Church of England had the highest proportion of upper-class members, whilst a much higher proportion of the adherents of the Baptist Church came from the ranks of the manual workers? This might reflect an unequal distribution of social and political influence, but did it necessarily indicate similar differences in the strength of the religious teaching or the vitality of the spiritual life of these Churches? These questions were neither asked nor answered by Booth, because the lack of precision in the definitions of basic concepts, especially those of the 'religious', the 'social' and the 'spiritual', prevented issues of this kind from arising out of his work.

So to write must not, however, be interpreted as in any sense a criticism of Booth's achievement. It is, of course, a matter of extreme difficulty to distinguish between the religious element and the social in human affairs, for man and his destinies are inseparable from the societies in which he lives. Social egalitarianism, for instance, must be regarded as a concept which is clearly distinct from Christian fellow-

---

[1] *Religious Influences* i, pp. 41, 86; vii, p. 152; *Final*, p. 75.
[2] Ibid., vii, pp. 118, 279, 423, 429.

ship, though the two are closely connected in our own society. Yet neither can be adequately understood unless each is considered apart, and the same applies to both religious and social life. A distinction therefore has to be made between the Church as part of a larger society, and as a religious body acting as a motive force within it.

Comparison of Booth's work with that of his contemporary, William James, illuminates both the subtlety and the importance of the distinction, and in so doing, demonstrates the considerable extent to which he in fact succeeded in penetrating what is still difficult and unexplored intellectual territory.[1] Like William James, Booth started with the basic assumptions that respect must be paid to religious truths, and the world of religion must be regarded as real, even if unseen. He stated that 'the investigation of organized religion in all its forms' had 'taken the first and largest place' in the Religious Influences Inquiry, although it was only supported to a small extent by studies of the religious experience of individuals, which were more or less taken for granted. This involved him in a confusion of thought because, although it is social behaviour which creates social institutions, and religious behaviour is in one sense also social, the essence of what is to be regarded as the 'religious' can only be found in a very special kind of individual experience. In truth, Booth was thus endeavouring to find in social phenomenon that which could only be traced in the personal lives rather than in the social experiences of individuals. William James, on the other hand, recognized explicitly that there was a 'great partition which divides the religious field', on one side of which lay the 'institutional', and on the other 'personal religion'. It was the 'more personal branch of religion', the 'inner dispositions of man himself, his conscience, his deserts, his helplessness, his incompleteness' which formed the centre of his interests.[2] He insisted, in fact, on the importance of the distinction between 'religion as an individual personal function', and religion as an 'institutional, corporate, or tribal product', asserting plainly and beyond possibility of misunderstanding that 'ecclesiastical institutions'

---

[1] It is strange that Charles Booth and William James appear to have been unaware of each other's existence. The similarities between the ideas embodied in the Religious Influences Series (of which the first volume was published in 1902), and in *The Varieties of Religious Experience* (First Edition, also 1902) may be explained on the ground that both authors reflected the outlook of the age and class in which they lived in regard to matters of religion.

[2] *The Varieties of Religious Experience*, Longmans Green & Co., Thirty-seventh Impression, 1928, pp. 28-9.

had hardly interested him at all.[1] But whilst the deeper significances of religion escaped Booth, because he made little or no contact with the religious life of individuals, James failed to grasp how it was that the religious life of individuals had been conditioned by the society in which it was lived, and he recognized at the end of his book that personal and institutional religion were more closely connected than he had assumed them to be at the beginning, being ultimately compelled to admit that they exercised a profound influence on each other.[2]

William James therefore saw with considerable perspicacity where the difficulties lay in the scientific analysis of religious experiences and behaviour. Had his clearer vision been available to Booth, the Religious Influences Inquiry might have succeeded in providing a much more sharply defined account of the structure of religious institutions, and a more penetrating and more useful explanation of their influences on the lives of individuals. If Booth's work had been available to James, he might have been able to develop a description of the religious life of the ordinary man that would have been much closer to realities than the account which he actually gave. Unlike James, Booth was able to develop a method of inquiry which was 'scientific' in so far as the evidence which was collected by using it was based on the statements, written and verbal, of the representatives of every religious body in London, and could therefore be taken at their face value as representative of religious life at large. But though this was an advance on James's methods, from the scientific point of view, it was not carried far enough to be decisive, enabling others to follow in his footsteps, to pursue his line of inquiry on a wider front, and to penetrate more deeply into the unknown.[3]

---

[1] William James seems to have considered that religion was endangered by social organization. As soon as ecclesiastical institutions came into being, they began to possess 'corporate ambitions of their own', and to become contaminated by 'the spirit of politics and the lust of dogmatic rule'. The common association that had arisen in men's minds between 'religion' and 'church' was, he thought, an unfortunate one. 'To some persons the word "church" suggests so much hypocrisy and tyranny and meanness and tenacity of superstition that in a wholesale, undiscriminating way they glory in saying that they are "down" on religion altogether.' Ibid., pp. 334-5.

[2] 'Men need formulas just as they need fellowship in worship.' The comparison between the institutional influences exercised on Protestants and Roman Catholics is very far-sighted. Ibid., pp. 459-61.

[3] James relied in the main on biographical and autobiographical accounts of the lives of very untypical people, supplemented by quotations from a wide variety of writings, theological, philosophical, and literary, believed by him to have a bearing on the subject of religious experience.

If it was the literary quality of *The Varieties of Religious Experience* which gave it its popular appeal and made it a classic source of reference throughout the succeeding half-century, it was the comparative success of Booth's methods of investigation which led all who gave serious consideration to his work to recognize the importance of the subjects with which he dealt. As one reviewer put it, he had demonstrated that those 'who exclude the mighty factor of Christianity from their sociological calculations are the victims of "childish obstinacy" or "unhistorical hallucinations"'.[1] On the other hand, it was perhaps the pessimistic tone of his writing and of his conclusions that prevented the use of the Series as he might be supposed to have hoped. As the same reviewer remarked, the results of the Inquiry could be sum-marized in a single phrase: it has revealed 'a decadence in ecclesiastical Christianity, unaccompanied by a corresponding decay of Christian belief itself'. Nevertheless, he had not made any suggestions whereby the more or less inarticulate goodwill of the masses could be translated into active support of one church or another, or given any reason for supposing that practical measures could be taken to stem the processes of decay. From the point of view of the churches, the argument of the Series appeared to end in a blind alley.

So far as its subject rather than its method is concerned, Booth's main contribution amounted to a demonstration that this decadence had in fact set in. This was especially true in so far as the working classes hardly came under the direct influence of the churches at all, whereas, at the time at least, they were very ready to follow the lead of socialist politicians, especially those at the head of the trade unions that were then rapidly growing in power. Furthermore, he was able to demon-strate in considerable detail that the decline in religious influence was due in some measure at least to social and economic factors. Religious institutions had become so disconnected from the wider society in the life of which they should have participated, that the endeavours of individuals of goodwill, intelligence and even of saintliness had ceased to exert anything like the decisive influence which might have stemmed the rising tide of disillusion. 'Taken as a whole', the 'efforts of the religious bodies to improve the conditions of life where they are lived (as in North London) fail'. 'In what sense London may be called "poverty-stricken",' Booth added, 'I have tried to gauge in many ways; so, too, in our present inquiry, we are gradually realizing in what sense London is "a heathen city".' Those who regarded 'all men

---

[1] *Journal of the Royal Statistical Society*, 1903, p. 398.

as open to receive the Gospel', were considered to be suffering from 'the optimistic delusion common among religious bodies'. The fact that the main features of Church work were shared by all denominations was simply explained, for 'what is done is just what can be done . . . amongst our population, since religious effort, no less than physical energy, moves along the line of least resistance'. There was no sign of a spiritual revival, and he found himself 'left to trace the Spirit of God working among many minds in many seemingly divergent ways'.[1] These were his last words, and the sentence may be regarded as the keynote of his work on the subject of religious influences.

His argument stopped at this point. He wisely refrained from prediction, and it is well that he did so, because his prophecies must have been falsified by the fact that his attention was directed towards the possibilities of improvement in the position of the churches, rather than the expectation of the onset of decay. It was not long before the whole scene began to change. A calamitous decline set in soon after the Religious Influences Inquiry was published, the origins of which were plainly evident in it. Fifty years later, the position of the churches at the time when Booth described them thus appeared to be one of 'terrific prosperity', setting a standard against which the potential strength of Christianity in England has since been measured.[2]

Although his somewhat negative conclusions can hardly have been what he had hoped for from his study of religious influences, Booth held firmly to the belief that religion could, and should, be made the object of sociological analysis. As he put it:

> Of the creation of man by God we know nothing. Of the creation of God by man we know almost everything. Not only are the records on the subject by far the best of human records, but the process in all its forms goes on today; intelligibly under our eyes. There is comparatively little mystery about it. We can watch men of all races struggling to find their God, as plants turn towards the light, and achieving faith in the reality of their own conceptions.[3]

His contemporaries agreed with him in his appraisal of the ultimate importance of spiritual values, and the publication of the Religious Influences Series placed him on the peak of his reputation. Few attempts have been made by sociologists since Booth's day, however, to describe and analyse the religious life of their own societies. His

---

[1] *Religious Influences* i, p. 156; iv, p. 23; vii, pp. 9-10, 415, 432.

[2] *Christian Newsletter*, 7 July 1948, pp. 8-9.

[3] Unpublished MSS., presumably drafted for the Religious Influences Series.

methods were, of course, novel, and because their use had not made it possible to understand the nature and significance of religious influences with any degree of precision, they were not utilized, still less improved on, by others, as had been the case with the Poverty Survey. This is, no doubt, partly due to the technical difficulties of studying so intangible an aspect of behaviour in the complex societies of the Western World, and it is a revealing fact that the investigation of the social functions of religion has been left to anthropologists working with non-literate or 'simpler' peoples. When, for example, the *New Survey of London Life and Labour* was being planned in the 1930s, it was decided only to examine the social as distinct from the religious work of the churches. It was recognized that the omission of any attempt to describe and measure the value of the latter left a gap unfilled, but it was also felt that:

such an attempt to weigh imponderables could not reasonably be expected to yield results fairly comparable with those set out in Charles Booth's volumes. Measurements of this kind are of all others the most delicate, and the most likely to be affected by the personal equation of the observer.[1]

Moreover, as has already been pointed out, no programme of action emerged from the Inquiry to help the leaders of the churches, as the old-age pensions campaign had resulted from the Poverty Inquiry, and the continuation of these researches therefore lacked the stimulus and support of practical need. Whether this tendency to ignore the Religious Influences Series is also to be attributed to the fact that there was a strong positivist trend in contemporary sociology is a moot point,[2] but there can only be general agreement with Lord Beveridge's comment made in 1948, that it was difficult to believe that any survey made at that time would have given space to the churches and their influences proportionate to that occupied by the Religious Influences Series in the Inquiry as a whole.[3]

---

[1] Vol. IX, p. 18.

[2] 'The knowledge which is supposed to be derived from revelation differs, it should be noted, in several important particulars from that which is based on science. . . . Revelation, if it is to rank as an independent extra-scientific source of knowledge, means something more than the emotions of awe or exaltation with which it is associated: it means those emotions, *plus* the overwhelming certainty of communion with God, and consequent conviction of his existence. A very considerable part of the human race shows no sign of having this experience in its totality.' Barbara Wootton, *Testament for Social Science*, Allen & Unwin, 1950, p. 102.

[3] *Voluntary Action*, Allen & Unwin, p. 224. It has also been suggested that the sociology of religion failed to flourish in England in the first half of the twentieth century as the

The Religious Influences Series has thus come to be regarded as an historical text providing an invaluable description of the organization and activities of the churches at the peak of their influence in London, rather than as a scientific inquiry which can be extended, corrected, and amplified by other researches. But at the mid-point of the twentieth century the social scientist has begun once more to study the network of beliefs in which the energy making civilized life possible has its origin.[1] Some of the more recent studies concerning religious beliefs and experiences have been carried out from a frankly rationalist standpoint,[2] whilst others, particularly those for which Christians have been responsible, have faced once more the fundamental problem that confronted Booth. Work of this latter type has rejected the positivist assumptions, the significance of which in the development of sociology is hard to exaggerate, and a new branch of sociology, the sociology of religion, has been making rapid progress.[3] In other words, there has been a reawakening of interest in the subject examined by Booth, in an age which can no longer take motives and objectives for granted. Since Booth explored with courage and energy those aspects of human experience of which the inner and fundamental realities are eternal, and endeavoured to develop methods of understanding their nature and significance in his own society, and since his writing is clearly related in historical perspective to our own, his work may well be regarded as of even greater importance in the second half of the twentieth century than was affirmed when it first appeared.

influence of the churches was steadily declining during this period, and the neglect of the Religious Influences Series may be accounted for in this way. See Norman Birnbaum, 'La Sociologie de la Religion en Grande-Bretagne', in *Archives de Sociologie des Religions*, 1956, No. 2, p. 16.

[1] As Hobhouse had put it a generation before: 'Social Science . . . cannot ignore the elements of idealism as a working factor, as one of the forces . . . among the other forces which it studies. . . . Thus the philosophical, the scientific, and the practical interest, however distinct in theory, tend in their actual operation to be intermingled, and it must be admitted that we cannot carry one through without reference to the other.' L. T. Hobhouse, *The Metaphysical Theory of the State*, Allen & Unwin, 1918, p. 15.

[2] In his study of the social psychology of religion, published under the title *Religious Behaviour* (Kegan Paul, 1958), Michael Argyle only mentioned Booth's work once, when referring to the relatively high degree of religious activity of the middle and upper classes (p. 130). This is disappointing, having regard to the special attention given in this book to the social factors connected with religious behaviour, such as social class and urban-rural differences, which were examined by Booth at considerable length.

[3] Earlier developments took place in France, under the leadership of Prof. Le Bras; for an example of empirical work carried out in England, see Conor K. Ward, 'Some Aspects of the Social Structure of a Roman Catholic Parish', *Sociological Review*, 1958, pp. 75–93; also *The Family in Contemporary Society*, S.P.C.K., 1958, especially pp. 2–3, 23.

12

Conclusion

THE final appraisal of Booth's work requires a discussion of his
contribution both to the social sciences and to social policy.
He would, in all probability, have been surprised if not rather
amused by the application of so seemingly pretentious a criterion to
the task of evaluating his achievements. He was, above all, a modest
man, and he regarded his work merely as a common-sense and
businesslike, if somewhat dull, effort to understand some important
social problems, and to get to grips with them. He did himself an
injustice, of course, but his self-appraisal is significant in so far as it
demonstrates that he did not regard himself as being in any sense a
competitor with his contemporaries for academic fame, able to produce the all-embracing (and verbose) concepts of Patrick Geddes, or to
indulge in the philosophical and somewhat remote subtleties of L. T.
Hobhouse. Neither did he want to do so. Unfortunately, however, the
world has tended to accept him at his own valuation. Booth's contemporaries were unable to appreciate his true originality, partly
because the issues which occupied the minds of the thinkers of his
generation were not directly related to the problems with which he
was concerned,[1] and partly because his work was not cast in a philosophical mould; its theoretical interest is by no means explicit, and
indeed, in no sense compels the attention of the unobservant reader.

[1] It must also be remembered that the chief philosophical interests which prevailed in
England at the end of the nineteenth century lay in the examination and criticism of the
metaphysical theory of the State. The significance of the work of the French philosophers
of the Enlightenment was obscured by the figure of Hegel; this loomed so large that
L. T. Hobhouse was still attempting to demolish it as late as 1918, as revivified by Green
and Bosanquet, when he published *The Metaphysical and Theory of the State*. The keynote
of the discussions which went on around Booth, and in which he played no part, was
a priori rather than empirical.

Half a century after the Inquiry was completed, however, it has become plain that it represents one of the first attempts to apply the methods of the natural sciences to the solution of the social problems of an industrial society.

It is perhaps surprising that so long a time should have elapsed since the onset of the Industrial Revolution before a serious endeavour of this kind was made. The very foundations of industrialism are built on applied science, and it might be supposed that the use of scientific methods of inquiry in the conquest of the material world would have been only too readily made use of in the treatment of the ills associated with the factory system. It has been suggested that the slowness of the growth of the social sciences has been due to the conservative tendencies which are deeply embedded in the organization of human society. 'From the point of view of the sociologist', writes Professor John Macmurray, 'the social conditions which determine the production of sociology are bound up with the effort of society to control its own organization and development through knowledge and understanding. The inhibition which has hitherto prevented this is the fear of breaking loose from traditional habits of social life.'[1] So far as England is concerned, it may be questioned whether a fear of this kind was a decisive force. From the beginning of the nineteenth century the influence of Bentham and the Utilitarians was profound, and one of their most striking characteristics was a contempt for tradition. History, in fact, meant little or nothing either to Bentham, or to Chadwick, the great administrative reformer of the day.[2] Mental inertia is an obviously untenable hypothesis if it is used to explain resistance to innovations in one respect, at a time when radical changes in both ideas and customs were being readily accepted in most other spheres of social life and thought.

Moreover, it was certainly not for lack of intellectual stimulus that scientific methods of social investigation and control were not evolved until so late in the Victorian era. The concepts had been formulated and the pathway ahead clearly signposted during the eighteenth century. The French Encyclopaedists had asserted the possibility of understanding the forces at work in human societies; Condorcet had thought it legitimate to apply mathematical techniques, in particular the calculus of probabilities, to the measurement and prediction of social phenomena. The belief was firmly established that social laws

[1] *The Boundaries of Science*, Faber & Faber, 1939, p. 68.
[2] See S. E. Finer, *The Life and Times of Sir Edwin Chadwick*, Methuen, 1952, pp. 14-15.

could be formulated on the model of natural laws, and human vice and misery be brought under control by obeying them.[1] These optimistic ideas were continued into the nineteenth century in the work of Saint-Simon and Comte. The positivist philosophy that ultimately emerged rejected conjecture in favour of the certainty that was expected to emerge from the scientific study of social phenomena; in particular, Comte repeated the assertion made a hundred years before that these phenomena could be described and understood in terms of natural laws.[2] The researches that were to establish this certainty, and formulate the laws on which it was to be based, never materialized, however. The work of the philosophers of the eighteenth century thus petered out, more or less, in a blind alley; the gulf between Comte's historical studies and the methods of the natural sciences was a wide one and was never bridged by the positivists. Comtism flourished for a period, it is true, but only as a peculiar religious sect. Despite its rationalistic tone, Comte's teaching had the emotional fervour of a missionary campaign; it was no more supported by generalizations that could be validated by appeals to evidence than were the dogmas and beliefs of the religion he sought to overthrow,[3] and if he rejected other people's *a priori* reasoning it was merely to replace it with his own.[4]

Though the positivism of the eighteenth and early nineteenth centuries provided more than sufficient intellectual stimulus for the creation of a science of society that could be applied to the task of improving social welfare, nothing of the kind emerged from it. On the other hand, the British philosophical radicals succeeded in some measure in overcoming the difficulties which the positivists had failed to surmount. Comtism was a conservative or, as might be said today, a reactionary philosophy, its starting-point being Comte's hostility to the Revolution; it embodied a fundamental contradiction in so far

[1] Eighteenth-century views on the nature and possibilities of the social sciences are discussed by C. H. Vereker, in *The Development of Social Theory*, Hutchinson's University Library, 1957, pp. 154-63. The influence of these ideas on the twentieth century is dealt with by F. A. Hayek, somewhat controversially, in *The Counter-Revolution of Science*, The Free Press, Glencoe, 1952, pp. 123-35. For a modern appraisal of the possibility of formulating sociological 'laws' see E. E. Evans-Pritchard, *Social Anthropology*, Cohen & West, 1951, pp. 57-9.

[2] Cf. G. D. H. Cole, 'Sociology and Social Policy', *The British Journal of Sociology*, 1957, p. 162.

[3] Ibid., p. 169.

[4] See Roger Soltau, *French Political Thought in the Nineteenth Century*, Ernest Benn, 1931, pp. 205-6.

as it was based simultaneously on the appeal to reason which had destroyed tradition in the eighteenth century, and an attempt to restore tradition in a new form, in the nineteenth.[1] Benthamism avoided this contradiction, for it was essentially forward-looking; having rejected tradition, the Benthamites sought to re-establish the polity and society of their day in accordance with rational principles. They accepted, rather than rejected, the Revolution, and sought to go forward from it, rather than retreat behind it. The future lay with them, and they created a lasting and influential school of thought. In two respects there were close similarities between the teachings of Positivism and Benthamism. Both were presented in the 'scientific' manner; both, moreover, showed the same weakening tendency to develop into a personal creed providing a motivation for action rather than a means of understanding social phenomena. Like so many sociological schools of thought that have flourished since, both Comtism and Benthamism ultimately became speculative systems that made use of facts concerning social life as illustrations of doctrines that were not open to question, rather than as supplying the philosophical context for inductive reasoning that might lead to the discovery of new knowledge, and the concepts in which this knowledge might be expressed.

If Comtism contributed little to the development of the social sciences, other than by way of keeping some of the ideas of the eighteenth century alive, and making one or two additions to our vocabulary, the Benthamites were active as the originators of reforms, and as the administrators who carried them out; to be effective as such they needed large quantities of precise evidence relating to the problems and the situations with which they were concerned. They thus created a demand for social information, and they produced much of the machinery for obtaining it. To a certain extent, therefore, the Benthamites laid the foundations on which the social sciences have been subsequently built; mainly as the result of their activities, the idea of painstaking inquiry into the social problems was by no means new when Booth first went to work.[2] The Census had already been begun in the first half of the nineteenth century, and was, indeed, a necessary prerequisite of the kind of inquiry which he developed; it provided him, moreover, with both the stimulus and the opportunity to undertake more detailed and more penetrating researches. It must also be

[1] Soltau, op. cit., pp. 206, 249.

[2] There was, of course, also a long-established tradition of social inquiry centred on the Poor Law, which has roots in reformist movements far older than Benthamism.

borne in mind that the expedient of the Royal Commission, so brilliantly exploited under Benthamite influences in the 1830s and 1840s, resulted in the production of a mass of information, and provided (as was intended) the basis for legislation on a large scale. The awakening of public opinion to what had come to be termed the Condition of England question had already stimulated the publication of a number of reports and surveys before Booth's Inquiry was planned, and he had, as it were, a ready-made audience to address. The ideas of extensive social investigations and the use of social statistics were, therefore, well established by the time his work began in the 1880s, and it is because of this that it is necessary to speak of it as 'one of the first', rather than 'the first' attempt to apply scientific method to the solution of social problems.[1] Nevertheless, there was too much that savoured of the doctrinaire in the work of the Benthamite administrators to make it necessary to deny Booth the bulk of the credit for the invention and first application of modern methods of social inquiry. Their objectives had been to propagandize rather than to inquire; their ideas were fully shaped in their minds, and ready to put into practice, before their inquiries began. The Royal Commissions of the 1830s and 1840s, for instance, had more often been influenced by the theories and beliefs of enthusiastic reformers than by the logic of hard facts, established by dispassionate methods of inquiry.[2]

The delay in the application of scientific method to social problems may therefore be attributed not to intellectual conservatism, but to excessive confidence in deductive reasoning as a foundation for social policy, and until the futility of this had become plainly apparent as the

---

[1] Booth's methods of inquiry were to some extent anticipated by the public health movement, particularly by the investigations into the social aspects of disease conducted by Dr. William Farr when serving as Compiler of Abstracts in the General Register Office. Sir John Simon praised his report on the cholera epidemic of 1848-9 as a 'classic in medical statistics', 'admirable for the skill' with which the information was analysed by districts and classes. (*English Sanitary Institutions*, Cassell & Co., 1890, p. 240.) His report on industrial mortality, published in 1875, was also of great importance as it laid the foundations for the Factory Act of 1878. (Sir George Newman, *The Building of a Nation's Health*, Macmillan & Co., 1939, p. 368.)

[2] As the Webbs pointed out, the Royal Commission on the Poor Laws of 1832-4 offended particularly badly in this way. All its active members, and practically all the Assistant Commissioners, 'started with an overwhelming intellectual prepossession, and they only made the very smallest effort to free their investigations and reports from bias'. (*English Poor Law History*: Part II; *The Last Hundred Years*. Longmans, 1929, Vol. 1, pp. 84-5.) Edwin Chadwick was, perhaps, the Benthamite who was most active in influencing the course of public inquiries. As the Secretary of the Royal Commission on the Health of Towns, appointed in 1843, he thought it his duty to 'precognize' all its witnesses, as well as draft its recommendations. (Sir John Simon, op. cit., p. 198.)

result of practical experience, no advance was possible. This experience arose out of acquaintance with the facts of slum life, and in Booth's day the tide had begun to turn against dogmatic theorizing of this kind.[1] He was, it is true, directly influenced as a young adult by British positivists, but the impression they made on his mind does not seem to have run very deeply. There was much talk of the discovery of the 'laws' which governed British society in his early writings, but, significantly enough, none of this was carried forward into his published work. In his maturity, he appears to have had no illusions as to the possibility of building any utopias on a foundation of reason alone; it is in the highest degree significant that he never used the language of 'enlightened' eighteenth-century thinkers. His belief in the possibility of accelerating progress and increasing virtue by the application of scientific knowledge was restrained, to say the least of it. He had, by the time he set to work on his Inquiry, dropped the notion that a materialist millennium was just around the corner, if he had ever entertained it. His initial objective was not to demonstrate the immense power of man's mind when applied to the reconstruction of society, but the much more modest one of using human intelligence to best effect in the identification and solution of a very practical problem; namely, the reduction of poverty to the smallest limits possible, and the promotion of social welfare by better administrative organization. To achieve this, he struck out on a line that was characteristic of him, and his own.

II

Victor Branford, writing just before the First World War, thought that though *Life and Labour* was the best known of the surveys of his day, it was 'perhaps the least used'.[2] So far as social philosophers and sociologists were concerned, there can be no doubt that the dictum was justified: the paradox it embodies may be explained by Booth's lack of interest in sociological theory, on the one hand, and on the other, by the equally marked lack of interest in social realities on the part of the sociologists of his day. It was these realities, and these only, that occupied his mind; his work was 'problem centred', as it would

---

[1] Booth's appraisal of the value of Royal Commissions is interesting, in this context. Though he considered them to be 'unwieldly as direct aids either to legislation or administration', they were 'admirable in the dialectical treatment of opposing suggestions and theories'. *Final*, p. 38.

[2] *Interpretations and Forecasts*, Duckworth, 1914, pp. 69-70.

now be described. For him, theories were only of value in so far as they threw light on social questions, and even then, only in so far as they could be used as a source of hypotheses which could be tested, and either validated or disproved. Nevertheless, there was more than enough theory implied in his work to give it force and significance as a sociological text, for his association with Comtean positivism had implanted a belief in his mind that it was possible to study these problems scientifically, just as his Unitarianism had left behind it an enduring interest in social welfare and the spiritual problems of mankind. But the theoretical foundations of his work were never made explicit, and his reputation as a social scientist still rests almost entirely on the practical results of the Poverty Survey.

If Booth has been recognized as 'the father of scientific social surveys', it is because of his analysis of poverty alone.[1] He has been classified with Rowntree and Bowley as providing the methodological basis of the social surveys of today, but only because of his calculations of the proportions of the population living in poverty and in overcrowded conditions.[2] His work has been acclaimed as a classic, and he has been adjudged the 'pioneer in local social surveys of the best accepted type carried out by private enterprise', without mention of either the Industry or the Religious Influences Inquiries as supporting evidence for the appraisal.[3] He has, in other words, come to be regarded as a superlatively successful statistician with an interest in social welfare. What has been said in the preceding chapters of this book leaves no doubt that, though this implies a tribute to him that is deserved, his work has nevertheless been grossly undervalued. Booth was, in fact, a great sociologist rather than a great statistician, even though the standard textbooks of sociology give him virtually no mention at all. Such recognition as he has been accorded in America comes either from the neo-positivists who are interested in his statistics as being what they regard as an elementary form of social measurement, or the social workers, who are interested in his work on poverty.[4]

---

[1] C. A. Moser, *Survey Methods in Social Investigation*, Heinemann, 1958, pp. 18-19.

[2] Mark Abrams, *Social Surveys and Social Action*, Heinemann, 1951, pp. 33-41. It is only the Poverty Series which is mentioned by A. F. Wells in his chapter on 'Social Surveys' in *The Study of Society* (Kegan Paul, 1939).

[3] D. Caradog Jones, *Social Surveys*, Hutchinson's University Library, n.d., pp. 34-53.

[4] His name does not appear in the indexes of any of the following: Ogburn and Nimkoff, *A Handbook of Sociology*, Kegan Paul, 1947; Kingsley Davis, *Human Society*, The Macmillan Company, Seventh Printing, 1955; Sutherland and Woodward, *Introductory Sociology*, Lippincott, revised edition, 1940; Logan Wilson and William A. Kolb,

In sum, the Inquiry has been classified as a survey designed to collect facts 'largely in order to form a basis for practical measures', rather than as one 'with a purely scientific aim'.[1]

This tendency to minimize the theoretical importance of Booth's work as contrasted with writings which contain all-embracing analyses and explanations of social phenomena, may have arisen to some extent from the fact that he neither built a system of thought himself, nor made any endeavour to show how his work could be fitted into anybody else's. Nor did he try to present a complete picture of the society in which he lived, for he left out of the discussion some of the more important social problems or questions of his day, such as birth control[2] and feminism, both intimately connected with the organization and functioning of the family as he knew it.

That this should have been so has been held to be due in some measure to the fundamental characteristics of his personality. Though Beatrice Webb credited him, for instance, with possessing 'the scientific impulse', she denied him 'the specific genius of Charles Darwin or Francis Galton for imaginative hypotheses and for verification by observation, experiment, and reasoning'.[3] The criticism is in any event an unfair one, having regard to the immense amount of work which Booth accomplished in the testing of hypotheses, but still more important than that, it fails to take account of his strongest claim to recognition as a scientist and sociologist, which lay in the formulation of questions which could be answered by objective inquiry. Had his mind been influenced more deeply than it was by systems, had it ranged more widely in the construction of 'imaginative' hypotheses, objectivity might have been sacrificed to theorizing, and his researches and their results would almost certainly have lacked the decisiveness and the compelling qualities that made them so profoundly influential in the formulation of social policy at the turn of the century. His interests were clearly 'scientific' in the sense that he attempted to provide an accurate analysis of the organization and problems of the society in

Sociological Analysis, Harcourt, Brace, 1949; H. E. Barnes, _An Introduction to the History of Sociology_, University of Chicago Press, 1948. The last book contains a chapter by Lewis Mumford on 'Patrick Geddes, Victor Branford, and Applied Sociology in England; the Social Survey, Regionalism and Town Planning', in which Booth's name is only mentioned once, when his work is compared unfavourably with that of Geddes.

[1] Wells, loc. cit., p. 434.

[2] This was given a very brief mention as an 'objectionable and ill-omened practice', which was 'filtering down' from the upper to the lower classes. _Final_, p. 46.

[3] _My Apprenticeship_, p. 220.

which he lived. His intention was not immediately 'practical' in the reformist sense, and if his Inquiry became the basis for administrative measures, that was entirely due to the power of the analysis and argument embodied in it.

Moreover, the suggestion that Booth's lack of interest in social theory made his work of small importance as a contribution to sociology ignores the special value of properly planned empirical studies in the development of the kind of theory that is directly applicable to social realities. As Professor Merton has pointed out, the process of empirical research undoubtedly 'raises conceptual issues which may long go undetected in theoretic inquiry'. It is also true that 'an explicitly formulated theory does not invariably precede empirical inquiry'; and it may be that 'as a matter of plain fact the theorist is not inevitably the lamp lighting the way to new observations. The sequence is often reversed.'[1] Basic research in areas in which problems are particularly evident can, then, advance theory whilst throwing more light on social problems, and thus satisfy both scientist and administrator simultaneously. It is because empirical research provides a peculiarly fertile ground for the growth of explanations concerning the nature of our societies, and because it provides the only way of testing them convincingly, that it must be recognized as essential to the advancement of sociological knowledge.

III

Booth's work might therefore have been expected to become the basis of an active school of empirical research in England. It may, indeed, have represented to some the dawn of a new era of sociological research, followed as it was in 1903 by the foundation of the Socio-logical Society.[2] His own position was, of course, essentially empirical. He asserted that he valued neither facts nor theories for their own sake; his conclusions had emerged after close study of relevant data and were evolved as a means of understanding their significance:

[1] Robert K. Merton, *Social Theory and Social Structure*, Free Press, 1949, p. iii.

[2] Booth appears to have played no part in the negotiations which took place in June and July 1903, leading to the foundation of the Society. He was away in Brazil at the time, but it is somewhat surprising that he was not sent a copy of the letter in which Victor Branford invited influential persons to give their support to it; the Inquiry was, however, mentioned in the general statement of aims, drafted by Branford, as an example of important sociological work. No other references to Booth can be found in the early records of the Society now deposited in the Library of the University College of North Staffordshire.

My own ideas have taken shape gradually in the course of my work. In beginning my enquiry I had no preconceived ideas, no theory to work up to, no pet scheme into agreement with which they would have to be squared.[1]

It soon became apparent, however, that these ideas were not well received by the English school of academic sociology which had been born at the turn of the century. Although there was no dogmatism in the ideas of this school as ultimately developed by Hobhouse, the latter adopted Spencer's methods, in so far as his theories were linked together into abstract systems, the relevant facts being treated as illustrative material rather than utilized as evidence whereby hypotheses could be validated or disproved. This point of view was the antithesis of Booth's own position; the classic example of it is that provided in 1858 by Spencer's account of his own methods of work:

> Within the last ten days my ideas on various matters have suddenly crystallized into a complete whole. Many things which were before lying separate have fallen into their places as harmonious parts of a system that admits of logical development from the simplest general principles. . . . In process of time I hope gradually to develop the system here sketched out.[2]

The sociologists of Booth's day thus tended to rely almost wholly on deduction, whilst he sought to blend deduction with induction, in a more truly scientific manner. A gulf thus came to separate them from him, and the dawn of the new sociological era proved to be a false one. This was tragic, because, surprisingly enough, the possibility of linking sociological research with the foundation of social policy was a theme that was common to Booth and the sociologists of the Hobhouse school.[3] The reason why this possibility was not pursued is open to speculation; the explanation appears to be that Hobhouse's attention was diverted from 'practical' activities of this kind by the sharp conflicts concerning the nature of sociological studies, particularly with Patrick Geddes and Victor Branford, which arose as soon as attempts were made to introduce them into the universities. There appears to be no evidence that Hobhouse ever gave any serious consideration to Booth's work, but he shared with Comte a belief that sociology should, as it matured, render increasingly possible an expansion of the area of

---

[1] *Poverty* i, p. 165. See, however, above, pp. 193, 214.

[2] *An Autobiography*, Williams & Norgate, Vol. II, 1904, p. 17. 'Spencer's idea of a tragedy', commented T. H. Huxley, 'is a deduction killed by a fact.' Ibid., p. 276.

[3] See L. T. Hobhouse, *The Metaphysical Theory of the State*, Allen & Unwin, 1918, especially pp. 14-15.

conscious control over the trends of human development,[1] and this was in full agreement with Booth's views. Had Hobhouse attempted to translate this dictum into practice, he would have found himself working alongside Booth, and the subsequent history of sociology in England might have been very different.

IV

When Booth's work was completed, a brief but bitter battle was about to be fought between what became two rival 'schools' of thought, represented by Hobhouse on the one hand, and, on the other by Geddes and Branford. The interests of the former were directed to the development of sociology as an academic subject, whilst those of the latter were chiefly in the direction of utilizing sociology as a means of advancing social welfare, especially through improving the planning of towns and civic services generally. The endowment by Martin White in 1907 of two chairs in Sociology at the London School of Economics necessarily involved the School in this difference of opinion. The appointment of E. A. Westermarck to one of these Chairs does not appear to have been the occasion of controversy. The other, it has been said, was intended for Geddes, but 'by some unhappy accident' associated with a lecture he had delivered, it went instead to Hobhouse.[2] The latter, however, soon found himself in collision with the more influential members of the Sociological Society,[3] and he resigned his editorship of the *Sociological Review*, after holding it for only three years, partly because of 'a divergence of view' as to its conduct.[4] From then on a split developed between the two schools which soon became permanent.[5] In the event, the academic school of

[1] J. A. Hobson and Morris Ginsberg, *L. T. Hobhouse*, Allen & Unwin, 1931, p. 101. As Professor Ginsberg has put it, 'the conception of a self-directed humanity is new, and as yet vague in the extreme. To work out its full theoretical implications, and . . . to inquire into the possibilities of its realization, may be said to be the ultimate object of sociology.' *Sociology*, Home University Library, Thornton Butterworth, 1934, p. 244.

[2] Lewis Mumford, loc. cit., p. 681. Out of friendship for him, Martin White had already endowed the part-time chair in Botany which Geddes occupied at Dundee. H. J. Fleure, 'Patrick Geddes (1854-1932)', *Sociological Review*, 1953, No. 2, p. 7. As to the peculiar terminology and construction of the lectures Geddes gave during this period in the London School of Economics, see Philip Mairet, *Pioneer of Sociology*, Lund Humphries, 1957, pp. 122-6.

[3] Geddes and his colleague Branford had played leading parts in its foundation.

[4] J. A. Hobson, in Hobson and Ginsberg, op. cit., p. 46.

[5] Booth associated himself in public with Geddes, when he took the Chair at meetings of the Sociological Society in 1904 and 1905, at which the latter read papers on

sociology took deeper root than that of Geddes and Branford, who were undisciplined thinkers; they did not, it has been said, suffer fools, 'particularly academic fools', gladly, and both were addicted to frequent and prolonged foreign travel. As a result, sociology gradually became, in the language of a follower of Geddes, 'another name for social philosophy',[1] in London and in British universities generally. The effect was to cut sociology, as a social science, off from its empirical roots.

Though Booth took no part in these academic disputes, they are of importance in the final appraisal of the value of his work, as their existence explains why attention was deflected from the Inquiry at a critical point in the development of sociological studies in England. It is plain that Geddes thought highly of Booth's work.[2] Booth, on the other hand, identified himself with Geddes,[3] but not very closely, for Geddes' ideas were those of a visionary who set out to save mankind from the evil fate of Victorian urbanism, a task which in no way

'Civics: As Applied Sociology' and 'Civics: As Concrete and Applied Sociology'. Geddes referred to the sterility of post-Comtean and post-Spencerian sociology as being explained by the lack of observation and analysis of living societies. Booth's work had, he said, been a 'fresh and freshening influence', 'as truly a return to nature as was Darwin's Voyage or his much more far-reaching studies in his garden and farmyard at home'. Booth replied to these polite remarks by saying that it was 'of the utmost value' to have large conceptions such as Geddes'. Nevertheless, he added that there was extreme difficulty in bringing investigations like Geddes' to practical conclusions. *Sociological Papers*, 1904 and 1905, Macmillan & Co., Vol. I, 1905, Vol. II, 1906.

1 Mumford, loc. cit., p. 686.

2 His comment on the Industry Series was that Booth was 'one of our . . . best Economists'. *Sociological Papers*, 1904, p. 135.

3 At the second of the meetings at which Booth took the Chair for Geddes when the latter presented a characteristically turgid paper, embellished with diagrams, Booth remarked, 'I feel always the inspiring character of Professor Geddes' addresses. He seems to widen and deepen the point of view, and to widen and deepen one's own ideas, and enables us to hold them more firmly and better than one can do without the aid of the kind of insight Professor Geddes has given into the methods of his own mind. I believe that we all hold our conceptions by some sort of tenure. I am afraid I hold mine by columns and statistics much underlined—a horribly prosaic sort of arrangement for everything. I remember a lady of my acquaintance who had a place for everything. The discovery of America was in the left-hand corner; the Papacy was in the middle; and for everything she had some local habitation in an imaginary world. Professor Geddes is far more ingenious than that, and it is most interesting and instructive and helpful to follow these charming diagrams which spring evidently from the method he himself uses in holding and forming his conceptions.' *Sociological Papers*, 1905, p. 112. This passage underlines the reservations in Booth's mind concerning Geddes' work; his doubt, though clear, was tactfully expressed, for he commented on Geddes' paper at the first meeting as 'one of the most complete and charming papers I have ever heard'. It seems possible that it was this paper which caused the dispute at the London School of Economics (*Sociological Papers*, 1904, p. 119).

appealed to Booth. 'Practical work', he stated from the Chair at one of Geddes' lectures, 'at present needs the most attention.'[1] On the other hand, Booth never made any use of the philosophical sociology of his age, though it is obvious that his work would have profited if he had given more adequate attention, for instance, to Spencer's historical perspective or to Le Play's methods of social survey. More intimate relations with academic sociologists might well have gone far to remedying some of the Inquiry's deficiencies.

As things were, his unwillingness to discuss the theoretical implications of his work had the unfortunate consequence of leaving his philosophical position suspended as it were in mid-air, between the 'science' of Comtism and the revelation of the Christian religion in one dimension, and in another, between the individualism of the classical economists and the socialism of his supporters in the campaign for old-age pensions. And so on. Still more important, Booth's isolation from academic sociologists had the effect of denying them the opportunity to discuss his work, and to appraise its true value. Had they become personally acquainted with him they would have found that he was no mere collector of facts or measurer of poverty; still less was he a doctrinaire doer-of-good of the kind associated with the Charity Organization Society. The discovery that he deliberately occupied a half-way position between concrete fact and abstract theory would have been stimulating in the highest degree to them. Moreover, as has already been pointed out, Hobhouse's sense of obligation in matters of social welfare needed no arousing; he might have been expected to meet Booth at least halfway in developing a common interest in such problems as those of poverty and old age.

V

In sum, Booth did not set out, like so many others, to build a pseudo-science designed to provide a complete explanation of the way of life of the world in which he lived. He did not pretend to understand this world without at the same time making an effort to evaluate what he observed, and, if need be, to criticize it and work for its improvement. His scheme of things was not an alternative to that which prevailed, as was the Comtean paradise, or the ultimate state of affairs envisaged by the apocalyptic teachings of the Marxists, or the Freudians. He was content to accept the current of his times as it

[1] *Sociological Papers*, 1904, p. 127.

flowed, rather than attempt to stem or deflect it into new channels; although he was inhibited to some extent by too ready an acceptance of individualist interpretations of social phenomena, he was un- hampered by the burden of dogmas and beliefs that would have brought him into collision with majority opinion. More positively, he accepted the values of his day and age explicitly, and sought to make them more effective by showing where and how they could be applied in everyday life. His influence was correspondingly great.

His ultimate objective was no less than to point the way ahead to the development of a valid study of social problems and organization which would take account of the presence in man of a wider and deeper nature than is implied in the mere fact of his existence as a 'social animal'. His work was done at a time when the understanding and control of the effects of advancing industrialism in England had be- come an urgent necessity. Information of an impressionistic type, such as had been collected together in Mayhew's *London Labour and the London Poor*, was of little assistance; the imaginative speculations of the utilitarian philosophers and others had outlived their usefulness. The latter had led to the formulation of oppressive and misleading doctrines concerning the condition of the poor, the former had produced nothing at all except perhaps sentimental misgivings and regrets. Before Booth's day, no serious attempt had been made to fit fact and theory together on anything like a large scale, otherwise than in the exposition of doctrine. It remained for him to try to place a firm foundation of evidence under theories relating to social structure and social behaviour, as had already been accomplished more than two centuries before in the natural sciences.

It is this endeavour to develop working hypotheses, and apply them to the conditions of a living society, that gives Booth his true signific- ance as a sociologist. History has shown that the task is a supremely difficult one to accomplish. Since Booth's day, the pendulum has swung from an excessive emphasis on theory, which carries with it the temptation to live a life untroubled by the cares of making relations with, and explaining oneself to, ordinary people, to the other extreme where an addiction to the pursuit of fact-collecting permits the sociologist to evade the anguish of original thought, and sometimes even the strains of elementary scholarship.[1] The mean between these

[1] The complaint that too much attention has been paid by British sociologists to 'fact- finding' can be justified only too easily. But Booth has been spoken of as having estab- lished a fact-finding tradition, against which Hobhouse led a 'revolt', and the Inquiry

extremes has proved to be so elusive that few have captured it for any length of time.[1] Moreover, although both British and American sociologists have on many occasions called for the carrying out of studies in which theory can be blended with fact, too few have themselves endeavoured to accomplish anything of the kind. Sir Alexander Carr-Saunders has, indeed, commented on a tendency to separate facts from interpretation, to emphasize the importance of the latter, and 'to suppose that the answer comes at the end, whereas in truth illumination comes in the handling of material and by the way'. Academic sociologists, moreover, are apt to pose large questions: 'They love to direct attack on a large front', but they have to face 'the immense complexity of social experience', with the result that

if a claim is made for any result of substance, it can usually be shown that relevant facts have been omitted or misinterpreted; or if care is taken to escape this criticism, the claim is for some generalization so thin, some formula so tenuous, that it provides no satisfaction.[2]

Booth's greatest achievement lay in the success with which he dealt with these difficulties. Operating on a broad front, he nevertheless penetrated it in depth, without sacrificing significance or accuracy in his results to any undue degree. He opened a door to further researches of this kind through which few have succeeded in passing, by reason of their lack of conceptual ability, technical skill, or the social qualities needed to make good relations with others. His line of approach was to select a series of problems which appeared to him, and to his fellow-citizens, to be urgently in need of examination, and then to proceed to examine them by whatever means seemed to be most appropriate, inventing new methods as he went on. The extent to which he shared the aspirations and the anxieties of his neighbours was one of his greatest assets; it gave him open access to the Englishman's home, and church, and indeed to the factory and the public-house as well; it gave him all the information he needed to write vivid descriptions of London neighbourhoods, of family life, and of Londoners at work.

has been found to be 'not only a milestone in the history of social surveys in England' but also 'symbolic of the turn taken by social research' in Great Britain. This seems to strain the evidence somewhat unduly. Booth was in no way addicted to the collection of facts 'for their own sake'. See W. J. H. Sprott, 'Sociology in Britain: Preoccupations', in Howard Becker and Alvin Boskoff, *Modern Sociological Theory in Continuity and Change*, The Dryden Press, 1957, pp. 607-9.

[1] See Nicholas S. Timasheff, *Sociological Theory*, Doubleday, 1955, p. vii.

[2] *The Social Sciences, Their Relations in Theory and in Teaching*, Le Play House Press, 1936, pp. 216-17.

It made it possible for him to blend extensive inquiries with intensive case-studies, and to build up a convincing argument, as in his treatment of the problems of old age, out of an amalgam of impersonal statistical information and the highly personalized social history of individuals, villages and Poor Law Unions. If Booth's work means anything at all to the twentieth century, it is because it demonstrates that there is an inseparable relationship between fact and theory which can be established as an essential element in successful social research.

Those who conduct such researches must start with an interest in a problem or a set of problems; this implies an evaluation of their relative importance according to a preconceived standard or criterion. They must also start with a conceptual framework in mind whereby the data they assemble may be analysed and ultimately understood; this implies the widest assumptions concerning the significance and nature of the knowledge they set out to acquire, which the philosophers may discuss *ad infinitum*.[1] As this is made explicit in Booth's researches it would be unjust to classify his work as that of an 'applied' sociologist, in the sense of a person who is supposed to do no more than 'shovel up the facts' needed by politicians and administrators;[2] it would also be impossible to comprehend it within these restricted terms. His achievement can, indeed, only be appraised as that of a scientist who seeks to gather facts in order to understand. It provides conclusive proof that in social research no clear cut distinction between theoretical speculation and practical application, such as is now frequently attempted, is either feasible or logically permissible.

VI

In addition to the contribution Booth made to the logic of the social sciences when he evolved a method of testing the truth of hypotheses, and demonstrated that his results could be verified by an appeal to the pragmatic test of their usefulness as a means of understanding social realities, he also added to sociological knowledge by extending the boundaries of social research to the point at which the more strictly 'social' became closely related to the 'moral' and the 'religious'. It was Booth's endeavour to link factual and statistical studies of social and economic behaviour with theoretical explanations

[1] Cf. Dorothy Emmet, *Function, Purpose, and Powers*, Macmillan, 1958, p. 13.

[2] T. H. Marshall, *The British Journal of Sociology*, 1953, p. 206; quoted Sprott, loc. cit., pp. 621-2.

of the same phenomena, rather than to keep the two apart,[1] which gives the Poverty and Industry Series their primary significance two generations later.[2] Though the theories they embody tend to be obscured by the facts which he collected in the course of his work, these Inquiries are essentially modern in outlook, if somewhat out of date in execution; their study involves no intellectual strain, no assimilation of new and strange concepts. In the Old Age Inquiry, however, Booth set out to demonstrate that an acceptance of certain basic moral principles made it necessary to adopt new methods of relieving the poverty of the aged; in other words, he linked fact, theory and obligation together in a single statement of explanation and evaluation. In the Religious Influences Series, moreover, he dealt with an aspect of human experience that he could only understand by the simultaneous use of social or psychological, and theological, moral, or philosophical concepts and methods; much of the language he used came to be foreign to later generations. The final outcome of the Religious Influences Inquiry was the conclusion that 'things hang together in a perplexing tangle of causation beyond possibility of unravelment'.[3] But the impossibility of unravelling this tangle was not, for him, only attributable to the inadequacy of the methods of inquiry at his disposal; for, as he put it when he was discussing the general problem of the improvements of social conditions, 'the moral question lies at the bottom. On it rests the economic; and on both is built up the standard of life and habit. Then all act and react on each other, and to be attacked, must be attacked together.'[4]

More often than not, when social scientists have attempted to study the problems of moral evaluation and religious belief, their labours have resulted in trivialities, or have failed to carry conviction with them. This is because they have assumed that the scientific method compels them to study the data as epiphenomena, and that their real nature can only be understood in terms of the operation of the unconscious mind, the influences of early upbringing, or the processes of social, economic, or institutional change.[5] Booth had to make up

---

[1] Or, as Barbara Wootton has remarked, 'carefully' segregating them, which she suggests was the practice of economists in the inter-war period. *Lament for Economics*, Allen & Unwin, 1938, pp. 113-14.

[2] Even as late as 1939, Barbara Wootton asserted flatly that, 'I can find very little evidence that the ability of economists to interpret concrete situations usefully has advanced appreciably during the past hundred years'. Ibid., p. 67.

[3] *Religious Influences* vi, p. 378.   [4] Ibid., i, p. 193.

[5] William James deals with these arguments, as stated at the turn of the century, in *The Varieties of Religious Experience*, pp. 10-25.

his mind when he decided how he was going to conduct the Religious
Influences Inquiry, whether or not he was going to assume that if a
rational element could not be found as the dominant factor in religious
life, then it had to be condemned as mere superstition. His decision
that what was truly religious could be distinguished from the super-
stitious and the crudely emotional, placed him alongside William
James, who adopted a similar point of view when he found himself
compelled to regard man's learning and science as only a part of his
mental life, and to assert that his intuitions came from more profound
sources than 'the loquacious level which rationalism inhabits'. The
rationalist account of human experiences was for him, indeed, only a
'relatively superficial' one.[1]

So far as social duties and individual motivations are concerned, the
point must be reached sooner or later by the social scientist who makes
them his concern (as Booth did in the Religious Influences Inquiry),
when ultimate ends or values are encountered which cannot be explained in terms of anything else.[2] Since his day, 'value-patterns' have
usually been dealt with by social scientists as part of, or as arising out
of, one form of social organization or another; although a certain
limited choice may sometimes be left open to the individual, the basic
pattern is, it is supposed, so firmly laid down that those who fail to
adjust themselves to it are regarded as misfits or 'cases', butts for the
censure of their neighbours, and perhaps in need of the care of a
social worker, or even of mental treatment. It is clear, however, that
this is an inadequate explanation of social realities. As Professor
Cole has argued, it leaves out of account the fact that 'changes in
value-patterns, if they occur, must come from somewhere, and cannot
be derived from the structure of expectations as it exists in the prevailing value pattern'. If the change ultimately stems, in one way or
another, from the mental processes of an individual or individuals,
rather than from the social processes of influence and interaction, then
the values of a society must be admitted to stem to this extent from an
extra-social source, and in the last analysis the positivist argument
falls to pieces.

As Booth found in religion a phenomenon that was both social and
extra-social, his presuppositions coincide with Professor Cole's argument. In so far as he accepted the reality of individual religious experience and moral responsibility, and in so far as the problem of

[1] Op. cit., p. 73.
[2] Cf. Wootton, *Testament for Social Science*, Allen & Unwin, 1950, p. 124.

poverty, as he studied it, called for action as well as understanding, the social world with which he was concerned was that of the ordinary man, rather than one created by the social scientist to make it possible to apply the methods of mechanistic science to human behaviour.[1] In brief, he attempted to achieve less than the Positivists in some respects, and more in others. Though, like them, he tried to show how religious institutions and behaviour were influenced by the social setting in which they were placed, he did not share their error of attempting to explain away religious behaviour by treating it as neither more nor less than a facet of social organization. It was, indeed, only too plain to him that mechanistic explanations were apt to lead into blind alleys of speculation rather than towards the widening of the frontiers of human knowledge. At the same time, he went further than the Positivists, in so far as he sought to show that a distinction had to be made between what was falsely claimed to be 'religion' or 'religious', and what was in fact 'true religion'. The former could be completely described and fully analysed in social terms; the latter embodied an element that transcended description and interpretation.

Booth's assessment of the religious content of social phenomena was the cause of the greatest difficulty to him, and his success in understanding it may appear meagre at first. He must nevertheless be given credit for having made an energetic attempt to widen the categories of social analysis so that they could be applied in some measure to the fuller and deeper realities of human experience, which had hitherto only been discussed in terms of the more abstract concepts of the moral philosopher and the theologian. In his work, social, moral, and theological thinking were brought together in a mutually supportive relationship with a success that has still to be equalled. In a few years' time, the greatest value of the Inquiry may well be found to lie in the fact that so successful an endeavour was made in it to mend the

---

[1] G. D. H. Cole, 'Sociology and Social Policy' in the *British Journal of Sociology*, 1957, pp. 162-3. The same problem is dealt with in a wider framework of argument in Lord Lindsay's *Religion, Science and Society in the Modern World*, Oxford University Press, 1943, pp. 39 seqq. See also Sir Alexander Carr-Saunders, *Natural Science and Social Science*, The Rathbone Memorial Lecture, Liverpool University Press, 1958, pp. 8-9. Speaking of the same problem, which arises in the discussion of the biological theory of holism, Sir Alexander Carr-Saunders adds: 'There is a suggestion of inevitability when social trends and movements are discussed and when the metaphors of growth, maturity and decay are used. It sometimes looks as though modern man had reverted to the state of mind of primitive man who believed that he was subject to forces which he could not control. But primitive man did believe that he could propitiate these forces by appropriate gifts and sacrifices. Modern man seems to think that he can do no more than detect the path and estimate the speed of the movements which carry him along.'

dangerous rift that had sundered scientific explanations of man's behaviour, from moral and theological discussions of human obligations. If this rift caused concern in the Victorian era, it profoundly disturbs both scientists and philosophers a century later.

VII

Though the value of Booth's work as a social scientist has too often been criticized, if not ignored, there is no division of opinion concerning the importance of his contributions to the formulation of social policy, and the praise which his work has received as affording the basis of, and pointing the way to, social reform has been unstinted and sincere. The standard histories of the nineteenth century have emphasized the significance of *Life and Labour in London*. 'Charles Booth', Professor Trevelyan has written, 'put the demand for old-age pensions on a scientific basis.' His 'scientific study of the London Poor ... did much to enlighten the world and to form opinion'.[1] Professor Ramsay Muir considered his work to be the 'greatest example' of sympathetic social inquiries; it was free from 'complacent pity', and refrained from advocating 'condescending and unavailing charity', for it dealt with 'maladies of the social order, which affected all classes, and which must be treated by communal action, based upon scientific study'.[2] In Booth's own day, Canon Barnett considered that his work had led to modification of public opinion. 'The facts, disputed or not, are preparing the public mind for reforms and for efforts. Perhaps this is the best result of any work. It is better to prepare the soil than pluck the flower.'[3] In sum, as it has been stated in *The Encyclopaedia of the Social Sciences*, Booth's influence in the field of social planning was 'as significant as that of the survey method in sociological generalization'.[4]

The widening of political responsibilities for the promotion of the welfare of society at large, involving the displacement of *laissez-faire* doctrines, has, indeed, been attributed by many authors to the impact on the public mind of the results of Booth's work. Both directly and indirectly, his influence was far-reaching; indirectly, in the effect he had upon public opinion and, in particular, upon the minds of young

[1] *British History in the Nineteenth Century*, Longmans Green & Co., Fifth Edition, 1924, p. 400.

[2] *A Short History of the British Commonwealth*, Vol. II, George Phillips & Sons, 1924, p. 683.

[3] *Canon Barnett, by His Wife*, John Murray, 1918, Vol. II, p. 54.   [4] Vol. XIV, p. 163.

men during their formative years; directly, in that he supplied the essential materials for schemes of practical reform.[1] Old Age Pensions were, of course, his own personal concern, but his influence can also be traced in the enactments and the administrative schemes which led to the establishment of labour exchanges, unemployment and health measures, trade boards and machinery for laying down minimum wages, and, ultimately to the break-up of the Poor Law.[2] The development of factory inspection and legislation owed much to his researches, which 'weakened the superstition about individual liberty as no amount of socialist theory could have done'.[3] 'The outstanding revelation came', Professor Beales has stated, 'with Booth's epoch-making survey.' It 'was the most notable product of systematic social investigation up to then attempted. It gained from its preoccupation with religion as well as social interests.' His demonstration of 'the social meaning of his statistics' was fresh and authoritative. Like the inquiries of the Poor Law Commission of 1905 to 1909, it was 'a massive landmark in the building up of our social code'.[4] A new line of thought was started, in so far as Booth's analysis of the conditions of poverty pointed away from the shortcomings of individuals, and towards the conditions in which poverty occurred. Over-emphasis on morals was thus replaced by more adequate attention to positive factors promoting the welfare of the people (such as education), or preventing destitution (such as the control of the 'sweated' trades).[5]

[1] When Lord Beveridge was an undergraduate at Balliol in 1903 the Master (Edward Caird) told him that 'while you are at the university, your first duty is self-culture, not politics or philanthropy. But . . . one thing that needs doing by some of you is to go and discover why, with so much wealth in Britain, there continues to be so much poverty, and how poverty can be cured.' Lord Beveridge adds that it was because of Booth's influence that Caird gave this advice. *Power and Influence*, p. 9.

[2] The background of this movement is described in Thomas Jones' *Lloyd George*, Oxford University Press, 1951. 'Throughout the eighties and nineties, at an increasing rate, the nation's awareness of what was comprehensively called "the social problem" had grown in width and depth. Charles Booth's *Life and Labour of the People of London* converted a vague emotional impression of metropolitan misery into facts and figures' (p. 33). See also Sir George Newman, *The Building of a Nation's Health*, Macmillan, 1939, p. 177: Booth's work 'illuminated the problem of public health, the effects upon it of destitution and of employment and unemployment, and furnished the medical officers of health with new data, method and ideal'.

[3] B. L. Hutchins and A. Harrison, *A History of Factory Legislation*, P. S. King & Son, 1911, p. 201.

[4] L. T. Hobhouse Memorial Trust Lecture, 1946: *The Making of Social Policy*, pp. 17-21.

[5] Lord Attlee has stated the opinion that Booth's estimate of poverty 'dispelled for ever the complacent assumption that the bulk of the people were able to keep themselves in tolerable comfort', and that 'poverty was mainly due to the moral deficiencies of individuals'. (C. R. Attlee, *The Social Worker*, G. Bell & Sons, 1920, p. 235.)

It may seem at first sight strange that although Booth contributed so much to the policies and practices of legislation and administration in his own lifetime, he should apparently have had so little direct influence on his outstanding contemporaries. Though Octavia Hill remained a lifelong friend, she was never able to approve of his support of the campaign for old-age pensions, and all that it implied.[1] Sir Charles Loch, again, was always his inveterate opponent. To him, Booth's definition of poverty was fundamentally unsound because it did not deal with the 'social habits' which, in his opinion, were the real cause of poverty. Although Booth had had no hand in their formulation, Loch attributed the recommendations of the Minority Report of the Royal Commission on the Poor Laws, which he thought would create a 'huge industrial villeinage', to the bad influence of 'social investigation'; this, 'divorced from social science' (or, in other words, from the theoretical preoccupations which were an integral part of the faith of the leaders of the Charity Organization Society) had 'led the people astray'.[2]

In general, it was the fact that Booth laid so much stress on the combination of socialism and individualism, which he referred to as 'limited socialism', 'a socialism which shall leave untouched the forces of individualism and the sources of wealth',[3] that prevented those who were officially identified with the cause of charity from welcoming his work. There was, in truth, nothing that was essential to his conclusions and recommendations that should have alienated him from the sympathies of those whose cause was the welfare of the individual, the righting of his wrongs and the alleviation of his sufferings. But there was at the time so deep-rooted a fear of Socialism, in some ways similar to that occasioned by Communism in the mid-twentieth century, that what Booth had to say could not be listened to dispassionately by many of his contemporaries. 'Socialism', 'individualism' and 'collectivism' are abstract conceptions the use of which by individual authors is frequently inconsistent and obscure, and when Booth used the expression 'socialism' he certainly did not attach to the term the meaning that it had acquired for the Webbs, for instance. However true this may have been, Booth's use of the term 'socialism' and his

[1] Thanking a friend for the loan of the First Edition in 1890, she told her that 'I know in my heart of hearts, what I think; and *that* is that it all depends on the spiritual and personal power; and *that* we must measure, if at all, in the courts, rather than in the book'. *Life of Octavia Hill as Told in Her Letters*, ed. C. Edmund Maurice, Macmillan & Co., 1913, p. 515.

[2] *Charity and Social Life*, Macmillan & Co., 1910, pp. 386-9.   [3] *Poverty* i, p. 177.

advocacy of old-age pensions aroused prejudices in the minds of his critics which never died down.

VIII

The confusion which surrounded the argument continued throughout Booth's life. For Dicey, probably the best-known of the Victorian authors who discussed the problem, collectivism was synonomous with socialism, which he defined as the school of opinion 'which favours the intervention of the State, even at some sacrifice of individual freedom, for the purpose of conferring benefit on the mass of the people'.[1] In this sense Booth was undoubtedly a socialist. But he was certainly not a socialist in the opprobrious terms of Dicey's more extreme definitions, as, for instance, when the latter stated that 'the weak point of the socialistic ideal is that it is a dogmatic or authoritative creed and encourages enthusiasts who hold it to think lightly of individual freedom, and suggests the very dubious idea that in a democracy the wish of the people may often be overruled for the good of the people.'[2] Booth, in truth, was an example of the kind of Conservative who came into much greater prominence in the generation which succeeded him, namely, one who was prepared to accept collectivist measures if he was convinced that they could be based on the established traditions of British public life, and would add directly to the sum total of the welfare of the nation as a whole. Dicey almost discovered this for himself, when he expressed the hope that 'we may carry the individualistic virtues and laws of the nineteenth century into the twentieth century, and then blend them with the socialistic virtues of a coming age', adding immediately afterwards that the views put forward by Booth in *Industrial Unrest and Trade Union Policy* as to the possibility of reconciling the conflict between capital and labour suggested 'the mode by which the end may be accomplished'.[3]

If, therefore, the social workers of Booth's day, such as Sir Charles Loch and Octavia Hill, had not been prevented by their dogmatic presuppositions and inflexibility of thought, they might have recognized that the way ahead towards social advancement lay in the direction which Dicey indicated,[4] and realized that Booth's work was

[1] *Law and Opinion in England*, Macmillan & Co., Second Edition, 1917, pp. lxxiv, 64. 'Collectivism', he added, 'is a hope of social regeneration.' Ibid., p. 69.

[2] Ibid., p. lxiii.   [3] Ibid., p. xcii.

[4] The first edition of *Law and Opinion* appeared in 1905.

SCB

an essentially constructive, and conservative, contribution to it. They might also have been able to understand, with less difficulty, that Booth's sympathies lay with the social workers and administrators who were bearing the burden of alleviating the sufferings of the masses of the poverty-stricken. Equally, his redefinition of poverty should have been made the beginning of a new phase in their work. As long as poverty was regarded as an infliction of Providence, the only realistic attitude was to preach resignation to the victim and charity to the more fortunate. By revealing the deeper nature of poverty, however, Booth demolished once and for all the philosophy of acceptance. By analysing the factors which contributed to poverty, he made both a cure of a large part of the disease possible, and, still more important, he showed how much of it could be prevented. The bogy of 'the poor' was reduced to a pathetic rather than a frightening figure, and the eradication of poverty became an obligation imposed on all responsible citizens.

Furthermore, Booth's talent for seeing the individual as an individual albeit in relationship to the society in which he lived, was in close accord with the desire of such leaders of social thought as Octavia Hill to regard the individual with respect. Not only did he approach his poorer fellow-citizens with a reverence which must have been a source of astonishment to many of his own class, but his genuine regard for their way of life, which he thought enviable in some respects at least, must also have been a cause of concern to many. His claim that there are both social and emotional compensations to be offset against the more obvious miseries of 'the poor' must be classed as a major contribution to urban sociology. It is one which has been consistently and regrettably overlooked by his successors, who have assumed far too readily that the middle-class way of life is intrinsically better than that of the classes 'beneath' them. The balance only began to be redeemed in the work of social scientists fifty years after he completed his researches. Moreover, he never posed as a 'detached' social scientist who persuades himself that, by keeping aloof from the world's affairs, he can maintain his objectivity. It has, indeed, been suggested that it was his active and energetic participation in the movement for social reform that was one of the signal qualities of his greatness as a social scientist,[1] and the concern which he felt for the problems of

---

[1] This, it has been said, has given meaning and purpose to 'a large proportion of the most memorable social scientists of the past century. . . . There is a strangely neglected uniformity in the aspirations of these great men. Comte's altruism, Le Play's paternalism,

poverty can be thought of as a source of strength to him rather than a cause of weakness. The person who by virtue of his investigations identifies himself with the troubles of his fellow-citizens, but who resolutely refuses to accept any responsibility for their alleviation, must in some measure be regarded as lacking in moral qualities. In such a person the strength of purpose which is required for the successful completion of research projects is also likely to be lacking in corresponding degree. This may account for the failure of many in the field of inquiry in which Booth was so successful.

Booth was also well aware that the point of view of the social worker could not be expressed in statistical language:

> It is difficult for those whose daily experience or whose imagination brings vividly before them the trials and sorrows of individual lives, to think in terms of percentages rather than numbers. They refuse to set off and balance the happy hours of the same class, or even of the same people, against these miseries; much less can they consent to bring the lot of other classes into the account, add up the opposing figures, and contentedly carry forward a credit balance. In the arithmetic of woe they can only add or multiply, they cannot subtract or divide. In intensity of feeling such as this, and not in statistics, lies the power to move the world.[1]

Booth claimed no more than that 'by statistics must this power be guided if it would move the world aright'. He never lost sight of the individual citizen as the ultimate reality when problems of social policy and administration were under consideration. It was perhaps this quality, more than any other, which made his work one of the most powerful forces which led to the creation of an imposing array of new social services in the decade preceding the outbreak of the First World War.

IX

Still more important, Booth's work represents a watershed in the history of British social policy in another and quite different sense. Until his researches had been published, policy rested on a basis of beliefs and of doctrines, only corrected to a limited extent by observing the results of applying them in practice. After his work had become

Booth's genuine concern for the relief of poverty, the fervid ecological propaganda of Geddes, for each of them the stimulus of social curiosity would by itself have been patently inadequate.' John Madge, *The Tools of Social Science*, Longmans Green & Co., 1953, p. 17.

[1] *Final*, p. 178.

SCB*

generally known, no amendment of social policy was possible without a carefully tested appeal to experience and the evaluation of proposals in the light of the relevant evidence.[1] In other words, a new attitude of mind was created towards the study of the problems of contemporary society,[2] which has had as deep an impact on the treatment of the mentally ill and the criminal, and the care of the deprived child, as it has had on the more restricted problem of the relief of poverty. It has proved, indeed, to be the most powerful tool which has been used in the creation of the Welfare State.[3]

In this way Booth provided the nation with a new instrument of government. His avoidance of the doctrinaire, and his determination to arrive at the truth irrespective of beliefs and dogmas led him to collect information and propound views which representatives of all schools of thought, even those with which he was entirely out of sympathy, could use. And they did so, in full measure. He thus introduced an element of continuity and stability into British social policy and public life, which made it possible for the British nation to undergo without signs of excessive stresses and strains, and in a common-sense and businesslike way, the social revolutions of the first half of the twentieth century.

It has been suggested that it was 'the coincidence of anxieties about the maintenance of competitive economic efficiency, the consequences of a widened franchise, the spread of socialism and the threats of war' which gave Booth's 'massive certainties their political cutting edge, and social policy its twentieth century setting'.[4] To say this is only to

---

[1] Though generally true, these statements require a certain measure of qualification. As has already been made clear, much had already been accomplished in the field of public health before Booth's day to relate policy to evidence (see above, pp. 244-5). Moreover, even today policy recommendations are still sometimes largely based on doctrine, as in the case of the Royal Commission on Marriage and Divorce of 1951-5.

[2] *The British Social Services*, Political and Economic Planning, 1937, p. 43.

[3] Booth's influence on the shaping of postwar social policy appears to have been potent, and at times direct if not explicit. For instance, Lord Beveridge's Report on *Social Insurances and Allied Services* contained the picturesque remark that 'Want is one only of five giants on the road of reconstruction and in some ways the easiest to attack. The others are Disease, Ignorance, Squalor and Idleness' (para. 8). The similarity to Booth's equally colourful writing on the same subject is too close to be merely coincidental. For him, 'East London lay hidden from view behind a curtain on which were painted terrible pictures: Starving children, suffering women, overworked men: horrors of drunkenness and vice; monsters and demons of inhumanity; giants of disease and despair.' First Edition i, p. 591.

[4] O. R. McGregor, 'Social Research and Social Policy', in the *British Journal of Sociology*, 1957, p. 157.

emphasize rather than to explain away the profoundly important contribution which he made to British social history. The nurture and conservation of the nation's strength in the conditions of a new industrial age, and its mobilization in two world wars, have been attributable in no small measure to the social unity and vitality that came from the practical application of his methods. It was the laying bare and the facing of unpleasant truths, which he accomplished almost single-handed, that has led to the eradication of so many social ills, and ultimately to the building of a new, a stronger, and a better community in the postwar world.

Appendices

Published Works by Charles Booth

1889.   *Life and Labour of the People.* Volume 1.
1891.   *Labour and Life of the People.* Volumes 2.
1892.   *Pauperism, a Picture, and the Endowment of Old Age, an Argument.*
1892-1897.   *Life and Labour of the People in London,* 9 volumes (Second Edition).
1894.   *The Aged Poor in England and Wales: Condition.*
1899.   *Old Age Pensions and the Aged Poor: a Proposal.*
1901.   *Improved Means of Locomotion as a First Step towards the Cure for the Housing Difficulties of London.* (Pamphlet.)
1902-1903.   *Life and Labour of the People in London,* 17 volumes (Third Edition).
1910.   *Poor Law Reform* (92 pp.).
      Reform of the Poor Law by the Adaptation of the Existing Poor Law Areas, and Their Administration (38 pp.).
1911.   *Comments on Proposals for the Reform of the Poor Laws,* with note by Sir Arthur Downes (23 pp.).
1913.   *Industrial Unrest and Trade Union Policy* (32 pp.).

All the above, with one exception, were published by Macmillan & Co.; the first edition of *Life and Labour* was published by Williams and Norgate.

Papers read before the Royal Statistical Society and printed in the Society's Journal

1886.   'Occupations of the People of the United Kingdom, 1841-81, being a re-statement of the figures given in the Census returns arranged to facilitate comparison' (Vol. XLIX, pp. 314-435).
1887.   'The Inhabitants of the Tower Hamlets (School Board Division), their Condition and Occupations' (Volume L, pp. 326-91).
1888.   'Conditions and Occupations of the People of East London and Hackney, 1887' (Volume LI, pp. 276-331).
1891.   'Enumeration and Classification of Paupers, and State Pensions for the Aged' (Volume LIV, pp. 600-43).
1892.   Presidential Address: 'Dock and Wharf Labour' (Volume LV, pp. 521-57).
1893.   Presidential Address: 'Life and Labour of the People in London: first results of an Inquiry based on the 1891 Census' (Volume LVI, pp. 557-93).
1894.   'Statistics of Pauperism in Old Age' (Volume LVII, pp. 235-45).

Specimen page from *Life and Labour*[1]

Flint Street The lady visitor to whose notes on this street we have had access makes it better than it looks, and better than other reports have led us to expect. It looks very poor, very bad, and above all, very uncomfortable. It is rather a wide street, and the houses are of three storeys. Its situation is retired but rather good; not too far away from the centre of things and very handy to a main thoroughfare, well served by omnibus and tram-cars. It is one of a group of streets; and all of them have gone wrong and become the habitations of a very low class, of which the individuals come and go while the types are constant. Many of the lowest quarters of London, however much we may deplore the existence alike of the places and their inhabitants, give an impression of ease in life, rather pleasant in its way, provided no outside standard be invoked. It is not so here; and after each visit to this place I have come away without any relief from its depressing influence, without seeing any of the more agreeable features of human life. I do not doubt that they exist; but all that usually can be seen is dull, miserable, ill-conditioned, squalid poverty. The houses are six-roomed, two rooms on each floor, and are all alike except two shops in the middle of the row. A sample follows:

No.		Rms.	Pers.			
15	ground front	1	1	(B)	Woman and 1 child.	Several children away. Girl at school.
	back	unknown				
	first front	1	empty	(D)		
	first back	2	3	(D)	Man, wife, and 1 child.	Man in regular work.
	top floor	1	empty			
17	ground floor	2	3	(C)	Man, wife, and 1 child.	Cab-washer. Boy at school. One girl in service. Nearly always starving.
	first floor	2	2	(D)	Man and wife.	
	top floor	2	8	(C)	Man, wife, and 6 children.	Bricklayer, decent man, often out of work in winter. Wife drinks. Eldest boy and girl go to work.

[1] *Poverty* ii, p. 88.

No.		Rms.	Pers.			
19	ground floor	2	2	(D)	Man and wife.	Middle-aged people. May have children but none here.
	first floor	2	4	(C)	Man, wife, and 2 children.	Casual man.
	top floor back	2	4	(A)	Widow and 3 children.	Big girl, and 2 little ones at school. A bad lot.

[The capital letters indicate the social class to which the household was estimated to belong. The street as a whole was allocated to Class B, mixed with A.]

Note on Booth's system of classification by Classes and Sections[1]

THE social Classes and occupational Sections were dealt with separately by Booth in his first Paper in 1887; the descriptions of the Sections were amalgamated with those of the Classes when the material in his two Royal Statistical Society papers was republished in Vol. I of the First Series. This may indicate a recognition on his part that social and economic conditions are inextricably interwoven. The 'double classification' was adopted in the first instance because 'no possible classification by employment' would 'serve also to divide the people according to means'; on the other hand, 'most sections contribute to more than one class, and each class is made up of many sections'. There was, however, a clear correspondence between the 'Classes' and the 'Sections'. The two classifications converge on the six divisions of ordinary labour, there divisions having been made to match the six 'Classes'. Thus Sections 1 and 2 (loafers and casual workers) were equated with Classes A and B respectively, 3 containing both 'very poor' and 'poor', 4 representing exactly the definition of 'poor', 5 being 'almost entirely above the line of poverty' whilst 6 corresponded with Class F.

The individual Classes were described by Booth as follows:

(A) The 'Lowest Class consists of semi-occasional labourers, street-sellers, loafers, criminals, and semi-criminals'. 'Homeless outcasts who take shelter where they can.' Casual labourers 'of low character . . . their life is the life of savages, with vicissitudes of extreme hardship and occasional excess. Their food is of the coarsest description, and their only luxury is drink. . . . From these come the battered figures who slouch through streets, and play the beggar or the bully, or help to foul the record of the unemployed; they are the vast class of corner men who hang round the doors of public-houses, the young men who spring forward on any chance to earn a copper, the ready material for disorder when occasion serves. They render no useful service, they create no useful wealth: more often they destroy it. They degrade whatever they touch, and as individuals are perhaps incapable of improvement; they may be to some extent a necessary evil in every large city, but their numbers will be affected by the economical conditions of the class above them, and the discretion of the "charitable world"; their way of life by the pressure of police supervision. . . . They are barbarians, but they are a handful, a small and decreasing percentage, a disgrace but not a danger'. 'Those who are able to

1 Based on *Poverty* i, pp. 33 et seq.

work the mud may find some gems in it. There are, at any rate, many very piteous cases.'

(B) *Casual Earnings.* This class included widows or deserted women and all those, even artisans and clerks, who 'failing to find a living in their own trade, compete at the dock gates for work'. Such men 'do not on the average get as much as three days' work a week, but it is doubtful if many of them could or would work full time for long together if they had the opportunity'. Many of the members of this class, except the poor women, 'are inevitably poor' 'from shiftlessness, helplessness, idleness or drink. The ideal of such persons is to work when they like and play when they like; these it is who are rightly called "the leisure class" amongst the poor—leisure bounded very closely by the pressure of want, but habitual to the extent of second nature. They cannot stand the regularity and dullness of civilized existence, and find the excitement they need in the life of the streets, or at home as spectators of or participators in some highly coloured domestic scene. There is drunkenness in this, especially amongst the women; but drink is not their special luxury, as with the lowest class, nor is it their passion, as with a portion of those with higher wages and irregular but severe work. The wives in this class mostly do some work, and those who are sober, perhaps, work more steadily than the men; but their work is mostly of a rough kind, or is done for others almost as poor as themselves. It is in all cases wretchedly paid, so that if they earn the rent they do very well.' 'Both boys and girls get employment without much difficulty.' The class 'is not one in which men are born to live and die, so much as a deposit of them who from mental, moral, and physical reasons are incapable of better work.'

(C) *Intermittent Earnings.* The workers 'are more than any others the victims of competition, and on them falls with particular severity the weight of recurrent depressions of trade'. It includes labourers, many of the poorer artisans, street sellers, and small shopkeepers. 'Here may perhaps be found the most proper field for systematic charitable assistance; provided always some evidence of thrift is made the pre-condition or consequence of assistance.' Some casual workers earn very high wages. 'These are men of great physical strength, working on coal or grain, or combining aptitude and practice with strength, as in handling timber. It is amongst such men, particularly those conveying grain or coal, that the passion for drink is most developed.' 'In this class the women usually work or seek for work when the men have none; they do charing, washing, or needlework, for very little money; they bring no particular skill or persistent effort to what they do, and the work done is of slight value. Those who work the most regularly and are the best paid are the widows.'

(D) *Small Regular Earnings.* This includes men at the better end of the casual dock and waterside labour, those having directly or indirectly a preference for employment. It includes also a number of labourers in the gas works whose employment falls short in summer, but never entirely ceases. 'The rest are men in regular work all the year round at a wage not exceeding 21s. a week. These are drawn from various sources, including in their numbers factory, dock, and warehouse labourers, carmen, messengers, porters, etc.; a few of each class. Some of them are recently married men, who will, after a longer period of service, rise into the next class; some old and superannuated, semi-pensioners; but others are heads of families, and instances are to be met with . . . in which men had remained fifteen or twenty years at a stationary wage of 21s., being in a comparatively comfortable position at the start, but getting poorer and poorer as their family increased, and improving again as their children became able to add their quota to the family income. In such cases the loss of elder children is sometimes looked upon with jealous disfavour. None can be said to rise above poverty, unless by the earnings of the children, nor are many to be classed as very poor. What they have comes in regularly, except in times of sickness in the family, actual want rarely presses, unless the wife drinks. As a general rule these men have a hard struggle to make ends meet, but they are, as a body, decent steady men, paying their way and bringing up their children respectably. The work they do requires little skill or intelligence. . . . The women work a good deal to eke out the men's earnings, and the children begin to make more than they cost when free from school: the sons go as van boys, errand boys, etc., and the daughters into daily service, or into factories or help the mother with whatever she has in hand. The comfort of the home depends, even more than in other classes, on a good wife. Thrift of the "make-the-most-of-everything" kind is what is needed, and in very many cases must be present, or it would be impossible to keep up so respectable an appearance as is done on so small an income.'

(E) *Regular Standard Earnings.* This includes the bulk of those with wages of from 22s. to 30s. in regular work, 'together with the best class of street sellers and general dealers, a large proportion of the small shopkeepers, the best off amongst the home manufacturers, and some of the small employers'. 'The bulk lead independent lives, and possess fairly comfortable homes. As a rule the wives do not work, but all the children do, the boys commonly following the father . . . the girls taking to local trades, or going out to service.' Those in this class 'take readily any gratuities which fall in their way, and all those who constitute it will mutually give or receive friendly help without sense of patronage, or degradation; but against anything which could be called charity their pride rises stiffly. This class is the recognized field of all forms of co-operation and combination, and I believe, and am glad to believe, that it holds its future in its own hands.'

(F) *Higher-class Labour.* This consists of the 'best paid of the artisans, together with others of equal means and position'. 'This is not a large section of the people, but it is a distinct and honourable one. These men are the non-commissioned officers of the industrial army. . . . They supply no initiative, and having no responsibility of this kind they do not share in the profits; but their services are very valuable, and their pay enables them to live reasonably comfortable lives, and provide adequately for old age. No large business could be conducted without such men as its pillars of support, and their loyalty and devotion to those whom they serve is very noteworthy. . . . The foreman of ordinary labour generally sees things from the employer's point of view, while the skilled artisan sees them from the point of view of the employed. Considered with this fact it is to be observed that the foremen are a more contented set of men than the most prosperous artisans.' The sons of those in this class 'take places as clerks, and their daughters get employment in first-class shops or places of business; if the wives work at all, they either keep a shop, or employ girls at laundry work or dressmaking'.

(G) *Lower Middle Class.* 'Shopkeepers and small employers, clerks, etc., and subordinate professional men. A hard-working, sober, energetic class.'

(H) *Upper Middle Class.* 'The servant-keeping class.'

Booth commented that 'an account of the life of each of the several classes that are grouped under the letters G and H would be very interesting, but is beyond the scope of this book'. (*Poverty* ii, p. 22.)

APPENDIX IV

Note on Booth's definition of 'Poverty'

THE phrases 'above the line of poverty' and 'on the line' were first used in the First Paper in 1887 (e.g. pp. 329, 339, 375), but Booth never achieved a clear definition of 'poverty'. His explanation of his use of the term has always been assumed to be much more precise than it was; it embodies a reference to a weekly income, but it is important to note (a) that the figures only gave the limits within which the wages of the 'poor' were supposed to fall, and these were fairly wide; (b) it was intended to apply to a 'moderate' family, which was never precisely defined; (c) it was only given for illustrative purposes and (d) no indication was given of the level of income of the 'very poor' family.

The full passage containing Booth's first definition is reproduced in Chapter 9, p. 184. In his Second Paper, delivered in 1888, Booth agreed that his 'division of the people into "poor" and "very poor"' was 'arbitrary' (a point to be reiterated in his *Final Volume*), but he saw no reason to alter the definition given in the First Paper; he did, however, rephrase it, repeating the estimates of income as an illustration, and adding that the ' "poor" are those whose means may be sufficient, but are barely sufficient, for decent independent life; the "very poor" are those whose means are insufficient for this according to the usual standard of life in this country. My "poor" may be described as living under a struggle to obtain the necessaries of life and make both ends meet; while the "very poor" live in a state of chronic want' (p. 278). He also elaborated his distinction between poverty, want, and distress. 'Want is an aggravated form of Poverty, and Distress is an aggravated form of Want. The distinction is relative: I recognize a degree of poverty that does not amount to want, and a degree of want that does not amount to distress.' In order to throw more light on the situation and in particular on 'the causes of distress', Booth undertook an analysis of 4,000 cases of the 'poor' and 'very poor', in which low pay was classified as only one amongst a total of nine causes of poverty (20 per cent.). (Low pay was combined with irregular work in the case of 'great poverty', which together amounted to 9 per cent. of the total, casual work accounting for 43 per cent. (p. 294).)

In Volume One of the First Edition, Booth reprinted the relevant section from the Second Paper without modification (p. 33). He also noted the fact that a man who earned a regular income of 21s. a week or less for fifteen or twenty years might be in a comfortable position at the start, and then find himself getting poorer and poorer as his family increased, his situation improving again as his children began to earn (p. 49, see also above p. 183). This is obviously evidence that Booth took a rough estimate of needs into consideration as well as income in drawing his poverty line. Moreover, in order to show exactly what he meant by poverty, want, and distress, and thus attach some positive value to the definition of 'poor' and 'very poor', Booth analysed the expenditure of 30 families in Classes B to F (pp. 132-46). As he found the average weekly expenditure for adult males below, on, and just above the line of poverty to be 5s., 7s. 6d. and 10s. respectively, this gave him 15s., 22s. 6d. and 30s. per week for a family of father, mother and three children. The difficulties Booth encountered in analysing these family budgets are discussed in Chapter 9; his estimate of the incomes demarcating the boundaries between the Classes seems to have been imprecise.

In Volume Two of the First Edition Booth returned to the problem of what would now be called 'secondary poverty', with special reference to the 'follies' of mankind. He also discussed exceptional needs, arising for instance out of sickness. It could be argued on the one hand that the poor were often really better off than they appeared to be, because of extravagances; on the other that follies should be disregarded. 'According as the one or other of these two points of view is taken, thousands of families may be placed on the one or the other side of the doubtful line of demarcation between class and class among the poor.' Though Booth might have swayed 'this way or that according to the mood of the moment', he was fully satisfied that 'the general conclusions were not very far from the truth'. If there was any 'general error' it would be 'found on the safe side; that is, in overstating rather than understating the volume of poverty' (pp. 18-20).

Booth added in *Industry* v (pp. 15, 25) that in view of the special circumstances of each trade, 'it is perhaps not surprising if nominal earnings of from 25s. to 30s. a week still fall within the lines of our measure of poverty'. Though this conclusion was made in an attempt to reconcile figures of earnings with statistics of overcrowding, it nevertheless demonstrated that Booth did not hold on to earnings as a measure of poverty with any degree of firmness.

In sum, Booth's poverty line must be regarded as being so drawn as to coincide with popular opinion, and all depended, in the last analysis, on the judgement of his interviewers. The key phrase is in the definition in the Second Paper; those families are 'very poor' whose means are insufficient *'according to the usual standard of life in this country'* (authors' italics); it was not his fault if his endeavour to translate this into shillings and pence for illustrative purposes was regarded by others as the main factor in his evaluation. No attempt to set a price on the necessities of life was ever made by Booth; this hazardous operation was conducted much later by his successors. Many misunderstandings, and many false comparisons have arisen, however, from Booth's use of estimates of family income.

This aspect of the Inquiry is of special interest as affording an example of the successful use of the judgement of field workers, which in this case produced data affording a reliable basis for simple statistical calculations.

Index